HOW
TO
LOVE
YOURSELF

ALSO BY TEAL SWAN

The Sculptor in the Sky

Teal Swan

HOW TO LOVE YOURSELF

Previously published as *Shadows Before Dawn*

WATKINS
Sharing Wisdom
Since 1893

Originally published as *Shadows Before Dawn* (2015)

This newly revised and updated edition, first published in the UK and USA
in 2022 by Watkins, an imprint of Watkins Media Limited
Unit 11, Shepperton House
89-93 Shepperton Road
London
N1 3DF

enquiries@watkinspublishing.com

Design and typography copyright © Watkins Media Limited 2022

Text copyright © Teal Swan 2022

2 3 4 5 6 7 8 9 10

Typeset by JCS Publishing

Printed and bound in the United Kingdom by TJ Books Ltd

A CIP record for this book is available from the British Library

ISBN: 978-1- 78678-700-2 (Paperback)

ISBN: 978-1- 78678-704-0 (eBook)

MIX
Paper from
responsible sources
FSC® C013056

www.watkinspublishing.com

*This book is dedicated to my 21-year-old self,
whose struggle to love herself
ultimately resulted in this book.*

*This book is also dedicated to each and every being
who is ready to stop wanting for a different life—
those brave individuals who are ready to transform
their suffering into joy and their hatred into love.
Therefore, this book is dedicated to you.*

*May you come to know the first, last, and only love
that ever is or ever will be . . . self-love.*

CONTENTS

PREFACE

DELIVERING LOVE
TO THE UNLOVABLE

We all know on some level that it is important to love ourselves. But when people say that "all you have to do is love yourself," it's kind of like telling a child in kindergarten that he or she has to solve a college physics equation. Like that bewildered child, we have no idea where to begin. We are standing in a place where we don't love ourselves and haven't for some time. We simply have no idea where to start and where to go from here.

On the matter of hating myself with a passion, let me tell you—I am an expert. My journey to a new life was long and complicated. I couldn't continue hurting myself; I had to find a way to love myself . . . or I knew I wouldn't make it.

So the book you hold in your hands contains both my gut-wrenching journey to self-love and the techniques and methods that enabled me to turn my life around. In Part I, I share my harrowing story and hold myself up as proof that self-love is achievable even for the most desperate person, in the direst of circumstances.

Then in Part II, I share what I call my Self-Love Tool Kit—30 techniques that I learned on my journey, which I trust will help you on yours. Anyone who enters this path is welcome. There are small steps and bigger steps, whatever you are ready for at this time. Enter slowly or jump right in. You have nothing to lose and a life full of love to gain.

PART ONE

Lost Love—Found Love

CHILDHOOD LOST

A Difficult Beginning

The journey from self-hate to self-love was one that I had no road map for. I started in the depths of emotional hell. I was suicidal with no hope left for my life. And I clawed my way, oftentimes on hands and knees, to this place of freedom, joy, and love that I stand in today.

Let me assure you: It was worth it. That's easy for me to say, because I am now standing on the other side. But it's my promise to you that if you keep placing one foot in front of the other in the direction of self-love, you will get there, too, even if you have faced the worst kind of pain, heartbreak, and despair.

I would not ask you to go on this journey with me with an open heart if I did not first open my heart to you and share with you the story of how I got to where I am today.

By society's standards, my mother and father were good, liberal people who spent their lives in the pursuit of higher learning, justice, equality, and environmental protection. Having grown up in the '60s and '70s, they were well-educated hippie activists. Unknown to them at the time, neither of my parents had healed from their own emotional trauma before I was born; but nonetheless, oblivious to this, they met, married, and started a family like so many of their peers.

While my father was fairly ambivalent about having children of his own, my mother, on the other hand, felt as if motherhood was one of her lifelong callings. She dreamed of having the perfect relationship with her children, and when she found out she was pregnant with a girl, she imagined exactly how this little girl would be. She felt that her daughter would be a carbon copy of herself; and she would have a friendly, happy child who shared her common interests and who would fit right into the family. Most of all, she imagined that her daughter would validate her as a person and as a mother.

It was therefore quite a shock to her when I began to grow into my own personality because it soon became obvious that I was anything but what she had imagined. I didn't fit the image that she had in her head of what her child would be like or what being a parent would be like. As a result, my mother felt invalidated, just as she had felt during her own childhood.

A Girl with Too Many "Gifts"

My parents professed to love me, but they often admitted that they did not know *how* to love me. They had such a hard time relating to me that there were two running jokes in the house when I was growing up, both of which I found extremely painful as a child.

The first ongoing story line was that one day an alien spaceship would arrive to pick me up. And the second line was "The Beeswaxes have our baby." This joke came about because when I was born in New Mexico, most of the hospital staff was Hispanic and therefore spoke Spanish; they had such a difficult time with the pronunciation and spelling of my parents' last name (Bosworth) that when they rolled me from the nursery into the postpartum room, the little label on my hospital crib said "Beeswax."

The gap between my parents and myself was increased one hundredfold by the fact that I was born extrasensory, with a number of sensitivities that no one in my family could understand. The best way I can explain it is to say that our sensory organs are a bit like filters. They filter out stimuli in the environment around us so that we can perceive solid objects and the usual things in our world. But to me as a small child, it felt like my filters were blown. I figured out when I was older that I suffered from sensory integration disorder, and I knew then why I struggled with my "abilities" so much throughout my early years.

Of course, it's always hard to explain how the way that I see differs from other people because I have very little idea how other people see. That's part of the beauty of individual perspective, but it's also what makes it hard to fully comprehend how different I view the world in comparison to what is considered "normal" by most people.

Here's an example: You and I could be calling the exact same color *yellow* when in reality we are seeing drastically different colors. Things that should be solid don't appear solid to me at all, but I didn't figure out until I was in elementary school that other people were *not* seeing the same things that I was seeing.

Really, it wasn't until I was 24 years old that I began talking to people to try to actually decipher what I perceive and how what I perceive is radically different from how and what other people see around them. It was a shock to me at first.

Experiencing the World in a Radically Different Way

I was born seeing everything that is in the world around us, not as if it is a solid object but as if it is a "vibration." The amplitude and frequency of energy is what determines how (and in what form) that particular energy will express itself in the physical. Everything in the universe is made of moving energy— what I call *"vibration"*—and everything that vibrates imparts or impacts information. This vibration is what determines the form in which energy will manifest. Since physical things are just expressions of energy, then solid objects are more or less an illusion that I do not have and cannot really see.

And from the time I was born, I could see auras, which are thought forms both transmitting and receiving information to and from the physical structure they are associated with, such as a human body. An aura around a person or thing exhibits shapes, textures, hues, sounds, and patterns; it emanates light as well. These effects colored my world as a child, they still do, and I naively thought everyone could see them.

I came to realize that the varied characteristics of an aura were able to tell me valuable information about the physical person or thing that the aura is associated with. They can at times tell me a nearly complete story of who you are. An aura will respond to a thought and change its characteristics to match that thought. Auras are also highly receptive to interaction, so I can use my own energetic field to manipulate the energy fields of others to help them heal, not unlike the way in which practitioners of Reiki are taught to do. Energy fields are as easy for me to feel with my hands as water is to most people.

I also see thought forms (which are thoughts that have enough inherent energy that they take on a configuration, shape, or visual appearance), and they may manifest to me in a nonstatic way. There are traditionally three types of thought forms: The first is energy that takes the image of the thinker; the second is energy that takes the image of a material object; and the third is energy that takes a form entirely its own, expressing its qualities in the matter it draws around it. So this allows me to see, interact with, and communicate with entities, which some people might call ghosts; and I also perceive guides and angels, usually around myself or people I meet. This has given me the ability to act as a "spirit medium" and bring messages from spirit to individuals on the earth plane.

I have a hypersensitive sense of hearing. I can even hear tectonic plates moving in the earth. I'm sure you're familiar with how the tide is pulled by the gravity of the moon. What most people don't know is that the gravity of the moon affects everything, not just water—it pulls at the earth, too, and I can hear it. This means that full moons are very, very loud to me. And I hate the sound of cotton balls (a sound I gather most individuals can't hear). People talking in other rooms, which would be inaudible to many, is not inaudible to me. I have hearing that is able to pick up the extremely high frequency of thought forms, so I also have clairaudience.

In other words, I not only see thought forms but can hear them, too. My senses all have extra levels to them, so I can actually *see* sounds and *taste* colors. You can only imagine how distracting and bewildering all this was to me as a child and to my parents, who had no idea what I was seeing, feeling, or talking about most of the time.

No Such Thing as Negative Space

It was truly enlightening to me when I fully comprehended that unlike other people, I do not see negative space, which is what many people call "air." Instead, everything looks to me like energy with no spaces in between. Every energy field bleeds into every other energy field, creating one huge existence of "inter-being." And because of this, I perceive how everything that *is* affects everything else that *is.*

Metaphorically speaking, then, a pebble dropped into this energy that makes up all that is would create ripples that affect the entire field. The only reason people seldom consciously perceive it that way is that, generally, our human senses—like sight, taste, and touch—give people the impression of objects being solid and finite with a boundary of separation between them and other things.

So, you quite likely see skin as a finite boundary where the body stops, but for me, the skin is a certain point of density within the energy that makes up a human. I actually see impressions of what is below the skin. When I meet a person, I am able to see their bones, organs, nerves, veins, and so on.

I am also able to see the energy channels within the body, which have been labeled by some people as chakras and meridians. I can see where a person's energy is not flowing properly and what physical ailments he or she has, and I can often see the vibration that is leading to *why* he or she has a particular energy blockage or a physical ailment.

Furthermore, I can see whole life paths, which basically means I can see the future. But the future is not decided. What I am seeing is lifepath potentials. These are outcomes—occurrences in the future that are a match to the current state that someone is in, which doesn't often change, because our thought patterns tend to be habitual. But it *can* change.

Thoughts are what create the world around us, so when we are able to change our thoughts, our entire physical reality shifts, and those new thought patterns create our future.

With my given abilities, I often see and emotionally feel our collective future as well, which comes to me as prophetic visions or dreams. In the past, I've had trouble with this, even to the point of having seizures in the days leading up to a natural disaster, a man-made catastrophe, or a war.

Confusion and Conflict as a Child

These special abilities might be called spiritual "gifts," but I considered them a curse when I was younger, and the mainstream medical community at the time diagnosed me with mental illness. The different way that I perceived the world was frustrating to me, and quite frightening to my parents, who had never encountered anyone who had such abilities or knew anything about them at that point in time.

I would get very upsetting reactions from people who met me as a child, once they found out that I could tell them what color they were because I could see their aura or when I would start conveying messages to them from their dead relatives. I would try to be helpful, and I would often feel the urge to lay my hands on someone's body and tell them they were sick and heal them, but I felt like something was seriously wrong with me when they backed away looking frightened of me.

I felt as if I didn't belong with my parents; or in this world; that I didn't really fit in anywhere. But that lonely feeling and isolation were nothing compared to what came next.

CHAPTER 2

NATURE, NURTURE, NOWHERE

Moving to an Unsettling Setting

When I was very young, my parents accepted a job as wilderness forest rangers in Utah. We lived in a tiny two-room guard station cabin with no electricity, no indoor plumbing, and an outhouse in the Rocky Mountain wilderness. My childhood was spent there, where those early summer days fed off of time, striping light and darkness alike from the sky in lazy cycles. Every morning the sun rose, kissing the tips of each rolling hill as if trying to suck life from them. This was a place where animals were not in cages and people were not stuck behind concrete and glass.

Utah is absolutely Idyllic. But there is also a flip side to rural Utah. The winters there covered the sagebrush and skin alike with a dry cold so deep that life itself turned numb and silent. I saw grown men turn as calloused as the hands they worked with, beaten into a state of crudeness where all elements of mercy were lost. Not surprisingly, the women were disintegrated in the face of this intense harshness. I could see them try to muscle up an impression of grace where it was better not to be born a girl in the first place.

I know now that those women and girls clung to religion as the only means to cope. From a very young age, I found out the hard way what those women already knew: to live without God in Utah was to live alone as prey.

Making the Wilderness Work

Nonetheless, I was a child, this was our new home, and I was blissfully unaware of what all was to come. When I was almost four, my brother was born, a gorgeous baby boy with platinum blonde hair and bright blue eyes. My brother was not extrasensory. Unlike me, he was happy, playful, never fussy, and insatiably outgoing. Unlike me, my brother did validate my mother both as a person and as a mother. He did fit in.

Unintentionally, his birth drove an even deeper wedge between my parents and myself. I felt more ostracized than ever, truly all alone, even when I was with my family. I felt like something was wrong with me, and like I was stuck in a family of people that I didn't belong with. I felt like a changeling child.

Had the conditions been different, I think that life at the wilderness cabin would have been a wonderful way to grow up. In fact, I loved it there. There is simplicity and a sense of undisturbed peace that comes from living a life removed from the static hum of electricity in the walls and absent of the distraction of modern technology.

As such, I found ways to love my surroundings despite the isolation. Nature was all around us. We made the most of the forms of entertainment that we had, enjoying family meals, games of make-believe, animals, and hobbies. Raising us in this way was the best decision my parents could have made, except for one thing: When my parents moved to Utah, they did not consider the pervasive religious atmosphere of the state.

Living Among People with Strict Religious Rites

The Church of Jesus Christ of Latter-Day Saints, also called the Mormons or LDS, had made Utah one of the most religiously homogeneous states in the nation. It's not a Sunday religion; rather, it's a culture that permeates every second of every day of its members' lives. As long as the doctrine is agreed upon and no questions are asked, it's a culture of family and community.

But the community we had moved into soon began to notice that they weren't seeing my family at sacrament meetings. Before long, rumors about my extrasensory abilities were spread by word of mouth around the town. Given that I was born to liberal hippies, I didn't conduct myself the way that a typical female child from the Mormons did. Long story short, I was not received well in the community at all.

After aggressive attempts to convert my family didn't work, the majority of the people in town just made it a deliberate point not to interact with us. In most cases, their children were not allowed to play with me, and they would not allow me to enter their houses. I was often singled out in the parking lot after school and informed of the consequences of following my parents' impious choices. I was told that the life my family led was an impure one without hope of salvation.

If it were left at that, I could have fared much better than I did, but there was another wrinkle. The Church of Jesus Christ of Latter-Day Saints professes to be the "one true church," and they believe God's true word and priesthood can only be passed down through its founder, Joseph Smith, making all other religions the religions of false prophets. Spontaneous healings and interaction with things "beyond the veil" were known and practiced in the Mormon faith. Any kind of extrasensory gifts were thought to be, in fact, a potential gift of priesthood, passed from God to Joseph Smith and from Joseph Smith to the baptized and devout.

Here's the catch: Priesthood could only be passed from God to Joseph Smith to a man. So when the rumors began to spread in the summer of 1988 that there was a young girl in town who was exhibiting these very same abilities, what I could do was *not* seen as a gift of the divine. My abilities were seen as a gift from the devil.

I will say that, for the most part, Mormons seem to subscribe to a turn-the-other-cheek philosophy when it comes to outsiders that they fail to convert. But like most religions, the LDS church has splinter groups. One example of a splinter group is the Fundamentalist LDS, who have been at the heart of a number of scandals played out in mainstream media, particularly given their beliefs about polygamy and how often those beliefs bleed into the practice of pedophilia.

Then there is a seldom-recognized splinter group called the Blood Covenant. The Blood Covenant believes that it is their God-given mission to rid the earth of evil. They believe in the LDS church's original teachings on blood atonement, and in the Blood Covenant it is accepted that sins should be paid for with the blood of man. These two beliefs lead the group to infiltrate local satanic covens with the intent of undermining them and holding counter rituals. It also leads the Blood Covenant group members to participate in sadistic and masochistic ritualistic acts under the belief that in suffering, you find the light of Christ and through bloodletting, you are cleansed of your sins.

The Dark Journey of My Soul Begins

In 1989, I was invited to visit the home of a girl who attended the same kindergarten class that I did. Her father was a member of a satanic coven in the area, and it was there that I caught the attention of Doc. Doc was in his 50s or 60s at the time. Unbeknownst to my mother, he was a member of the Blood Covenant, and he had infiltrated a local satanic coven.

Years later, when I was older, I came to realize that Doc was a sociopath with multiple personalities, but the only personality that most members of the community saw, including my parents, was a superintelligent, charismatic, and successful do-gooder type. Because of his multiple personalities, however, Doc lived a double life. On the one hand, he was a likable, smart, local health expert who was obsessed with the study of the human mind; on the other hand, he was a sadistic psychopath who attended cult rituals in his spare time.

Doc quickly developed an obsession with the idea of possessing me. He followed me in his truck when I was riding my pink Huffy bike alone one day, pulled me off the bike, and raped me for the first time inside a local Mormon stake house (church house). He placed me back on my bike, but I was bleeding and I was in so much pain and shock that I couldn't ride the bike straight.

I pulled the bike off to the side of the road and ran into a field, where I sat, watching my reality collapse. I figured that what had happened was punishment. I thought that I was in trouble for riding my bike around the stake-house parking lot.

Until that moment, I had believed that my parents were like Santa Claus and would swoop out of nowhere to rescue me from danger. But that day, I realized that my mom and dad couldn't protect me from everything, and that I was alone in a very dangerous and brutal world. That was the day my childhood ended and some distorted version of adulthood began; I was only six years old.

From that point on, Doc set up a plan to gain access to me. When I was still six, he managed to corner me at a horse lesson and turn my world upside down again. He held me by my throat up against a wall of a stable and told me that he was my real father. He said that I was a demon that had taken the place of my parents' real child, and he warned me that if anyone found out that I had done this, I'd be taken away from them and that no one could save me from that fate but him.

Doc informed me that if I told anyone about who I really was or what he had said to me, my whole family would be killed. Even at that young age, I was a silent, strong, personally accountable type of child, so I assumed that it was all my fault and I had done something wrong that day to deserve the interaction. I said nothing to my parents about it because I had no reason to disbelieve what Doc had said. I was terrorized by the idea that he would in fact retaliate against my family, as he had promised, if I were to tell anyone about the interaction.

Mentor or Opportunist?

Later that week, the vice principal of my grade school came into my classroom. She said the school had received a note from my parents saying I was going to be picked up after roll was called. They asked me if I needed someone to walk with me out to the parking lot to get picked up. I said no, and once roll was called, I took my backpack and walked out of the school to the parking lot. Lo and behold, it was not my parents waiting in their car. It was Doc waiting in his truck.

That was the beginning of 13 years of ritual, mental, emotional, physical, and sexual abuse. I can see now that it was all carefully orchestrated by Doc. He had already systematically gained access to me without my parents' knowledge, so all he had to do then was capitalize on the already preexisting emotional gap that existed between my parents and myself. Pedophile sociopaths are opportunists who target ostracized children.

The unfortunate emotional dynamic between my family and myself opened the door for Doc to widen that gap between us further. He gained regular access to me, unfettered, by reestablishing a friendly relationship with my mother, which was easily done because he already knew her. He managed to convince both my parents that he knew everything about the extrasensory gifts I was exhibiting and that he was the perfect mentor for me.

Under Doc's sick plan, I very soon developed a dependence on him and on his approval of me. This is a syndrome that has often been referred to as Stockholm syndrome, and I truly believed he was my real father. I believed everything he said. My parents felt I really did need help and here was an intelligent man offering his assistance—an expert in these matters and someone who was passionate about helping me. That's why my parents trusted him.

My parents continued to worry about me and had grown quite distressed about how chronically unhappy I was, and they knew I had no friends whatsoever. They had begun to accept that something was seriously wrong with me but had no clue as to what was really causing it or what more they could do. They saw most of the red flags but misinterpreted them, and during my years with Doc, I exhibited many telling symptoms.

I was injuring myself by cutting, so any time I arrived home with injuries caused by Doc or another member of the cult, it was excused away as self-injury or an accident that I had had with the horses. When I was acting as if I was in an altered mental state because of the drugs that Doc had been administering to me, or if my mind or mood was off because of my extrasensory abilities, it was explained away as schizoaffective disorder.

When I displayed extreme separation anxiety well past the appropriate phase of development in childhood and withdrew socially, making no friends at all, it was explained away as shyness. When I would hoard food in my room, my parents explained it away as a personality quirk. When I wouldn't play like other kids, but preferred to be obsessively perfect in whatever task I was set on performing, usually an athletic one, they explained it away as me being a talented perfectionist.

When I wrote dark, disturbed poetry or drew disturbing pictures, they assumed I was overly sensitive and had been affected by someone else who was being abused at my school. When I kept getting bacterial infections and urinary tract infections, stomach pain so bad I was hospitalized, and migraines, they attributed it to a weak immune system or a hormonal imbalance.

When I was 13, a friend of my mother's who was an RN examined me, only to discover that my hymen was not intact. After asking my mom if I was sexually active and being told no, she explained it away as potentially being the result of years of horseback riding.

How Could Such Horrendous Abuse Be Missed?

Sure enough, all the symptoms that I showed as a child and teenager, which were caused by the abuse, were attributed to something else, in the ways described above, or to me being mentally ill. My parents thought I had a mental illness that no psychologist or psychiatrist could diagnose. Don't get me wrong—psychiatrists and psychologists diagnosed me plenty; it's just that they all disagreed on my diagnosis because my symptoms didn't fit the mold of any one form of mental illness.

Sexual abuse was mentioned several times as a potential issue by psychologists, but upon seeing that neither of my parents were perpetrators, they were forced to move on to other potential explanations. The idea that I could be getting abused by someone whom my parents trusted was simply outside of everyone's reality. I don't know if they even considered it at the time. It was a notion that seemed as far-fetched to them as alien abduction.

All this time, I was terrified to admit to anything that went on with Doc. I was completely under his control. The sicker and more unhappy I got, the more Doc would "come to the rescue," suggesting that I spend more time with him and that he knew what to do to help me. From my parents' perspective, it seemed that all the adults around me in my childhood, including them and Doc, were sincerely working together to try to figure out what was wrong with me and fix it.

In this way, my parents would let Doc spend more and more time with me because they were desperate about what could be done to help me, and they were desperate to find someone who could show me how to cope with my unusual brain. I think in some way, the idea of having so much control over me and that he could do all of it right under my parents' noses was what gave him even more excitement. Like an addiction, Doc had to keep increasing and increasing the level of deception and risk to get the same high. The same went for his need to increase the level of his violence, and that put me in situations of ever-increasing danger and terror.

To spare you the graphic details, I'll just summarize quickly what happened from age 6 to 19. I was tortured physically and sexually in cult rituals, raped, deprived of food, and forced to undergo three abortions (all performed by Doc himself, who was also the father). I was photographed for sadomasochistic pornography, sold to men for sex in outdoor gas-station bathrooms, and kept in basements and in a hole in the ground in Doc's backyard. I was also exposed to electroshock programming, forced to undergo isolation torture, and left overnight tied up in lava caves in southern Idaho.

During this time, I was drugged chronically by Doc with anesthetics, all of which he had unlimited access to due to being a veterinarian by trade. I was chased through the Idaho and Utah wilderness by Doc "playing" tracking games in which he would hunt me, and I would undergo consequences (like him "counting coup" by cutting my rib cage or being raped) if I was caught. And I was used as a lure to other children who ended up being hurt and on occasion killed.

Finally a Mistake Opens Up to an Escape

By the time I was 19, I was a shell of a person. I was a cutter, and I was dissociated most of the time. I had attempted suicide and was still suicidal. I had believed for 13 years that my family was in fact not my real family, that my life with them was a facade. I lived with the guilt of the belief that I had stolen the life of their real child. I believed that I was evil. I believed that if I told any of them about my "real life" with Doc, they would all be brutally murdered.

After exhausting every single option they could think of to try to get me help, my parents were so confused about what was going on with me and so utterly powerless about what to do with me that they had all but given up.

But then when I was 19 years old, Doc made a mistake. It was the first mistake he'd made in 13 years. He made a mistake with the dosage of an anesthetic drug that he was administering to me. He had intended to drug me to the point that he could convince me that I had done something that I hadn't done. But the misdosage resulted in me retaining memory that I didn't do what he said I had done.

Finally my head was clear enough to think to myself, *If Doc is lying about this, what else has he lied about?* I couldn't come up with any reason for him to convince me that I had done something that I hadn't actually done, other than to scare me into total, powerless dependency. That realization, which came on the heels of his mistake with the dosage, afforded me the chance to escape—and I did.

I escaped that very same night to the sanctuary of a man whom I had met only twice. His name was Blake. I had met him as a result of my mother trying to expand my nonexistent social circle as a teenager. She had connected with a family whose son (not Blake, but another boy) was diagnosed with bipolar disorder. It was my mother's idea that perhaps if we found another teen with a mental illness, I might feel some kind of connection and be less alone.

I had attended a party with this new acquaintance of mine, and as I went to open the front door of the house where the party was being held, a willowy-looking young man, full of enthusiasm, said hi as he propelled himself over the railing and into some bushes. I thought to myself, *What an idiot.*

But when he came back inside, and we made eye contact for the first time, I found his eyes and his essence to be so familiar and so pervasively kind that we were inseparable that night. We ended up going skinny-dipping in a reservoir with a group of other teenagers, and something in me felt a palpable camaraderie. I knew that he was so pure and innocent that I could trust him.

The night I fled from Doc's control, the only safe place I could think to go was Blake's house. I had been there only once before when he said he wanted to show me his Hacky Sack collection. That night, Blake wasn't home and neither were his two roommates. But I was in such a state of distress that I broke in through a window and knew no other way to cope with the distress than to cut myself.

When Blake returned, he was shocked to find me in his bathtub with blood spilling down the drain. He cleaned me up, bandaged my cuts, and told me to stay with him. And so I did. I had no real plan to run away from Doc forever; I didn't think that was an option. But I stayed with Blake for a day, and a day became two days, and two days became a week, and by the end of a month, I never wanted to return. I was hiding.

Blake didn't know at first why I was so obviously disturbed and tortured, and mercifully, he didn't even ask. But he was so devoted to my every whim that I started to get better, gradually emerging from my emotional hell.

CHAPTER 3

MY GUT-WRENCHING JOURNEY TO SELF-LOVE

In a Prison of My Own Making

I eventually explained the entire story of my childhood and Doc and the cults to Blake, which only seemed to deepen his dedication to my healing process. When I landed safely with Blake and was hiding out, I knew that neither Doc nor any other cult member would come looking for me at first because that would violate the rules of the "bonding" and "call back" programming that they had implanted over the years. If they had to come looking for me, it was a liability and also it meant that I was the one in control. They were relying on my programming to cause me to return willingly like a runaway dog. But I did not. I slowly took steps to regain my life. I found people and activities that I used to develop my own self-esteem for the first time, but it was not an easy or straightforward process.

As for Doc, some years after I escaped, a case was opened against him. However, as with so many other abuse cases, many years had passed between the time of my escape and the time that the case was opened, which left little physical evidence. Faced with scarce tangible proof or witnesses, the district attorney decided there was not enough hard evidence to prosecute, and the case turned cold. For any further action to be taken through the justice system, additional evidence would have to surface or witnesses would have to come forward.

You might think that this is where the story ends, but I can tell you personally that the road to healing extends much further than simply escaping a situation physically. I may have gotten out from under the control of my abuser, but I was still a shell of a person. I didn't have a life. All I had were the tattered remains of a life that could have been. As a young woman, I had no idea how to cope in society. I had no life skills, I had severe post-traumatic stress disorder (PTSD), and I hated everything about myself.

Truly, my abuser had not disappeared when I got away from him; instead, he set up shop inside my head, taking up residence in me, and I was the one continuing the pattern of abuse on myself. I was addicted to cutting, and I was still suicidal. Nearly every life choice I was making at that time was self-sabotaging instead of self-loving. I was convinced that if I stopped abusing myself that the bad in me would triumph over the good and I would become a terrible person, just like the abusers from my childhood. I was convinced that the only thing that made me different from them was that I punished myself.

As for Blake, who was so pivotal to me at the beginning of my healing process, he went on to become the right-hand man in the career that I forged. For 11 years, we worked together facilitating positive change throughout the world. I have come a very long way, and that journey to my new life wasn't easy. I had to discover a way to love myself, and this book holds a Tool Kit of the techniques and methods that enabled me to turn my life around.

Rebuilding My Life Through Therapy

I was forced into therapy at age 21 by a man I was dating who could no longer stand trying to be in a stable relationship with me. The aftereffects of my abusive childhood were making it too hard. He looked me in the face and said, "This is not normal. The stuff you went through is not normal, and you need to understand that. I'm not going to be with you anymore unless you get some help from someone professional."

He brought me to a rape crisis center and said to the women at the front desk, "She needs to be here." They called the director into a room with me, and she asked me why I thought that my boyfriend's opinion was that I needed to be there. I began to open up about the things I went through as a child. I remember watching her facial muscles becoming tight, and I remember her fidgeting as I let her in on only a few of the details of what had occurred.

She assured me that I did indeed need to be there, but she also said that the kinds of things that I was talking about were way over her head and way beyond what they usually deal with at the center. However, she knew someone who specialized in childhood ritual abuse and said that she would call her up to see if she would take my case.

Later that same week, I met with the specialist for the first time. She was warm and affectionate, which was in stark contrast to the psychologists I was used to. That affection, combined with her extensive knowledge of trauma recovery, broke down all my walls, and together with her I began the process of rebuilding my life.

Therapy brought me to the point where I could admit that I didn't deserve the abuse I endured as a child and that it wasn't my fault. But I reached a point at age 24 where I realized that therapy had taken me as far as it was going to take me. I knew somewhere deep inside me that there had to be something beyond the feeling of being a victim, beyond pity, and beyond trying to cope with PTSD.

It may sound grim from where you are sitting today reading this, but suicide had become my exit strategy. I lived through each day by reminding myself that I could always kill myself tomorrow. I found that this allowed me to really focus on what I could do today to feel better. I did whatever I could to feel better and made feeling good the most important thing in my life.

So I dedicated myself to being a professional winter sports athlete, experimented with cooking, found places to live that felt safe, and started meditating. Slowly I found that the mantra changed from "I can always kill myself tomorrow, so what am I going to do today?" to "I can always kill myself in a week, so what am I going to do this week?" Then it became "I can always kill myself next year, so what am I going to do this year?"

Eventually I realized that I didn't really want to kill myself anymore. Even though I still struggled on occasion with suicidal feelings, those feelings were temporary instead of a permanent fixture of my life.

After I escaped the abuse, I wanted nothing to do with my extrasensory abilities. I threw myself into competitive winter sports in order to avoid them. I tried to become as grounded in the physical world as possible. I still helped people by using my extrasensory gifts once in a while if someone was in a desperate state, but as far as I was concerned, my abilities were to blame for all the pain that I had experienced, and I remained tortured by the fact that I could not get rid of them. I was still desperately afraid of the world.

Seeking Love for the Wrong Reasons

When I was 22, I married a man I didn't love because I wanted to be kept safe and I wanted to be taken care of. That marriage fell apart and was annulled after six months. Then, that very same year, I married for a second time; I got married for a sense of safety again. What I did not realize then is that on top of a never-ending desperate search for belonging, I was really trying to use men to run away from myself. I wanted to be kept safe, not only from the world but also from my self. On the inside, I was still living in an atmosphere of self-hate so pervasive that I couldn't trust myself.

Then, when I was 25, my son was born. Having gone through infertility treatment and having lost three pregnancies as a teen, I felt a deep need to experience the magic of belonging and of actually being able to have and hold a child of my own. Contrary to my fantasy, I experienced an extremely traumatizing pregnancy and birth.

When we found out the baby was a boy, I had imagined that I would have a physically active jock for a son, a sports enthusiast, who would never have to suffer from the pain that I did. The love I felt for my son was unparalleled by any other love that I have ever felt in my life. But to my dismay, when he was born, he had a clear-colored aura, an aura that looked like a prismatic crystal light. These auras, which, because of their color, have been referred to as *crystal auras,* belong only to people with innate extrasensory abilities.

Lo and behold, as usual, the universe had given me the very child I needed. I cried for a solid 40 minutes because I was so afraid that because of who he is, he would suffer like I had suffered. Then it dawned on me that if I was going to teach him to embrace his own inborn abilities, I would first have to embrace my own.

Scrat and His Acorn

The year was 2009. My six-month-old son was taking a nap. I was sitting on the black-and-white-checkered linoleum floor of my kitchen, in a state of despair. Since becoming a mother, I had ventured into the land of children's entertainment, including a film called *Ice Age*. The movie featured a saber-toothed squirrel named Scrat. The entire theme of the Scrat character is that he is constantly trying to find and hold on to his precious acorn.

The Scrat character is on a perpetual, yet ill-fated, quest to keep his acorn. Just when you think he has it at last, his bad luck strikes and some improbable turn of events rips it away from him once again. Scrat is haunted by Murphy's Law, which simply put means that anything that can go wrong, will go wrong, to prevent you from having what you want.

When you are a full-time mother, it starts to feel like your adult brain goes away and is replaced by Disney. Sitting there on the kitchen floor that day, I couldn't get the character Scrat out of my mind. The humor of watching him on the screen was tainted for me by some kind of deep grief and identification with his dilemma. Scrat was me. His acorn was happiness.

My life was nothing but an endless, ill-fated quest to find and keep my happiness, and here I was on the floor, feeling defeated because it never worked out. "Why doesn't it ever work out?" I silently asked myself. I knew the answer. The answer was that I didn't want *me*. Living in my own skin felt like a prison sentence instead of a choice. I kept thinking to myself, *How am I supposed to commit to something I don't even want?*

I Am Where I Am

It became obvious to me that I hadn't loved myself for a long time, if ever. I didn't love myself, and I didn't have the slightest idea *how* to love myself. I hated the idea of self-love. Having grown up in a family that prioritized selflessness, self-sacrifice, and service, I felt like the concept of self-love was a villain. Self-love seemed like the devil coming to destroy my goodness and destroy all the chances I had of being loved by someone else.

It felt like I'd hit rock bottom. I imagined that this was how people feel when they are so pathetic and so destroyed by life that there is nothing else left for them to do. I had chased myself into a corner. All other attempts at feeling good in my own skin had failed. That was the moment that, like a person admitting to being an alcoholic, I admitted to hating myself.

Admitting to where you are feels simultaneously like pain and like relief. It's not fun to realize that you are living with an enemy within, but at the same time, admitting it feels like finally accepting something you have been resisting for years. The energy required to resist where you are is exhausting. Admitting to where you are feels like letting yourself float downstream after swimming upstream against river rapids for years. With that relief I found a sudden determination: I had to figure out how to love myself. I would try anything and everything.

There seemed to be lots of theories. People in the business of self-help talk about self-love all the time, but most don't know what self-love really means. They can tell you all day long that you need to love yourself and list reasons why you need to love yourself and even give you reasons why you're lovable. But no one taught about *how* to love yourself, or what self-love *looks like* on a practical level.

Thus my search for self-love left me even more frustrated than I was to begin with. Ultimately, I was left with the question, *What makes people who love themselves different from people who don't?* I knew that those differentiating qualities and behaviors would spell out in certain terms what it would take to love myself.

Many of the stereotypical self-help techniques for improving self-worth simply didn't work for me. It felt like I was trying to chip away at an Alaskan glacier with a grapefruit spoon. Affirmations made me feel worse. I would sit down at the kitchen table and try them. I'd write "I love myself" 100 times on a sheet of paper and try to feel the words as I wrote them. But as I wrote them, it was as if my brain was saying back to me, "You don't really think I'm this stupid, do you?" I could repeat the words *I love myself* all day long, and they would still be a lie. But later that year, I had my very first self-love breakthrough.

The Water Glass

Being an extrasensory, I can actually visually observe the effect that thoughts have on things and the effect that the frequency of one thing has on another thing. I can literally see how thoughts like *I am never going to be good enough* feed right into the stomach area and create conditions like gastritis and ulcers.

I choose not to drink tap water if I can help it because I see the way the chemicals and the pipes affect the energy of the water. As I mentioned in the beginning of this book, the line between thought and reality, physical and nonphysical, does not exist for me. Even so, in the powerlessness of my self-hating condition, I had overlooked an amazing opportunity.

One night, I decided to go to the city library to stock up on movies. I've always loved documentaries, and that day I was drawn to one called *Water: The Great Mystery.* In the film, they talked about the idea of "structurizing water." The documentary demonstrates what I have always observed, which is that everything that is around the water influences the water, and that your body, being such a high percentage of water, works the same way. In the documentary, they took the structurized water and poured it into an ocean with the idea that the structurized water would positively affect the water in the ocean.

I paused the movie halfway through and flew around the house looking for a pen and paper with all my bells and whistles going. I couldn't believe I had missed something so obvious. I knew I couldn't focus positively toward myself enough to love myself, but I could focus positively toward something else. The idea of finding things to like about myself turned my stomach; however, I could look at my son and find a zillion things I loved about him. It stood to reason, then, that I could take a glass of water and think about everything I love about my son and direct that heart-bursting affection and positive focus that I feel for him into the water. Then I could drink the water.

I felt like a war general who had just conceived of the "self-love Trojan horse." Like a reverse poison, I could restructurize the water in my body that had been programmed with self-hate by inundating it with the vibration from the glass of water that I had infused with love. I wasn't sure what reaction I would have, so I was too afraid to try out my little experiment that night. But during my son's nap time the very next day, I gave it a try.

Teal, the Guinea Pig

History is filled with great minds such as Benjamin Franklin, Jonas Salk, and Albert Hofmann, who tested their hypotheses by performing experiments on themselves. I have always taken the same approach with my own ideas. The day after my hypothesis took shape, I stood in the kitchen in a state of mild panic. Granted, I wasn't going to fly a kite in a thunderstorm like Benjamin Franklin did, but everything in my body was screaming, "Run away!" as if I were about to make a major mistake.

An internal tug-of-war raged as I poured the water and started to focus on it all the things I loved so much about my son. When the timer went off at five minutes, I lifted the cup to my lips and, as if I was taking medicine, drank it as fast as I could. I expected that I would instantly feel good, like being full of internal delight. I was wrong! I immediately started shaking. I felt sick to my stomach. My whole body flushed, and instead of throwing up, I started sobbing. My body started purging grief that had been suppressed within me for years.

I lay in the fetal position on the kitchen floor, crying for a good 20 minutes. As my crying subsided, I felt this overwhelming sensation of relief. I felt grounded. I took a walk and realized that I felt the hint of inner peace for the very first time. I didn't feel ecstatic, but I also wasn't desperate to find an escape from myself. So I decided that I would carry on with my little experiment and do it every day for a month at the same time each day.

For the first week, I had the same reaction. Drinking the water felt like a chemical reaction, like two violently repelling energies were at war within my body. After that first week, the reaction I had to the exercise gradually decreased. I was acclimatizing to the unfamiliar frequency of love.

Then funny things began to happen. External changes started taking place. I complimented my own cooking in front of a friend, something that would have thrown me into a guilty self-hate spiral before, but this time it didn't feel wrong. I tried out affirmations and discovered that they weren't as hard to believe as they had been before. I could say, "I like the color of my skin" and really mean it. The angry voice in the back of my mind that would say things like, "You're too difficult for anyone to love" or "Like you're one to talk" or "Nicely done, stupid"—that voice started to grow quiet. And my anxiety started to decrease.

I was reminded of a time when I was randomly listening to a radio interview many years ago while driving across the country, and I will never forget what the person being interviewed said about the letters in the word *anxiety*. If you reorder the letters, you end up with "any exit," which is essentially what anxiety is. It's the state of trying to find any exit you can to get away from something. I could see how my anxiety was caused by the fact that I had been trying to find any exit to escape from myself. As my rudimentary self-love practice progressed, my desire to get away from myself slowly began to fade away and with it, so did my anxiety.

By coming in the back door of my own self-hate through this practice of drinking water that was infused with love, all the other practical how-tos of self-love became easier to do. By coming through the back door, I had broken down the heavy walls designed to keep love out, and from that point on I found I could take a front-door entry approach to self-love. I set out on a mission to find every single ingredient that I could in order to design the perfect recipe for creating self-love.

Calling Off Cutting

One of the most debilitating physical consequences of my self-hate was my addiction to cutting, and I knew that this would be my next huge hurdle. From the time I was 11 years old, self-harm had become a full-fledged addiction. Endorphins block pain and also play a part in our ability to feel relief and pleasure. They affect us much like codeine or morphine does. When endorphins reach the opioid receptors of the limbic system, including the part of the brain called the hypothalamus, we experience relief, pleasure, and a sense of satisfaction. We also feel calmer and positively energized.

When your body experiences pain, your brain releases endorphins. Endorphins both soothe and energize you so you can get out of harm's way. For this reason, cutting myself soothed my negative emotion. It is a coping mechanism that provides temporary relief from intense feelings, such as anxiety, guilt, depression, stress, and emotional numbness, as well as a sense of failure, self-loathing, poor self-worth, or the pressure of perfectionism.

People can become addicted to the chemicals that their own bodies produce in response to certain things with the same voraciousness that they become addicted to a street drug. So as soon as we associate the action of cutting with the corresponding feeling of relief, we create neural pathways in our brain that automatically compel us to seek relief when we feel negative emotion, and we do that by cutting.

Like a caged animal, the cutter is in a prison where negative emotion, especially despair, hatred, and rage, cannot be expressed. So those emotional states are internalized. There is nowhere for the energy to turn but inward, toward the self.

When I was growing up, the burden of my life was that I had to keep a very large secret. I was living a double life: one life with my parents, and one life without my parents in a sick and twisted reality created for me by a psychopath who was supposed to be my mentor.

Very early on, I was taught by my abuser that the calm feeling caused by punishment, either inflicted by someone else or by the self, is the light of Christ absolving you of sin. Cutting became my go-to coping mechanism. I used it whenever I felt trapped, guilty, desperate, or angry; and most especially, I cut myself whenever I felt like something was wrong or bad about me. I also used the excuse of self-injury to cover up other injuries that were caused by my abuser. I had spent the better part of my life up to that point, using cutting as a method to get away from and prevent myself from drowning in emotional pain.

It's Just a Phase . . . or Is It?

Unfortunately and unintentionally, my parents added fuel to the fire with regard to my cutting. At home, my emotions were invalidated and I was labeled "mentally ill" because my parents thought that I had no good reason to feel as miserable as I so obviously felt. They thought the only possible explanation was that something was wrong with me. It's a logical conclusion that many parents make. But it turned me against myself. All the adults in my life reinforced the idea that something was wrong with me because I was cutting, but by doing so, they only added weight to the reason why I was cutting in the first place.

The psychologists and psychiatrists didn't help because they kept telling my parents that it was a phase. They kept promising that it was a "teen thing" and that I would outgrow the habit by the time I was 18. But when I turned 18, I was still cutting. Then they promised I would stop cutting by 25. But when I turned 25, I was still cutting. I tried every suggestion I came across to try to stop cutting. All of them proved unsuccessful. And I might still be doing it, but then I met my inner child.

One of the leading techniques that is used in trauma integration involves a person meeting and re-parenting their childhood self.

After I went to the police with my case, I was given a small amount of crime victim's reparation money, and it allowed me to see a leading trauma specialist. She was the warmest woman I've ever met. The first time she led me through a visualization to interact with my childhood self, I couldn't stop crying. I could see how little and vulnerable I was and also how pure I was. I had felt so dark and tainted for so long that it was a shock to see this vulnerable and innocent side of myself.

A Shocking Meeting with Myself

I was actually afraid of my inner child self at first. When I would mentally go to connect with my childhood self, I was too afraid of her to touch her. I'd have to imagine other things, like angels or warrior princesses helping her or comforting her. Over time, I gained the confidence to imagine myself holding my childhood self. I began to connect with my own inner child, and I began to love her. I now think that inner-child work is revolutionary. By doing inner-child work, you are not merely addressing a symptom. You are altering the very causation of emotional trauma. But my respect for this work was about to go up yet another notch.

Some years ago, I had realized that the inner child didn't go away when a person (such as myself) grew up physically. The inner child doesn't go away for any of us—it's resident within us always. It occurred to me that anything I do to myself now, I'm ultimately doing to my inner child. Like most cutters, I had a "ritual spot" that I would go to when I wanted to cut myself. My spot of choice was the bathtub. I rifled through my stacks of old pictures in the garage, looking for the most adorably innocent picture of myself that I could find from my childhood, and I taped it up on the tile wall beside my bathtub.

Sure enough, the day came once again when I felt the frenzied craving to cut myself. I went into the bathroom, locked the door, broke a glass cup, and picked up the most intact piece of glass I could find. I stepped into the bathtub and saw the picture of myself as a little girl. At first I was almost angry at the weight of responsibility I felt when I looked at that picture. I needed relief, but this little child in the picture was staring at me with trusting and innocent eyes. Trust that I was about to betray. Innocence I was going to destroy.

I started thinking about what I was doing in the context of "everything I do to myself I do to the child within me." I began to get images of her playing and giggling. I saw myself grabbing her tiny little arm and drawing the broken glass across her arm so that it bled. I imagined her crying and pulling her arm back from me, not understanding what she had done to deserve it.

It made me feel like a child abuser. I started crying instantly at the tragedy of such an action. It was as if I reconnected with the innocence and trust that was destroyed within me as a child. I could hurt myself, an adult. But I couldn't hurt a child. I dropped the glass in the bathtub and cried while looking at that picture. My body still craved injury, but I could not bring myself to do it.

I realized the tragedy of my own life by acquainting myself with my inner child. As a result, I began to see myself as *hurt* instead of *bad*. After years of thinking that I was a lost cause and that I was unfixable, I saw that my innocence didn't go anywhere. Like the tiny flame on the end of a matchstick, it may have flickered, but it didn't die.

I found my inherent goodness again. I found the part of me that couldn't be harmed by the people who found a way to harm everything else about me. Gradually, I began to reparent myself. By loving and caring for my inner child, I learned how to love and care for myself. It ultimately resulted in the end of an addiction that I had struggled with for more than two decades.

CHAPTER 4

FINDING MY OWN PURPOSE

The Great Shortcut

Earlier in my journey, when I started observing people who loved themselves, jealousy would often get the better of me. I would find myself sitting in front of them with a giant scowl on my face. When you hate yourself and hate your life and you come across bright-eyed, bushy-tailed individuals who are happy to be alive and happy to be themselves, the first thing you want to do is kill them. It may sound a bit harsh, but you know what I mean.

I resented the way that they would just make their decisions on a whim according to what made them feel the best, as if it was as easy as that. But then it occurred to me: Maybe it *is* just as easy as that. Maybe the rest of us were going about it the hard way. It occurred to me that, at that point, I had been taking the long road to feeling good. Instead, these people who loved themselves took the shortcut. I was *chasing* happiness, but they were *choosing* happiness.

I had no idea what would make me happy, and I also didn't know what my purpose was. But now I know the truth: It's impossible to make a wrong choice on the path to happiness and on the path to finding your purpose because it's not just *one thing*. Becoming happy and finding your purpose are about every decision you make and everything you choose to do. To explain what I mean by this, I'll use a few examples from my own life.

When I was younger, I decided to be a professional model. At first glance, it was a decision that made absolutely no sense whatsoever. I was a deep thinker and a tomboy. I was extremely introverted and spent most of my free time writing.

It was a cruel, shallow, nasty business. Trying to fit myself into the world of modeling was like trying to fit a square peg into a round hole. But I know now that there are no mistakes, so this step, as ill fitting as it was, was still valuable to me in many ways. But it surely wasn't my life's calling.

Choosing Between College and a Root Canal

In 2006, while still seeking my path, I decided to go to college and had settled on a major in philosophy. Having come from a highly educated family, I was convinced that if I got a degree, I would gain more credibility and respect . . . but there's just one problem. I *hate* classroom learning. I would sit in the dark auditoriums and listen to the lectures, feeling as if I'd rather be undergoing a root canal.

I'd stare at the faces of the other philosophy students, wondering if the only people who care about philosophy are like me—depressed, passively suicidal, and trying desperately to find some kind of meaning in life. It dawned on me after my first month that no good was ever going to come out of a degree in philosophy. Once we graduated, no one was ever going to pay us to sit in a room and *think*.

When I asked myself, *Why do I want credibility and respect anyway?*, the answer I received was that it would feel good to have credibility and respect. Suddenly I made no sense to myself. Here I was sitting in college, miserable and hating every minute of it because I wanted to feel *good*? In other words, I'm feeling bad now because I think that feeling bad now is going to make me eventually feel good? It was mixed up.

Granted, because I have a philosophical mind, I usually knew how to make these mental riddles make sense. But no matter how you spin it, this one didn't make sense. Instead of being brave enough to go straight for what felt good, I was trying to feel good in a roundabout way. So I asked myself, *What would someone who loves themselves do?*

I knew the answer immediately. I'd do what made me feel good right here and now. What made me feel good? Winter sports. I loved the feeling of freedom that arose from gliding over the frictionless surface of the ice to the clapping sound of long-track speed skates. To be honest, skiing was my true love. A year earlier, after making the U.S. Telemark Ski Racing Team, but finding no sponsors to support my ski-racing career, I had officially traded in my skis for speed skates. I thought I would become a competitive long-track speed skater.

I figured being any kind of winter sports athlete is better than not being one at all, but I wasn't the best speed skater in the world. I didn't start speed skating at age three, and I didn't start speed skating after a lifetime of in-line racing like most of the other professional speed skaters did. I had potential and that was all. But I still loved every minute of it.

Seeking Another Shortcut to Happiness

When I had asked myself, *What would someone who loves themselves do?*, the answer was, *Quit school and dedicate yourself to speed skating full-time, and don't ever look back.* So I did. I took the shortcut to happiness and began to live my life according to the question, *What would someone who loves themselves do?* That was when I started to really enjoy my life. I was following my passion, and it was great.

But not long after, I found myself at a decision point again. I was putting myself into premature menopause with my grueling training schedule, and the physical damage done to my reproductive organs during childhood meant that my window for having children was very slim already. I had a sit-down talk with two separate gynecologists, who both concurred that if I continued training at that pace, I might never have children.

I was faced with a serious decision. Is it more important to have a child, or chase my Olympic dream? In my teens, I had lost four babies in total, one set of twins and two other pregnancies, to forcible abortions performed by Doc himself. I felt a deep need within me to know what it would be like to actually hold my own baby instead of lose it. I felt like some part of me would not be complete if I never experienced it going right at least once.

At the time, I was also newly married and so together my husband and I decided that it was more important to both of us to have a child. Still, it was difficult to conceive. I had to work with an infertility specialist, but we managed to have a healthy baby boy.

When my son was born, I was faced with another decision: Do I want to live a quiet, private life and remain a stay-at-home mom, or do I want to come out about my past and help other people to improve their own lives by offering what I know, and what I've learned, to the world?

You already know the answer I gave to that question.

But here's the best part about all this: I can't help but laugh when I think about how it all came together. When I was modeling, I learned how to present myself in an extroverted way. I became comfortable with the camera and with crowds. Now, most of my life is spent in front of a camera and in front of crowds.

When I was doing professional sports, I realized that I couldn't excel at them unless I faced my inner demons and began to heal them. I was rehabilitated and empowered by sports. I had to live a healthy life in order to succeed. As a result, I got better and better. I got healthy. I learned how to deal with pressure. I became brave enough to step into the public eye. It was the perfect preparation for the career I have today.

Having my son caused me to embrace my extrasensory gifts, which are the platform of my profession. And best of all, those years ago in philosophy class, I dropped out after realizing that no one was ever going to pay people who graduated with philosophy degrees to sit in a room and think. But now that I have taken the direct route to happiness and live according to what someone who loves him- or herself would do, people actually do pay me to *think*!

Leading Others to Self-Love

I slowly started to take on clients—or, rather, clients started finding their way to me. It surprised me that the things I knew about this universe and the people in it, things I took for granted, were unknown to the vast majority of people. It surprised me even more that the things I knew had the capacity to genuinely help people. After a year of seeing clients, I realized to my surprise that I actually loved this life of healing-oriented work.

My greatest love had sprung from what I always considered to be my greatest hate.

I remember one particular Monday morning when I was sitting cross-legged on my bedroom floor, preparing for my first client of the day. One of the mixed blessings about coming into this life the way that I am is that it takes more effort to be physically present in my body with all of my consciousness. I astral plane instantaneously and sometimes unintentionally. I had no control of it at first and would sometimes become unconscious and collapse, but I have since developed the skill of remaining present and embodied by choice. To "astral plane" is to consciously or subconsciously shift consciousness from the perception of physical to the perception of nonphysical, which is not limited by distance and time.

My open and conscious connection to my nonphysical self (what many people call the higher self) was not lost during childhood. Because of this, I did not lose memory of what was before I came into this life, nor what will be upon death.

So I came into this life endowed with objective universal truths, and one of the benefits of this gift is that I can access the Akashic records. The Akashic records are the totality of information about all that ever was and is, which is encoded in the nonphysical plane of existence, also referred to as the Mind of God. It is a collection of unlimited information that can be accessed from a state of source-like consciousness, such as when one is in meditation, or astral planing, or under hypnosis.

This means that depending on my state, I have accurate awareness of past lives. It is a form of retrocognition. When I meet people, quite often flashes of images from their lives and childhoods and even past lives flood into my awareness, which can serve as either a tool or a hindrance when I am trying to focus on them here on this earth, standing before me. To overcome this, I have to consciously ground myself before meeting with people one-on-one, especially when all my conscious focus is required in the here and now.

So on this particular Monday morning, I was just completing my process of becoming grounded, when the doorbell rang at 11:00 on the dot. On the other side of the door stood Linda, a 43-year-old woman who, despite her age, was the size of a middle-school student. Her rusty pickup truck was parked outside the house, and it was still smoking. Her hair was falling out, and underneath her skinny frame that looked as thin as a willow sprig, there was a resident sadness protected by a haphazard, masculine demeanor.

Exploring the Roots of Blame and Self-Loathing

As she stepped through the door, I was inundated by images of her as a child lying in a crib and crying with no one to pick her up. I saw an image of her sitting on the wooden stairs in her house, feeling as if she didn't belong, her mother chastising her for not picking up her toys. I saw the emotional deprivation of her childhood, and I also saw images of her father coming to her bed at night when she was a young teenager to proposition her for sex. As usual, having trained myself to do it, I took the information and, without reacting to it, put it to the side of my mind so I could observe her various energy systems and her body and allow her to open up to me.

We sat in my therapy room, and Linda started off by informing me that she didn't know why she was here. She didn't believe in all this spiritual woo-woo stuff, but she had been diagnosed with MS and it was affecting her job so much that she felt desperate enough to give it a try.

I began by asking her what she was having trouble with exactly, and she explained that she was a construction worker so she had to stand on the side of the road every day. She would experience dizzy spells and then her legs would begin to tingle and go numb; if she didn't sit down, she would collapse and be unable to walk for the remainder of the day unassisted by a cane.

At this point, Linda asked me if I was going to do energy healing because she heard that I could do that. I told her maybe eventually, but I don't like to treat the symptoms of an illness— I'd rather treat the cause. She looked uncomfortable. I asked her if she was really willing to dive deep inside herself to figure out what the problem was. She nodded her head in the same way that someone does before they are about to bungee jump.

I asked her to pretend that she lived in a world where physical conditions were caused by difficult emotional and mental problems that people were facing. I then asked her, "What difficult mental or emotional thing are you facing or have you faced around the time that you started feeling the symptoms of your MS occur?" I wanted to see how conscious she was of the effect that her past had had on her emotional condition.

She replied, "Well, I have a feeling that I'm dying. It's like my body isn't absorbing any food anymore. I get skinnier and skinnier and I don't know why."

I gently asked her, "Do you *want* to live?" She looked at me with this shocked expression and stayed silent for a few minutes, trying to suppress her emotion, until she finally started weeping.

"No," she wailed. I kneeled beside her chair, holding her while the emotion escaped her in great heaving sobs. When she started back up again, she told me that she was so lonely, but that she just couldn't get close to anyone and that she had even thought she was a lesbian for a time because she was so afraid of men.

I asked her, "Do you know why you feel that way about men?"

"Well, my dad used to sleep with me when my mom was pregnant."

I told her, "That's enough to do it, right there." Linda started crying again and explained that that was the only time that either of her parents ever gave her approval and that she felt so guilty because she actually wanted to feel that way. Her father would sleep with her and then tell her that because she was so pretty, he just couldn't sleep in his own bed. He told her that she was his favorite, and so this was their little secret.

After I explained to her that her reaction of wanting his affection, despite being scared, was a perfectly normal reaction to sexual trauma, I asked her how she felt about herself.

"I'm okay," she replied.

"Do you want to know what I think?" I asked. "I think you hate yourself and wish you were never born." Again, Linda started sobbing.

"Yes, you're right," she admitted. As is common with so many abuse survivors, the blame is internalized, and self-loathing becomes second nature.

How Disease Takes Over

Over the next hour, I informed Linda of every perception I had about her and proceeded to tell her that she was correct about the feeling that she was dying. I explained that when someone doesn't really want to live because his or her life is so hard, the body begins to give out. It is a form of passive suicide. On top of MS, her body was slowly starving itself to death.

I went on to explain that MS is a disease that belongs to people who try to be all things to all people because they're convinced that that is the only way to be loved. The stress and the pressure is too much, and since they won't ask for help, their bodies eventually give out, forcing them to cut back and get help from others. I told her it was a message to let other people take responsibility for their lives and for her to focus on her and only her.

Linda's problem was self-love. She had none. And because she had none, she couldn't accept love from other people either. On an energetic level, living without love is like the body trying to live without water. Together, we designed a manageable program with day-to-day practices around the core of self-love. Maybe because she was ready or maybe because she was desperate, Linda saw me every other week for six months. She applied every process I have outlined in this book. She learned to base every decision on self-love. And just one year later, she was like a different person. Her entire life had changed.

The Powerful Impact of Self-Love

The week after our first visit, Linda called to inform me that she had gone through her wardrobe and realized that the only colors she wore were black and brown. She told me that she sat down on her bedroom floor with a printed picture of a color palette. She asked herself, *What would someone who loves themselves do?* while looking at the color palette and immediately felt drawn to the swatch of pastel pink.

She confessed to me that she always thought she hated pink. But actually, she had associated it with girlie girls and she knew that girlie girls were vulnerable. She didn't want to be vulnerable, so she rejected pink. Because she didn't ever want to feel vulnerable again, she also rejected men and she rejected any aspect of her own femininity. She rejected her own personality, and she even chose what she considered to be a masculine job.

Two weeks after our first visit, Linda confessed to me that she had discovered that she had always hated her job, standing in the hot sun and pavement fumes, being yelled at by drivers. So she quit. She determined that her true passion was plants.

Three weeks after our first visit, she came to my house and started crying the minute I opened the door. She said, "This is the hardest thing I've ever done in my life. I've had to change everything—I mean *everything*—and I'm starting to realize that I don't even know who I am."

It's a normal reaction to have. At first, it feels good to finally honor yourself after years of self-neglect. But then, honoring yourself means thrusting yourself into a world of uncertainty and discarding nearly everything you thought you wanted, trading it in for a brand-new life.

Starting over isn't easy. It can be downright torture. But as Linda found out, the pain of rewriting your life in the name of self-love will never compare to living the half life of being disconnected from your true self. Over the course of the first year we worked together, Linda moved to California to be near the ocean. She took out a loan to buy a little plot of land, which she lived on in a walled tent. She started growing medicinal herbs and eventually opened an online store where she sold her natural body products.

Two years later, a chain of health food stores started carrying her products, and because she could afford it, she bought a little farm. Her hair started growing back, and after she settled on a diet that felt right for her, she began to gain some weight. She started dating a man who used to come to her farm to buy fresh herbs for his small local restaurant. They were married, and despite Linda's doubts about being able to conceive, they recently had their first baby. And to the astonishment of her doctors, she has not had a single MS symptom for over a year.

Linda's case is just one example of what can happen when you start to love yourself enough to care how you feel, and care how you feel enough to make the right choices for your life. Linda did not turn her life around because someone else did something to heal her. She didn't find a miracle cure. She turned her life around because she was brave enough to begin to allow herself to have what she had always thought she had to be given by others. She was brave enough to risk everything in the name of learning to love herself.

CHAPTER 5

SYNCHRONICITY

A Point of Life Transition

My life had turned around. I had enjoyed the experience of being a professional athlete, I was living the life of an organic health advocate, I had a husband, and our son was two years old. At that time, I was seeing private clients for one-on-one sessions as a medical intuitive and spiritual guide. One day, I was driving down a road in Salt Lake City, and stopped at a light. To my right, I saw a man digging through a trash can. Every time I see someone who is homeless, I feel as if I am watching a life parallel to my own.

Many people feel a wide degree of separation between themselves and society's "untouchables," but I feel that there is only a gap about the width of a hair that separates the life that I am living now from the life that they are living; only a handful of circumstances that panned out differently. As I watched this man rifle though the garbage, I thought, *That could be me. That might still be me, given a few more misfortunes.*

The Sculptor in the Sky

As I pulled the car away that day, a desire was born within me: the desire to reach a larger audience with my message. I didn't just want to teach individual clients; I wanted to teach the world, and I had to find a way to make life-improvement knowledge accessible to those who couldn't afford a personal session. With that passion burning within me, I sat down that night to begin my first book.

It's as if I sat down with the pen and paper with my past self in mind, the self that was sitting in that train station high on a forced injection of heroin. I kept thinking, *What would I want to tell that 18-year-old girl about the world? What would I tell her about life that might change her perspective enough about this universe that she could begin to improve her situation?*

Within three months, I had written my first book, *The Sculptor in the Sky,* which is about the universe, how it works, why happiness is important to the universe at large, and how to find happiness. That same year, I held my very first Synchronization workshop. Twenty people attended. People started writing articles about me for small periodicals. Some of the articles were flattering; others were libelous and left me under the covers of my bed, crying. But within a very short amount of time, I developed a following.

Every time I would ask myself, *What would someone who loves themselves do?* I was directed to do another interview, another article, another guided meditation, another workshop, and as a result, my career took off. I began an online series on YouTube called *Ask Teal.* Every Saturday, I select a question or a subject from the thousands of submissions that I get, and I answer the question and talk about my perspective on the subject in video format. In the first year, the series gained millions of views.

I also started painting energy on canvas, and I called these art pieces *frequency paintings*. Because of the extrasensory abilities that I came into this life with, I am able to perceive the energetic vibrational reality that makes up the physical world you see around you. My frequency paintings represent the energetic vibrational frequency of whatever that specific subject matter is that I decide to paint.

I created these paintings because I knew that by focusing on these frequencies and having them in their living space, people's energy would start to "entrain with" and "resonate with" the same frequency and amplitude of the vibrations I drew, which would in turn help them amplify and manifest the presence of the subject matter into their lives.

I have since created more than a hundred of these paintings, and they became part of a "Frequency Billboard Campaign." This campaign is designed to use these frequencies to positively impact the collective conscious. We select populated areas that have an overall low vibration and that many people pass by on their commute, knowing that these frequencies will work in their select areas like a giant homeopathic remedy for the human race, positively affecting anyone who shares the space with them or observes them.

A Glimpse of Reality

When I showed up at my first international workshop in London, England, and looked out into an audience of more than 400, I had no idea, at that point, the impact I had made on people's lives. At home, I feel like a nutty professor, tinkering around with my theories and processes. At home, I don't feel like the icon of spiritual truth that I have ultimately become.

Yet suddenly, here I was being embraced by men and women in tears because they felt like my material changed their lives. Sitting in the hotel room after that first overseas workshop, I kept thinking, *This is so much bigger than me.* The big picture of my life began to make sense. Like a first-edition puzzle that had no picture on the box, for years my life gave no clue about what it was all adding up to. Still one piece fit into another piece, until the picture of my life made sense.

The overall path was not a pretty one. I came into this life bent in the direction of torture and hell. I was the very definition of a victim. But my choice was to either die or commit to life completely. I chose life. I pieced the bent and broken shards of my life together to make a new life. I walked out of hell, and I left bread crumbs along the way so I could show other people how to do it, too. And here they were, listening. Here they were doing it.

Now I realize that I couldn't stop doing this job if I tried. Looking back and reading the journals I wrote when I was young, it's obvious that writing, speaking, and giving rise to philosophies about life is something that I have always done. It is second nature. My purpose fell in my lap, like it always does, as if there was never any other way that my life could have gone.

Some people call my vision for this world lofty, but then I remind them that I am no stranger to beating the odds. I believe that the odds are not as stacked against me as people would believe. I believe that people all around the world are ready for lasting change.

Bringing Synchronization to Life

Hundreds of people file into their chairs the hour before one of my Synchronization workshops begins. Sitting in the greenroom, sometimes I can hear the murmur of their voices.

I listen to music to get myself into the mood for the group experience. I greet my security team. When the time comes to step onstage, I make my way backstage through boxes, props, and lighting equipment and stand behind the curtain while my microphone is being fitted.

Through the crack of the curtain, I can see the faces of the crowd. I can hear the heavy sound of the introduction that calls me onto center stage. I sit down in one of the two chairs that are positioned onstage. The spotlights are bright and they make the room appear to glitter, bathing me in a surreal warmth that I have come to love. Looking out across the crowd, I can see their energy fields diffusing into one another. I can see the patterns appear in their auras as they react to me. The most dominant patterns in a person's energy field stand out to me as clear as day.

Whenever I visit a new city, the people there want to know two things, so that is what I usually start my session with. They want to know what the strongest collective positive vibration of the city is, and what the most prevalent negative vibration is. In the same way that a food critic critiques food, I have become well respected as an "energy critic."

For example, if I visit a town like Boston, where people adhere to the philosophy "Mind your own business," I often see the pattern of loneliness in the energy there. With loneliness, the aura field folds in on itself, not allowing itself to merge with anything on the outside of itself.

And in Los Angeles, the dominant negative vibration is poisonous ambition, which makes it one of the most cutthroat cities in the world. But interestingly enough, the dominant positive vibration is ambition, which is ironically the positive flip side of poisonous ambition.

A Synchronistic Group Experience

As I look out into the crowd at any of my workshops, I can see the vibrations that the participants share, both positive and negative. I then decide what I am going to teach about based on what I see. I choose the dominant negative vibration that people are collectively holding as my theme for the day. I do this for a very good reason. The positive vibrations that people hold are already working for them, so I don't need to focus on those.

Instead, they come to me seeking help for what troubles them, for what isn't working, and I can see it in the collective energy fields in the room. So, for example, if I see that the collective vibration that people are struggling with is loneliness, I open by talking about loneliness and togetherness.

Reading the energy and choosing an overall theme are both exciting and nerve-racking because I cannot prepare for my own events. I don't know what I will teach about until the minute I am sitting in front of my audience. I don't know what questions I will be asked until they are asked live in front of everyone. But this is also how the greatest healing occurs.

For people to take part in the same experience within reality, they have to be a vibrational match. This means that they have to have enough in common to be drawn together in that specific place and time. This is grand-scale synchronicity, and it's why every Synchronization workshop that I host is unique and is a creation in and of itself. People often fly from countries around the world to attend, and no matter how far apart they live from one another or what language they speak, one thing is sure: If they are able to physically attend, their vibrations match those of each of the other participants in the room perfectly.

Even though the majority of my Synchronization workshops take the shape of questions and answers, they are above all a collective healing experience. I have people raise their hands if they have a question, as if they were in grade school all over again. The energy around the person whose question most closely matches the collective subconscious of the group will light up visually as if a light source is being projected through his or her aura. I call them to the stage and they sit opposite me so they can ask their questions in front of the crowd.

With these workshops, I have created a way for men and women who feel isolated in their beliefs and struggles to come together with each other and to unite with a group of people who accepts and welcomes them exactly as they are. They find out that they are not only acceptable, but also lovable even with their shadowy aspects in tow. I may be the reason they have all come together, but like any facilitator, I am enabling something much bigger than myself to take place.

As I mentioned, at these Synchronization workshops, everyone in the room is a vibrational match to one another. Therefore, anything that I say to the person with me applies to the rest of the audience as well. As I lead the person sitting with me through the microcosm of their own predicament into a state of awareness and improvement, the macrocosm experiences the same awareness and improvement, which serves as a mass healing for everyone there. The vibration within the room increases each time a new participant steps up onstage.

CHAPTER 6

Living a Life of
Self-Love

Celebrate the Little Things

When I was young, my closest neighbor in the summers was more than 16 miles away. I was isolated and did not relate to anything except my horses. Now, the path of self-love has built me a community of people. We are friends who have become family. Sleeping in my little room, I can feel their presence filling up the house, which is so lived in it is worn. I paint my frequency paintings on the easel in my healing room. I sit cross-legged on my bed, recording my latest insights on my laptop computer.

It's not the extraordinary aspects of my life that cause me the most pleasure. It's the fact that dawn has come to my life. Years ago, when my life was shrouded in shadow, I could not see the light at the end of the tunnel. Nothing held joy for me. In fact, the things that other people enjoyed, like sunsets or parties or vacations, used to cause me pain. It was like I lived my life behind a prison of glass. I could see out, but they could not see in. I couldn't touch joy like they could.

Now listening to big-band jazz while I'm stuffing green peppers in the kitchen, with the cross breeze floating through the room and the homey scent of rhubarb pie in the oven, and hearing the distant sounds of laughter and play from the people that I love, who are all sitting on the back porch, I am thinking, *This is joy*. I finally know what it feels like.

Even so, my life is not perfect. It would be a lie to say that everything is wonderful now. I still struggle with the aftermath of the trauma that happened. I still struggle with people who think that I'm a fraud and that I made up the story of what happened to me to make money. I even receive death threats in the mail from individuals who hate me and hate what I'm doing.

Fame is like living under a magnifying glass, as it amplifies all aspects of life. It amplifies the good things and also amplifies the bad. Needless to say, joy is not something that I feel all the time. The sun has not come up completely in my own life yet. But now that dawn has come, I can feel its rays against my cheek from time to time, and I can taste the promise that my future holds.

I cannot say that I would do it all over again if I were given the chance, but I can say that the light that has come with this new dawn has revealed the beauty of the shadow to me. I can see now that there were immense gifts contained in the darkness I endured. It took seeing the light to see the beauty inherent in the darkness.

A Path of Ease

I had to claw my way through my life, oftentimes on hands and knees, to this place of freedom, joy, and love that I stand in today. Upon reflection, it has become clear that I didn't get here because of effort or because I clawed my way here. I got here by virtue of *learning to accept and learning to love.*

Once you begin practicing some of the techniques in the Tool Kit, I hope you accept and understand, as I do, that the painful parts of our lives don't come up to torment us and ruin our lives. They appear so that we can learn how to embrace ourselves with compassion and be healed. When we struggle against part of ourselves, we cannot heal. Your love will always be conditional as long as you are excluding any part of yourself from your love, including your pain.

Pain cannot be healed by hating yourself; it can only ever be healed by loving yourself. Self-hate is like quicksand: When you struggle, it just causes you to sink deeper and deeper until you cannot breathe. But if you stop struggling, you can set yourself free.

Self-love, then, is not a destination we need to struggle to get to, but rather a state of being that is available to us in each new moment. We simply need to let it in. Allow it.

You will reach the essence of who you are and that is love. Your inner essence can't be harmed or lost. The most you can ever do is prevent it from flowing through you, but even that you can turn around with self-love.

Each moment you take one step forward is a brand-new moment, and you are a brand-new you. Be gentle with yourself. You are a precious piece of this world. This world could not be complete without you. You are priceless not because of what you do; you are priceless because you exist. You don't know it yet, but with time you will come to know that you are, in fact, the love of your life.

Recognizing One's Own Most Amazing Shift

My own bent and broken life finally reads more like a success story. For the first time, like looking at a completed puzzle, I can see the full picture of my life. I know the reasons why I experienced what I did as a child. I feel my purpose, and I finally know what I am really here to do. Some years ago, I experienced the most amazing thing. For the first time in my life, I turned to someone and said, "I *love* my life."

So what did I do that caused this miraculous shift to occur— moving from wanting to commit suicide, which is the ultimate act of self-hate, to the point of loving my life? The answer is quite simple: *I had incrementally taught myself how to love myself.*

What I've discovered is that no matter what kind of childhood someone had (unless they were raised by wolves), they always struggle with self-love. As suffering often does, it opened the door within me to an enlightenment experience. I walked through that door, and now it is my belief that my extrasensory abilities, coupled with the depth of self-hate that I experienced as a result of my childhood, have enabled me to guide anyone from the starting point of self-hate to the experience of self-love. And that is how I created the lessons and techniques that form the rest of this book, my Tool Kit to Self-Love.

PART TWO

The Self-Love Tool Kit

INTRODUCTION

USING THE SELF-LOVE TOOL KIT

Cultivating Flowers of Self-Love

Have you ever heard of the saying "If you want to kill a weed, you have to pull it up by the roots"? This is exactly what we need to do with self-hate. We need to pull it up by the roots and replace it with self-love. When you replace self-hate with self-love, the weeds of your life disappear, and they are replaced by flowers. Every single external circumstance of your life improves. Self-love is the highest state of all. If you have it, you have happiness. If you begin to cultivate self-love, everything you have ever wanted for yourself and your life will come to be.

So how do you do this? In the field of self-help, there are a million and a half modalities and techniques that can help you live a better life. There are so many ideas and techniques we can use to improve our life that it can become overwhelming. But in truth, they could all be abandoned for one thing: *learning to love yourself.* That is why I often say that self-love is the great shortcut. If we learn to love ourselves genuinely, we will embrace the whole universe.

There is only ever one single thing that we are working on in this life: self-love. When you say, "I love you," it is actually self-love. In this world of apparent duality, you may see a difference between yourself and the world around you. But in reality, this separation doesn't exist. Everything in your life is, in fact, a projection of yourself.

Cultivating compassion is cultivating self-love. Helping others is self-love. Forgiving someone else is self-love. You can't hold one tiny shred of resistance toward anything and truly love yourself. But if you are reading this book, it is highly likely that you don't know how to love yourself.

Virtually all of you reading this have been taught that to love yourself is selfish. You have been taught that people who love themselves don't care about other people. You have been taught that you are imperfect and that the purpose of your life here on planet Earth is to find out how to be *better.* And you have been taught that to be loved, you must be good. In fact, you have been led to believe that your only hope of being loved is to reach the standards that people around you consider "success."

And perhaps most damaging of all, you have been taught that in order to be a good person and to be loved, you must punish yourself when you don't meet those standards. This book is built upon the premise that this simply is not true.

One of the biggest collective human disorders is the belief that *we are not enough.* It is this belief, which we can call a pure lack of self-love, that permeates out to create lack in all other aspects of a person's life. Most people do not truly love themselves. If you are one of these people who believe you are not enough, and therefore do not love yourself yet, you are not alone. And this book is for you.

Where Does Self-Hate Come From?

To start with, I want to explain how we ended up this way. None of us were loved perfectly as children. That is the task of our lives here. We have come to this earth to learn how to love ourselves. It doesn't take an abusive childhood to develop self-hate. Self-hate is cultured by the very society we live in. It is reinforced even by "good parents."

The process that teaches us self-hate is called socialization. No matter how healthy your childhood was, chances are that as a child, you heard at least some of the following statements, and they were imprinted on you: *Shame on you; look what you did. Stop that; put that down. No, no, no. I can't believe you sometimes—didn't you learn your lesson? You know better than that.*

You can probably still hear many negative refrains in your head: *Bad girl. Bad boy. I told you so. Because I said so. Who do you think you are? How dare you? Don't you talk back to me. You shouldn't feel that way. Serves you right. Don't you ever think about anyone but yourself?*

The adults in your childhood didn't do this to deliberately hurt you. They were simply socializing you the only way they knew how. They raised you the same way that they were raised and the same way their grandparents were raised and the same way their great-grandparents were raised.

When you were growing up, your parents probably felt like everyone else: powerless to their own lives. They couldn't live with themselves if they thought of themselves as selfish, so they wouldn't admit that the real reason they were doing things "for you" and wanted you to behave in certain ways was really *for them*. Not for you.

Parents and adults in our society found a way to preserve their own self-concept, and that was through feeding themselves, as well as you, with the belief "It's for your own good." We are fed this lie from day one. Even those of us who grow up in the most loving households are fed this lie. We make our children sit through hours of lessons in the prison-like environment we call school and tell them it's for their own good. We discipline them in ways that are painful to their minds and bodies and tell them that it's for their own good.

Furthermore, we tell our children that their desires are inappropriate and that they need to choose other desires, and we tell them that it's for their own good. But herein lies the problem. As children, we begin to believe that maybe our parents are right. We start to think, *Maybe it is for my own good.* We believe our parents must know more about the world than we do since, after all, our parents seem to control our very survival.

Confusing Messages That Stay with Us for Life

In this way, we are influenced into believing that something that causes us pain is for our own good. We begin to believe that pleasure is bad for us and that pain is good for us. When our parents kept saying, "I love you, and I'm doing this for your own good," at the same time that they were causing us pain, we started to believe that love *is* pain. We started to think that we can't trust ourselves.

We naturally feel that our internal, emotional guidance system is leading us astray. After all, it's telling us we feel joy, when we are doing something that Mom says is bad for us and it's telling us we feel pain when we are doing something that Mom says is good for us. Is it any wonder, then, that after a while we think something has gone wrong if we are experiencing ease or pleasure? We distrust our desires. We let go of the idea that our own happiness is important.

The minute we believe that pain, suffering, and self-hatred make us good and get us love, we can't let go of pain, because we actually think that pain serves us. We become dedicated to perpetuating pain and defending it within ourselves. We become convinced that if we let go of pain and go in the direction of pleasure and self-love, we will be a menace to society, bad, forsaken, *unlovable.*

Again, your parents did not deliberately do this to hurt you, but they didn't understand that this kind of treatment would lead you to come to a very sad conclusion: "I am not good enough." You concluded that if you were not getting the love you naturally needed from them, it must somehow be your fault. Even though this assumption was incorrect, this assumption was the beginning of the cycle of self-hate in your life.

Punishment and Reward

Socialization is designed to keep societal order and keep people "good." The problem is that society thinks in terms of punishment and reward and therefore teaches us that in order to be loved and accepted, we have to be good. And it teaches us that in order to be good, we must punish ourselves. We are taught that good people look for the flaws in themselves and others, judge those flaws, and then punish themselves or others for those flaws until they change. You can see how this model for socialization works not only in our homes but also in the education and justice systems.

At this point, self-hate is such a normal condition in our world that we don't even realize that nearly everyone does it. Self-hate is not just a part of the lives of people who are addicted to drugs, cutting, overeating, starving themselves, prostituting, or committing crimes. Those are just examples of behaviors where self-hate is acting in overt ways instead of covert ways. Self-hate takes many forms, many of them just as harmful but not seen.

By the time we are adults, we hold a firm, untouchable belief that we are inherently bad, and that without punishment, the *bad* in us will triumph over the *good* in us and we will be unlovable.

Self-hate is an autonomous, endless process of self-conditioning and is the result of standards that you will never meet. It ensures that as long as you exist, you will always find something to hate about yourself—until you break the cycle.

But it's a hard cycle to break, and here's why. We are taught that to love ourselves is selfish and therefore bad. Our only hope of getting love is from other people, and to get it we must meet the standards of what others consider to be "good." We adopt their expectations as our own and punish ourselves if we fall short of them. But we will always fall short of them because those expectations are not our *own* real expectations, and they do not mirror our actual desires.

Furthermore, the kind of love we get from reaching other people's expectations is not real love because we had to change ourselves to get it. Society tells us we must be flawed, then, and once we start to focus on our flaws, all we find are more flaws. We then do the only thing we can think of, which is to try harder. And so the cycle continues.

Not surprisingly, then, we get more lost, more confused, and our lives get worse, mired in self-hatred and hopelessness. Trying to move forward in our lives when we hate ourselves is like trying to drive with the parking brake on. We are caught between a rock and a hard place. The only way to break free is to recognize the cycle of self-hate that we're caught in.

How to Use the Tool Kit to Self-Love

Once you recognize that you are stuck in an endless cycle and admit to yourself that your life isn't working, you can begin to examine the faulty beliefs about love you are holding on to. When you begin this process, it may feel like you are going down the path to certain doom. After all, you've been taught that only bad people love themselves, but be patient with yourself. The reason you are most likely reading this book is that you have already recognized that you can't keep doing things the way you have been doing them.

I applaud you for deciding that it's worth the risk to at least try something new, on the off chance that it might work. Open your mind and heart and remember that if anything set forth in this book doesn't work for you, you can always go back to doing what you have been doing.

I've constructed this section like a tool kit to help you. Each chapter will provide you with a different tool or technique, a new way to view things, which you can use to teach yourself self-love. Don't expect to apply every suggestion and institute every change that I am suggesting at once, or you will soon become overwhelmed and give up. Instead, choose only one or two things (techniques, tools, or ideas) to work with at a time. As you try even small steps, you will gain confidence in yourself and the process.

You may find that after you read through the whole book once, you'll want to focus on one specific chapter at a time and integrate the information contained in that chapter into your life. You will intuitively feel drawn toward making the changes that will benefit you most at any given time.

Another good way to use this book is to wake up in the morning and allow the universe to decide for you what you need to focus on for the day or the week. To do this, simply hold the book in your hand and allow it to fall open to any page. Allow your eyes to be naturally drawn to a sentence, paragraph, or page that you see. Take what you read as guidance from the universe, and reflect on what you have read throughout the day or week.

Don't be afraid that you won't know what to do with the information you have learned throughout this book. It is my promise that you will find a way to integrate it into your life. You may reread this book only to find that you have made some of these changes entirely on your own, as a result of other things that you have begun to do.

As you can see, there is no right or wrong way to use this information or apply it to your life. The fact that you even picked up this book in the first place guarantees that you are already committed to finding a way to love yourself.

365 Days of Self-Love

One Whole Year of Self-Love

Right now, for you to say "I love myself" might feel more like lying to yourself than telling the truth. For you to say this statement would contradict your own sense of intelligence and therefore make you more aware of where you *aren't* rather than making you feel good about where you are. But the best thing you can do for yourself if you don't love yourself yet is to begin to *act as if you do*. This will start to undermine the power that self-hate currently has over your actions.

For this reason, the journey from self-hate to self-love begins with a commitment. I call this commitment 365 Days of Self-Love, and it is a stepping-stone to helping you close the gap between wherever you are now and self-love, which is where you ultimately want to be.

In the current life you are living, you most likely struggle with making decisions and commitments because the basis on which you make your decisions is not one of self-love. Instead, you likely make your decisions based on things like principle, wanting approval, or symptom relief. But in order to live the life you were meant to live, you have got to get back in touch with your own personal truth and your own personal joy. Those two things need to become the principal motivations for any decision you make. Self-love needs to be the foundation that you lay first, and then the second step is to build the details of your life upon it.

To make this commitment, get a calendar and mark the day you plan to begin. Then, mark the day you plan to end, 365 days later. Once you have done that, it is time to make the actual commitment. For exactly a year, every single day, you are going to commit to live your life according to this mantra: *What would someone who loves themselves do?*

This sounds simple but it would benefit you to say it out loud right now: "What would someone who loves themselves do?" Get used to it, because you are going to be saying it all the time. You are going to ask yourself this question any time you have to make a decision, no matter how small or large.

Basically, then, all day, every day for an entire year, you will live your life according to this one simple question. When you ask this question, the answer will come to you immediately, as a flash of intuition. Intuition is defined as a sudden insight or under-standing without conscious reasoning. It comes as a knowing, gut feeling, thought, image, emotion, or bodily sensation.

Many of us have learned to tune out or ignore our own intuition, but by practicing this simple mantra, you can get back in touch with your natural gift of intuition, a gift we all have. The good news is that even if you may have shut out messages from your core self for years, the core self continues to give them, so it is impossible to completely lose your intuition.

Listen Well and Take Action

To truly listen for intuition means to listen with all your senses. Intuitive messages come in many ways, and they come differently to different people. Ask yourself a question inside your head, and you may hear or see the answer. You may just *know* the answer. You may get a physical sensation such as a chill or hot flash or feel the answer emotionally. As you practice listening and honoring your intuition, you will get better at recognizing the ways by which you receive intuitive information, however it might appear.

Whenever you ask yourself, *What would someone who loves themselves do?*, you are going to receive the correct answer for you personally in the form of intuition. The answer will come to you immediately. It will pop into your head. And then you will be ready for the next part of the process, the part where you take action.

The action part of this process is where you are going to act on the answer you receive. You are going to heed your intuition and go in the direction of whatever is in line with self-love.

For example, let's say you are at home and you have a million things you could be doing, but you can't decide what the priority is. You're going to ask yourself, *What would someone who loves themselves do?* Listen to your internal response. If the answer is to go take a bath, you're going to go take a bath. If the answer is clean the house, you're going to clean the house.

For 365 days, you are going to ask this question whenever you have to make a decision. Use this process if your decision is as pivotal as "Should I keep my job or quit my job?" But even if your decision is as mundane as "Should I eat an apple or an orange?" keep asking the question. There is value in being consistent and training yourself to do the loving thing, regardless of what is going on around you.

Simple Actions, Profound Changes

When you begin to apply this process, you will quickly find that you make decisions constantly throughout the day. The power behind this process is that by the end of the 365 days, it will be a habit for you to live your life in alignment with self-love. Ideally, you will be incapable of living your life any other way!

This particular process is much more profound than it may seem. When you ask, *What would someone who loves themselves do?*, it allows your intuition to deliver the answer. And when you act on that answer, everything that is preventing you from living the exact life that you want to live will be exposed.

Making this commitment will be the foundation for this journey from self-hate to self-love. Like a foundation, everything that is to follow in this book will be built on top of this commitment. In my opinion, everything contained in this book comes second to living your life according to the question, *What would someone who loves themselves do?*

If you take nothing else away from this book, that will be enough.

Tool #2

Discover That You Are Deserving

The Wicked Habit of Withholding

The biggest roadblock to achieving a state of self-love is feeling as if we don't deserve love. This pattern normally begins in childhood. This is because childhood is when we come to the conclusion that if we aren't getting something, we must not deserve it.

A baby does not come into this world with the concept that it does not deserve to have its needs met or be taken care of. A baby doesn't come into this world thinking that it doesn't deserve to have its diaper changed, be fed, be cuddled, or be nursed to sleep at night. And we as adults don't look at a baby with the idea that it doesn't deserve those things either.

But all too often, parents don't encourage personal empowerment and positive self-image in children in a loving, supportive way. Instead, adults participate in their children's dependence for a time, only to later draw an arbitrary line in the sand where they feel "put upon" by their children because they are expected to provide everything for them.

At that point, parents have a very hard time distinguishing between deserving and entitlement, and they have a tendency to suddenly give the child the impression that he or she does not deserve what the parents used to provide for them so freely. The child then comes to the only logical conclusion that can be drawn: "I must have done something wrong to deserve this." Or even worse, "Something must be wrong with me." This translates to the child feeling that he or she must be *bad*.

In fact, we make a special point in society of letting children know that they are bad and they do not deserve good things. It's a form of punishment called *withholding,* and it happens partly because people don't really understand the difference between being entitled to something and being deserving of something.

Are You Deserving or Entitled?

For those of us who can't quite shake the belief that to think you deserve something automatically makes you an entitled, selfish person, it is very important to distinguish between entitlement and deserving.

Deserving is the deep, internal knowing that one is worthy of what one needs and wants. Therefore, the belief that you don't deserve something is an issue of *not* feeling worthy. In other words, it's a self-worth issue. The person who believes that they deserve something has internal self-worth. And that is a good thing because a person who feels as if they deserve something also has the self-worth to trust that they can get whatever they want without having to take it from anyone or anything else.

Entitlement is something else entirely. Entitlement comes from the belief that one has a right to claim what one deserves from others. Therefore, entitlement is not a belief that has anything to do with true deserving. Those who feel entitled have a deep insecurity about their own ability to get whatever they want, and this leads them to cover that insecurity with pride and with the arrogant thought that they deserve to have what they want provided for them by others.

Entitlement is a form of deep suffering, while deserving is a form of self-love. It is very important to spend time differentiating between entitlement and deserving because in order to love yourself, you must first decide that you deserve love. If something is preventing you from feeling as if you deserve love, you will always sabotage yourself when it comes time to get love.

Developing Deservability

When you are trying to encourage the belief that you deserve love, it is important to first look at your life objectively and discover the ways that you treat yourself as if you don't deserve your own love. Start by taking note of all the ways in which you treat yourself as if you don't deserve your own love and attention.

For example, do you give yourself enough attention? Do you settle for second best? When you look in the mirror, does your attention immediately gravitate toward flaws? When you are sad, do you tell yourself to "get over it"? Do you try to suppress or silence your feelings by being passive-aggressive or indulging in an addiction? Just take some time to look at your life, and write down all the ways in which you treat yourself as if you don't deserve love.

Now with that list in front of you, I want you to imagine treating someone else the way that you have just discovered you treat yourself.

For example, you may be the kind of person who tells yourself to "just get over it" if you're feeling sad or frightened. Imagine that a friend of yours called you crying. Imagine saying, "Just get over it," to her or him. Notice how bad it feels to think about saying that to your friend. It feels bad because saying that is the same as saying, "You don't deserve love." And yet as you can see, you've been doing that to yourself all along. You've been poisoning yourself from the inside out. The lesson in this exercise is that we have been taught to love others and not ourselves.

Now I would like you to take that list you've written down, and for each and every example of how you treat yourself like you don't deserve love, decide how you would rather treat yourself.

You can do this by making sure every statement you write down begins with *I am ready and willing to*_____. Fill in the blank for each item on your list—and remember, there is no right or wrong answer. The answers are going to be different for everyone. You just want to make sure that the idea of how you would rather treat yourself feels really, really good.

For example, if your original statement was, "I tell myself to just get over things," then the way you would rather treat yourself might be, "I am ready and willing to allow myself to feel the way I feel, to take the time to listen to my emotions, and to prioritize how I feel."

When you are done compiling this list of ways that you would like to treat yourself, I would like you to write down a list of five practical commitments that you can make in your life right now that line up with the new way you would like to treat yourself. They don't need to be big commitments. They just need to be commitments that you feel capable of keeping right now.

For example, if one of the statements that you came up with was the one above, "I am ready and willing to allow myself to feel the way I feel, to take the time to listen to my emotions, and to prioritize how I feel," then a commitment you could make is that every time you feel a negative emotion, you're going to get a journal and write about how you feel and why you feel that way, instead of suppressing it.

Using Visualization to Soothe Your Inner Self

The mind seems to like to adopt all kinds of beliefs that, when we take a deep look at them, seem ridiculous. The idea that you don't deserve something is one such belief. To help counter this belief, and replace it with a more positive and truthful view, I suggest that you find at least 20 minutes to sit down, close your eyes, and use the process of visualization to help you.

As you sit quietly, I want you to imagine a safe, wonderful place. This place can be real or imagined, sort of like a personal heaven inside your own mind. Now inside this safe place, I want you to imagine yourself as a child. Just let the image come into your mind, allow it to be whatever it is. You may see a child who is very young, or a child who is older. I want you to just observe yourself as a child.

Take note of what this child self is doing. Take note of how he or she looks and how it seems like he or she is feeling. Now I want you to think about whether that child you are looking at deserves happiness. I want you to think about whether that child deserves to be loved. Does that child deserve to be unhappy? Does that child deserve to be deprived? Does that child deserve to be alone and unloved?

What you will find is that you can never look at your childhood self and say that that child deserves to be unhappy, deprived, and unloved. You know better than that when it comes to a child, any child.

Now I would like you to continue to stay with this visualization and scan back through your life between the age that this child sitting in front of you is and the age that you are now. I want you to try to identify the point in your life when you suddenly became undeserving of happiness and love. Can you find it? The answer is always no.

I want you to now scan back over your life and try to find a point at which that child ceased to exist. Is there a point when that child died and suddenly an adult took its place? The answer to that question is also always no.

Now imagine going up to that child and introducing yourself. I want you to tell this child that they don't have to be strong anymore. That you're all grown up and that it's time for them to just have fun. I want you to tell this child-you that they deserve to be loved and deserve to be happy and deserve to have anything they need and want.

I want you to tell this child that you will give it to them because you are all grown up now, and you are ready to take care of them. Tell them that you love them so, so much. Tell them what you love about them.

And then I want you to imagine giving this child a big hug. Hold your child. If your child begins to cry when you do this, just let them cry. Comfort them the way you have always wanted to be comforted. Feel for the sensation of relief.

When you and your childhood self are ready, you can tell this child that you will be there to comfort them and talk to them whenever they want. Imagine that this child has *a warm bed and a favorite food to eat and a companion to play with in this safe place inside your mind. Show the child where they are and tell them that you are going to do adult things for a little while.*

When you feel as if the child is ready for you to be able to leave, hug them once more and tell them that you love them and always have and always will. Imagine tucking them into bed or watching them eat something they love to eat or running off to play with their friend.

And now, I want you to slowly direct your attention back into the room. Wiggle your toes and fingers. Take a deep breath, and open your eyes.

You've Always Been Deserving

If visualization doesn't work for you, try to find a picture of yourself as a small child. Stare at that picture and ask yourself whether that child you are looking at deserves happiness. Ask yourself whether that child deserves to be loved. Does that child deserve to be unhappy? Does that child deserve to be deprived? Does that child deserve to be alone and unloved?

Think back over your life between the time that this picture was taken and now. Try to identify the point in your life when you suddenly became undeserving of happiness and love. Can you find it? The answer is always no. Now think back over your life and try to find the point at which that child in the picture ceased to exist. Is there a point when that child died and suddenly an adult took his or her place? The answer to that question is also always no.

What these exercises reveal is that it is easy to look at a child and see that they deserve happiness and love. Every time you think thoughts that are in line with, "I don't deserve something [fill in the blank]," and every time you speak words or take actions that are in line with, "I don't deserve something [fill in the blank]," it's the same as telling that child, who still exists within you, that he or she doesn't deserve those things.

Since you would never tell a child that they don't deserve to be happy or to be loved or to have their dreams come true, why are you telling yourself that? The lesson to take from this exercise is that there was never, is never, and never will be a time in your life where you deserve anything less than your childhood self deserves.

Tuning In

The universe that we live in doesn't operate in terms of deserving or not deserving. Your deserving was not, is not, and never will be in question. It is an absolute given. There was never, is never, and never will be a time that you did not deserve love and happiness. You deserve to have anything you could ever want the minute that you want it. The reason we do not get what we want in life has absolutely nothing to do with whether we deserve it. It has to do with whether we *believe* we deserve it. It has to do with whether we are a vibrational match to what we are wanting.

The universe loves you more than you could ever know, and it operates by the law of mirroring (often called the law of attraction). This law dictates that you can experience the physical manifestation of *only* that to which you are a vibrational match.

To understand what this means, we can imagine a radio tower. The radio tower is always broadcasting the radio channel 90.1 FM. But in order to receive that station, we must first tune our own radio dial to 90.1 FM. Sticking with this analogy, the universe is the radio control tower. It is always broadcasting the channel you want. For example, it is always broadcasting the channel called *love*. But to receive *love*, you must first tune your dial to *love*.

So if it's that simple, what dictates your vibration? The answer is: Your thoughts, words and actions. What does this mean? It means you cannot be thinking thoughts like *I'm such a failure* and be a match to success. You can't think thoughts like *I'm bad at everything* and meet the people who will make you feel good about yourself or the opportunities that will make you feel self-confident. Instead, thinking thoughts like *I'm bad at everything* guarantees that you can meet only people who make you feel bad about yourself, and you'll only find yourself in situations that reinforce that you are bad at everything. You can't experience kindness if you speak cruel words. You can't have companionship if you take actions to isolate yourself.

The universe never looks at you with the eyes of doubt, disappointment, or judgment. It will only ever look at you with the knowledge that you can have anything you ever wanted the minute you turn your attention and words and actions to it, instead of resisting it or focusing only on the lack of it.

The chips are overwhelmingly stacked in your favor the minute you begin to accept that you *deserve* to be the recipient of what you are asking for, and you will find that the universe does not withhold anything from you. The minute you change your thoughts, words and actions you will experience just how fast this universe yields to you the exact physical reflection of your new thoughts, new words and new actions.

Just remember, whether you deserve something was never in question. You deserve it all. That is a given of your very existence. The universe wants you to succeed and wants you to experience abundance, freedom, and joy. But this is not the kind of universe that treats you as if you are incapable of creating those things yourself. And this means that it loves you more than you want it to sometimes!

Tool #3

The Most Important Decision That You Will Ever Make

Deciding on Happiness

Now you are ready to learn the most important part about loving yourself. But it is not knowledge that you will gain. Rather, it is a decision that you will make. It is the decision that anyone who wants to love him- or herself must make. All you need to do is decide to make how you feel the number one priority in your life—in other words, make the number one goal of your life *happiness.*

If you want to love yourself, you have to care how you feel and make how you feel the most important thing in your life.

This will allow you to go in the direction of your joy, regardless of the risks you think you will be taking.

People who love themselves make happiness their number one goal. They know that everything else falls second to that. They realize that the only motivation for anything that any person does in this life is that the person thinks it will make him or her feel better and lead to happiness.

Upon first reading this, it may not make sense, but I ask you to look deeper. This is an exercise in understanding and compassion, which may begin with other people but will eventually end with you:

Why does a mother sacrifice her own lifestyle for her children's once they are born? Because based on her beliefs, she thinks it will make her feel better to do that rather than to live selfishly for herself.

Why does a junkie shoot up drugs? Because he thinks the drugs will make him feel better than how he currently feels.

Why does a person ask someone to marry him? Because he thinks it will make him feel better if the other person says yes.

You see, anything we do, whether it is selfish or unselfish, whether it is "good" or "bad," is done for one reason and one reason only: *We think it will make us happier.*

Happiness is the only motivating force in this universe. To love yourself means to cut out the middleman. If we realize that the "how" we think we will get happiness is the middleman, we can let go of the "how" and just make happiness the goal. When you look at the various scenarios above, the sacrificing of one's lifestyle is the "how" in the mother's life. The drugs are the "how" in the junkie's life. The marriage is the "how" in the groom's life.

What's Your Motivation?

To really get this important message, we need to understand the topic of motivation. Most of us believe that the best way to motivate ourselves and others is with external, extrinsic motivation. By external motivation, we mean external rewards like money and external punishments like jail time. We can call this the carrot-and-stick approach. It can be summed up as the "If_____, then_____approach." For example, as a child, if you do the dishes, then you get your allowance.

But the carrot-and-stick approach is not the best way to create motivation. In fact, it is detrimental because this kind of motivation destroys true motivation. True motivation is internal, intrinsic motivation—the deep, intrinsic human need to direct our own lives, to learn and create new things, and to find purpose by seeking improvement.

Intrinsic motivation comes from inside because personal gratification comes from inside. We get trained away from this internal, intrinsic motivation and toward external, extrinsic motivation when we are children. We begin to abandon our intrinsic motivation because we decide that the reward of other people's approval is more important to the success of our lives than our own intrinsic motivation.

Rewards make us temporarily happy, so ironically, for the sake of our own happiness, we are externally motivated to abandon our own personal gratification for the rewards that the adults around us provide. As children, we became externally motivated to seek external rewards (like approval) and avoid punishments (like spanking). While this decision of ours was a very intelligent one as far as self-preservation is concerned, it did not—and does not—bring us true happiness. We cannot find true, internal enjoyment by this model. Instead, we feel empty because we have no internal motivation and no internal enjoyment.

Instead, we seek things outside of us to try to fill in that emptiness. As adults, we find ourselves in jobs that we hate, just because of the reward of the paycheck. We stay in relationships that are unsatisfying just because we want to avoid the disapproval of others, which we would experience if our relationship failed. We find ourselves running the rat race only because of a promise of cheese at the end, not because actually running the rat race makes us happy. It's all a matter of external incentive.

Cutting Through to Your Own Truth

We need to be completely honest with ourselves about what our true incentive and motivation is. If you are reading this book, it means that you have decided that you want to learn how to love yourself. We know now that to love yourself means to prioritize happiness over every other motivation in your life.

But what kind of happiness do you want? Do you want the temporary happiness of achieving external rewards and avoiding external punishment? Or do you want the permanent happiness of admitting to and living according to your own internal, intrinsic motivation?

Do you want a life where you are continually trying to fill up the emptiness inside you with external substitutes, or do you want a life where the emptiness is not even there, because you are living according to what brings you enjoyment and personal gratification?

Let's consider that we all want a happy life with no emptiness. The question to ask yourself, then, is, *What would I do if I had all the money in the world?* Another way to ask this question is, *What would I do even if I never got paid to do it?*

You don't need to worry about the answer to this question being something like "I'd do nothing," because that defies the nature of existence. This is, in fact, the lie we've been telling ourselves for so long: That if it weren't for the external motivations of reward and punishment, people would do *nothing*. This could not be further from the truth.

All beings are born with intrinsic motivation. Our true nature is the desire to direct our own lives, to learn and create new things, and to find purpose by seeking improvement. This is our true nature because doing this causes all beings in existence to feel enjoyment. It is its own internal reward.

Living Your Own Priority

Therefore, the most essential ingredient to prioritizing happiness is to live your life according to intrinsic motivation and not extrinsic motivation. If you prioritize having a career and doing things that are their own reward because it makes you happy to do them, you will feel good about yourself. You will begin to love yourself. Any external reward you get, like a paycheck, will just be a bonus.

The question to ask yourself is, *What is happiness worth to me?* It may take bravery to exchange our external motivations for what we know in our hearts are our internal motivations. It may take bravery to prioritize our own enjoyment over wanting to gain rewards and avoid punishments from others, but in the end, it is the only way to find lasting happiness.

When you first came into this life, you intended for happiness to be the number one goal, because it's the only motivation that there is. You knew that if you followed your own happiness throughout the world, you would run smack-dab into your purpose. You knew that if you prioritized happiness from the get-go, you would never find yourself at the point in life where you were buried so deep that hurting yourself or someone else would feel better than where you are now.

It is okay for you to want anything you could possibly want, whether that is the freedom of wealth or the freedom of a world that is not run and ruled by money, whether it is a happy marriage or the ability to roam the world uncommitted to anyone but yourself, or whether it is a mansion or a life of simplicity.

Loving yourself starts with the decision to live for your own individual happiness. Happiness and love are not finite commodities. They are infinite. Getting happy and loving yourself doesn't mean that you are taking away from anyone else's happiness. You are not hurting anyone if you prioritize happiness. Instead, that happiness will overflow within you, and the light of your happiness will lead those who live in darkness out of it. You will show other people how to find their own happiness. You will show them how through the clarity of your example.

So true self-love comes on the heels of the realization that anything other than happiness is a "how." Any desire other than happiness itself is a desire brought about by thinking about how you think you are going to get happiness.

TOOL #4

FILLING UP
YOUR OWN CUP

The Elixir of Love

It won't take forever to learn how to love yourself, but self-love is a lifelong process. When you love someone, you never ask the question, How long am I going to have to love this person? You just love them. It's no different for the relationship between you and yourself.

For the relationship between you and yourself to flourish, it needs to be maintained with love. Most of us spend our time trying to give love to others, but we never seem to take the time to give love to ourselves. This is a recipe for unhappiness in all of its many forms. We are all trying to get love from each other, but all of our "love tanks" are empty. In essence, we are like beggars who are begging from each other.

For this reason, I want to introduce an analogy to you called the cup analogy. Let's pretend that every being on this earth is a cup. So this world is made up of nothing but tightly packed cups. Love is the fluid that these cups desire to be filled with. But in this world we live in, these cups don't tip. So every attempt to show love to others by spilling our love fluid into their cups is done in vain. It doesn't work in a world where the cups do not tip.

So in this world, how would you go about filling up other people's cups? You would fill up your own cup to such an extent that it overflowed. This is the way every commodity actually works. When you fill yourself up to the point where you have enough of any commodity, the commodity overflows, and the spillover nourishes the world.

Treating Love as a Scarcity

But what about the people who base their lives on greed? At face value, they are scrambling to fill their cups with love as well, but it doesn't work. It doesn't work because greed is not a natural human condition. In fact, it's not a natural condition of any being in existence. Greed occurs only when someone feels as if they do not have enough, and that person becomes focused on lack, and convinced of the lack in their own life. It's a condition that causes deep suffering. Greed tends to occur in someone's life if they are the kind of person who *doesn't* focus on filling up their own cup. And it's most likely to occur if a person doesn't feel capable of filling up their own cup and thus feels that they need to take things from others in order to fill up their cup.

On the other hand, when we as human beings feel as if we have enough, we are naturally drawn toward sharing. In fact, sharing becomes our joy. Our feeling of abundance fills our being. But it doesn't work to tell someone else that they have enough and need to share; they have to feel that abundance themselves. If you try to tell them your truth, all this does is make them feel as if the commodity, which they have precious little of, is being taken from them.

In other words, asking someone to share what they feel they do not have enough of is no different than asking a starving child to share their food. *Scarcity is in the mind.* And scarcity of love is no different. So the moral of this analogy is that when you are starting to learn how to love yourself, you need to think in terms of filling up your own cup.

In order to help you accept this analogy of the cup, I must first address the most common resistance that people have to it. When people first set the commitment to learn how to love themselves, a feeling of sadness usually follows that very commitment. The reason for this is that most people, those who do not love themselves, desperately want to be loved by others. Therefore, committing to self-love often feels the same as having to accept that no one will ever love you and that instead you have to give up on getting love and give it to yourself instead. This is not the case at all. I do not agree with sayings like "everything you want or need can only come from within" or "no one will love you until you love yourself." The journey of self-love has nothing to do with being loved by others or not. It has to do with your relationship with yourself. The point of self-love is not to get to a point where you do not need other people. As a species, people need other people to be in a state of health and happiness. If anything, the point of self-love is to heal so as to line-up with loving relationships. The analogy of the cup is simply intended to cause a shift in perspective that will cause you to feel less of a scarcity of love in your life.

Like Flowers Opening to the Sun

If I were to ask you right now to list some ways that you could show love to someone else, you could most likely give me some examples. This is because we have become accustomed to the idea of giving to others.

But now I want you to come up with a list of ways that you could show love to yourself. Scan your life and ask yourself, *what are some ways that I can think of to show love to myself?* Write down your list or key it into a file. Record all the ways you can think of, and make this list as personal as possible. The more creative you get with this and the more ideas you come up with, the better. Here are some examples you might find on this list.

WAYS THAT I CAN SHOW MYSELF LOVE

Asking myself, *what would someone who loves themselves do right now?*

Telling the truth (especially to myself).

Honoring my feelings and responding to those feelings.

Remembering that feelings are important signals.

Making my happiness and how I feel the number one priority of my life.

Honoring myself and who I really am because no one knows what makes me happy but me.

Recognizing that the universe is literally made of love. If I open myself to receive, like a flower opening to the sun, then everything is possible.

Spending my day scavenger hunting my environment and people I'm with for things I enjoy about it or about them, and then focusing on what I'm grateful for.

Writing a list of positive aspects about myself, which I really believe.

Admitting to my desires and why I want them, and recognizing that it's my right to want the things that I want. Letting myself go in the direction of my bliss no matter how crazy or risky it seems.

Admitting to what scares me.

Reading books that make me feel good about myself.

Finding ways that I can make myself feel safe and making them a priority no matter what is going on or what is pressing or urgent, especially when I feel unsafe.

Watching movies that have feel-good or inspirational stories.

Laughing, and seeking out things that make me laugh because laughter is fuel for my soul.

Eating foods that are in line with my highest good.

Prioritizing my own health and happiness above anything else. I can't be of service to someone any other way than by teaching by example.

Forgiving myself for having made mistakes.

Not letting fear keep me from what I want.

Realizing that it's okay to not be okay.

Not doing things that I don't want to do.

Allowing myself to admit when I'm wrong or have made
    a mistake.

Trusting in my higher self, and that if I "let go and trust,"
    I will flow in the direction of what is best for me.

Praising myself instead of being critical. For every criticism,
    I come up with three compliments for myself!

Allowing my enjoyment of things to be more important
    than my "principles." For example, if I think I have to
    get something done but I'm miserable doing it, I stop.

Allowing myself to have slipups without thinking I'm all
    the way back to square one.

Keeping only beliefs, which are useful and beneficial to me.

Communicating my true feelings to those around me.

Making a list of the reasons other people may want me for
    a friend and like being around me.

Not comparing myself to those whom I envy.

Not spending time around people who make me feel bad
    about myself.

Asking others for physical touch when I want it.

Allowing myself to accept affection from others.

Paying attention to what my body is telling me and *heeding* it.

Stop living life by other people's values, beliefs, desires, or priorities, and start living by my own.

Letting go of what does not serve me anymore, including beliefs, patterns, actions, addictions, and thoughts.

Treating myself how I believe others deserve to and want to be treated.

Realizing that it's okay to ask for help and then . . . asking for help.

Picking the path of least resistance.

Recognizing when I'm living according to fear instead of desire.

Meditating.

Stopping smoking.

Going out to dinner when I want to.

Cooking when I want to.

Going shopping occasionally to show myself that I care enough about myself to have things that I like around me.

Saving money so I can allow myself to feel secure.

Expressing my creativity in ways that I enjoy, such as painting, drawing, making collages, or writing.

Keeping a journal.

Writing down a list of what makes me happy (from the smallest things to the biggest things) and committing to doing one thing from the list every day.

Keep Up Your Efforts

The more that you learn about loving yourself, the more you can add to this list. You can go over the list on a monthly basis and ask yourself if you are still living in accordance with the things you have written down. If not, look for the ways you're contradicting the things on your list by living your life the way you are. Then decide what *one thing* you can do, with what you have, from where you are, in order to live a life that better reflects self-love. I am suggesting that you pick just one thing because I want you to be able to commit to it without being overwhelmed.

When we do not love ourselves, we have the tendency to be very good at coming up with any way we might be failing and piling that on top of our heads until we can't move. When we look over the ways we aren't living in accordance with our self-love list and pick just one thing we can do to live more in accordance with it, we are giving ourselves somewhere to start.

If you do find yourself feeling bad, just stop where you are and ask yourself, *What is one thing I could do right now to fill up my cup?* Then act on the answer you receive. Regardless of what you think or what you have been told, you *do* have the courage to do something revolutionary. You do have what it takes to act on behalf of your own happiness.

The goal of loving yourself isn't to become a little isolated universe in and of yourself, where you no longer need or want anything from anyone. The goal is to get you to a space where you are attracting into your experience the kind of people and things that add to your happiness so you can be loved in the way you've always wanted to be loved.

TOOL #5

DEVELOPING SELF-WORTH

Wondering about Worthiness

Lack of self-worth is a by-product of lack of self-love. But conversely, lack of self-love is also a by-product of a lack of self-worth. To understand how lack of self-worth leads to lack of self-love, we have to first look at the idea of worth in and of itself. *Worth* is defined as the quality that renders something desirable, useful, or of quality. And worthiness is the quality that renders something desirable, useful, or of enough quality to have *value*.

So many people are walking the surface of the earth with terribly low self-esteem. The core of this poor self-esteem is the feeling of not being valued. When we value something, we regard it as having worth to us because it is useful, important and beneficial. And it is this understanding that gives rise to the realization that can change your entire life. The realization is this: *Value is entirely based on needs and preferences.*

This means that value and worth is a very subjective experience. If a man is a car salesman and someone brings him a horse, he will not value the horse. But that does not mean that someone else won't value the horse infinitely more than a car. If a parent values logic and knowledge, that parent will prefer a child who is academic rather than artistic. If that parent has a child who is artistic, this child may feel as if he or she has no value. But that does not mean that another parent won't value an artistic child more. In this scenario, the child is the horse being brought to the car salesman.

So worth is based on desirability, usefulness, quality, and value. But the question is: to whom? Most of us define the worth we have to ourselves by how much worth we have to others. If you are filled with self-hate, then you likely believe that you are undesirable, useless, flawed, and are of no value to yourself. But this is actually impossible because you live with yourself, inside your own skin, every single day. Because this is the case, obviously you are of tremendous value to yourself.

But just saying it doesn't make self-hate go away. The roots of self-hate grow weeds in two opposing directions: the direction of *pride* and the direction of *shame*. Insecurity is at the heart of both conditions, where you start to see the world comparatively. We call this comparative worldview *vertical thinking*. This is an important concept to grasp. People who think vertically tend to experience the world through a perspective where they are either better than or worse than (on top of or beneath) the people, things, events, and circumstances in their life.

People who are described as "prideful" are often vertical thinkers. They have terrible self-worth because they cover over their deep insecurities by becoming arrogant. The substitute for real self-worth in their life is the thought that they are better and more important than others.

People who develop shame also have terrible self-worth. They are stuck in their insecurities, seeing themselves as dust of the earth. They never focus appreciatively toward themselves. The substitute for real self-worth in their lives is the thought that they are humble.

Authentic Self-Worth

True self-worth, on the other hand, stems from the understanding that imperfection exists alongside the perfection. They know this imperfection doesn't mean that they have more or less worth than anyone else. They view other people as objectively different but equal to them with regards to worth and so, in this way, they view existence on a more horizontal plane.

If we take this worldview a step further and accept that the world around us, including the people in it, are all projections of ourselves, we find that there can be no superiority and no inferiority. All that exists is . . . *our self*. When we can do this, our war with the world ends and when the war with the world ends, our war with *our self* ends.

When it comes to the concept of self-worth, you might want to consider throwing it away. "Worth" is a completely abstract concept. You cannot objectively determine the value of something. Worth has no basis in reality because it's entirely subjective. The criteria created to determine a person's worth is entirely dependent upon the society he or she is born into. Think of it this way. The quality of *being present* is worthless in a society that values *doing*. The quality of external beauty is worthless in a society for the blind. Perhaps the reason that you feel like you have no worth or value is because the very real qualities which you came in with (qualities that would have held infinite value to other people) were not considered valuable to the people that comprised your family or the culture or society you were born into.

For example, if you were born with artistic talents but landed in a family that valued the quality of scholarly intellect above all else, they may not consider your gifts valuable and therefore you would have received the message that *you* were not valuable. However, if you would have been born into a family of artists, your gift would have been instantly recognized as valuable and therefore, you would have felt as if *you* were valuable. The sad reality is that you can be born into a society, culture or family that is incompatible to you because your own innate value is not in alignment with their specific needs and therefore values.

True human worth is impossible to determine. Another way of looking at value, rather than to say that value doesn't inherently exist is that *value is inherent in all things, but value is not going to matter in certain situations or to certain people.*

If you are going to look at value as being inherent in all things, you can think about self-worth as a kind of light that is always there. It can't be taken away from or added to. It can't be earned or lost. It simply exists. It's an unchangeable, untouchable light that is always flowing. The things that you confuse with worth, like positive personality traits, achievements, or talents, are nothing more than a stained-glass window that you have erected in front of that light so the light can express itself in beautiful ways.

Likewise, the things that you confuse with worthlessness, like negative personality traits, failures, and shortcomings, are nothing more than cobwebs you have spun in front of that light, preventing it from expressing its beauty. No matter what you put in front of that light and no matter what you do to enhance or suppress that light, the light of your own worth is always there.

Try to accept that it is pointless to try to get someone to change their needs. It is a much better strategy to find someone who has a need that is compatible to you. And it is a guarantee that you will be seen as valuable to someone. Who might that someone be? If value were entirely based on needs and preferences, the most important question to ask yourself is: who needs and prefers *me*?

Recognizing Your Own Self-Worth

Lack of self-worth begins with the idea that we are not good enough exactly as we are, and therefore we can't be loved exactly as we are. So if we don't think we are good enough, how can we possibly love ourselves? There are two plausible answers. The first is to reach a state of perfection, and the second is to let go of the belief that we are not good enough.

In order to understand your true self-worth, you must begin looking for the quality inherent within you already—the things that make you desirable, the ways in which you are useful, and the value that you *do* have. Self-worth stands on the tripod of present endowments, potentials, and contributions and successes.

A present endowment would be a part of your nature that is enjoyable, such as, "I am a person who cares deeply about the well-being of those around me." A potential is an innate capability or capacity within yourself, such as, "I have the capability to convey love to others." You can focus on past contributions or successes by thinking of ways in which you have contributed to the well-being of others, of the world, or of yourself. An example might be, "When I was six, I saved a baby bird from dying when it fell from its nest," or "I got a promotion two years ago at work."

The key here is that in order to find self-worth, *you have to look for it*. Your focus has to switch from looking for the ways in which you lack worth to looking for the ways in which you have worth already. If your focus has been pointed at lack for many years, it may take some effort to retrain yourself to focus on what is there instead of what isn't there. But it's my promise to you that you *can* retrain yourself into your natural state, which is one of self-appreciation. Self-appreciation is the fertilizer for self-love.

Cultivating Love

The word *love* has been used to describe so many things that it has become a catchall term. But what is love? *To love something is to take it as a part of yourself. The reason we cannot say that we love ourselves is because we do the opposite of this. We push parts of ourselves away.* We try to become happy by pushing our sadness away. We try to be good by pushing any part of ourselves we see as bad away. We try to become successful by pushing any parts of ourselves that we judge as a failure away. We try to become self-loving by pushing self-hate away. The exact opposite vibration of love is fear. To fear is to separate something from yourself. Fear is exclusive. When you fear something, you push it away and dis-include it from you. When we experience self-hate, what we really mean is that we fear parts of ourselves because we feel those parts of ourselves are going to create pain for us in some way. To be in a space of self-love, you must end this process of pushing parts of yourself away. Instead, you must re-own them.

Love, then, is the emotional reflection of the vibration of oneness, and it exists only in the present. The emotion of love is your indication that you are holding the exact same perspective toward what you are looking at that the eternal consciousness within you holds, namely that consciousness is what you call your soul or higher self. In this way, love is the state of perfect alignment with your soul.

Cultivating self-love means to retrain yourself back into alignment. For this reason, it's a choice. You can choose to direct your attention positively toward yourself, or you can choose to direct your attention negatively toward yourself. Self-love is a commitment to practicing positive focus and an appreciative attitude toward yourself. It's a skill that you develop. When you direct your focus positively toward yourself, you will feel the emotional reflection of love toward yourself. It is a moment-to-moment choice that you become more skilled at doing the more you practice.

Creating a Personal Inventory

To begin cultivating your own self-worth, it's good to start by compiling three lists. Make these lists as long as you can possibly make them. If you want to keep adding to them over a period of time instead of completing them in one sitting, feel free to do so.

For the first list, you are going to begin an internal scavenger hunt for your present endowments. You're going to compile a giant list of your positive traits and talents. One good tool to use when you're doing this is a thesaurus. You can scan a thesaurus for positive personality traits and copy down the ones that fit you. You can also call other people and ask them to contribute to the list by telling you what they consider your endowments to be and what they value in you. Here are some examples of things that you might find on this list.

My List of Endowments

I am a good cook.

I persevere.

I am introspective.

I care.

I have a good ear for music.

I am the kind of person people feel comfortable telling
their problems to.

I have good sense of humor.

I am honest.

I am loyal.

It means a good deal to me that people around me feel
loved.

For the second list, you are going to compile a list of your
capabilities and potentials, which are expressions of what you
can do and what you could do. Examples of things on this list
might include the following.

My List of Capabilities and Potentials

I always have the potential to let go of what no longer
serves me.

I am capable of doing something even if it scares me.

My body is capable of taking food and turning it into energy.

I have the potential to find hope.

I can convey love to other people through my actions.

I can recognize my thoughts.

I have the capacity for self-awareness.

I could choose to quit and just end my life, but I haven't yet.

I could learn to be in the present moment.

I'm capable of understanding both sides of a story.

For the last list, compile a list of your past contributions and successes. These are examples of times when you have contributed to the well-being of yourself or others, and successes you have had in your life. Here are some examples.

My List of Contributions and Successes

I befriended the girl in my school who had no friends.

I won my grade-school talent show.

I discovered a way to attend college despite being born into a family that was poor.

I donated money to an animal shelter.

I remained on good terms with my ex-boyfriend or ex-girlfriend.

I baked a birthday cake for my best friend.

I put bugs outside instead of killing them.

I told my grandmother I loved her before she died.

I got a promotion at work.

I quit smoking.

Reinforcing Your Worthiness

It's important for you to realize that it's impossible to be worthless. But it's equally important for you to realize that if you have ever contributed to the well-being of yourself or any other being in this universe, it's even more impossible than "impossible" to be worthless.

I suggest that you keep these lists somewhere where you can refer to them every night before you go to sleep. If writing isn't a process that appeals to you, you can record yourself speaking these lists out loud and then listen to a replay of your lists before you go to sleep. Sleep is an opportunity to extend positive focus from a ten-minute exercise to an eight-hour exercise with no effort. When you wake up, you'll be on the same note that you drifted off to, which will guarantee that you'll start your day off on the foot of self-love instead of self-hate.

Because self-worth and self-love are so intertwined, they feed each other. As you work on recognizing your own worth, you will naturally begin to love yourself more. And as you begin to love yourself more, your self-worth will naturally increase. So don't feel as though you have to "tackle" your self-worth issues to the ground and find self-worth before you can love yourself. You can work on the process directly, the way we just did by writing the three lists, but self-worth will also appear as the result of the love you are beginning to show yourself.

And the good news is, the fact that you are even reading this book right now means that you have already decided you are worthy of self-love. If you didn't think you were worthy of self-love, you would not have put forth the effort to seek out a way to discover how to love yourself in the first place.

TOOL #6

JAIL BARS OF BELIEF

The Birth of a Belief

Our minds are generating thoughts all day long. But our thoughts are not the problem. The issue is that we *believe* those thoughts, the ones our mind generates. Some beliefs become like jail bars that keep us permanently stuck; other beliefs are freeing and allow us to soar.

If we are always thinking a thought like *I am so stupid,* a manifestation of that thought might be failing a test at school. Before we become fully aware that it is our thoughts, words and actions that are creating our reality, we tend to look at such manifestations as proof that the original thought is true. It becomes a belief.

If you start to deliberately think different thoughts , speak different words and take different actions often enough, different things will manifest and serve as physical proof. Soon you will be looking at proof that the *new* thoughts are true.

The first step to changing your beliefs is to change your thoughts. It's easy to say, a little harder to do, but you can do it. Let me show you how this prison break works.

It's Time for Some New Beliefs

As people, we hold tight to the idea that a reality exists that is separate from us, a reality we have to discover and own up to in order to be happy. We are obsessed with the idea of discovering what is "true." But the truth is that our physical dimension was designed like a giant holographic mirror. It was designed to become the physical reflection of our thoughts. So the reality we experience is the reflection of our most predominant thoughts, which we, of course, can call *beliefs.*

This is why no one's reality is the same as anyone else's. Most people can experience only the manifestations of their own thoughts. They can encounter only their own projections. We naturally want to like the reality we live in. But think about it: if your reality is only a projection of your beliefs, you can't really enjoy your reality if you are still holding beliefs that make you unhappy. Thus, it's time for some new beliefs.

This process is tied in with self-love because people who love themselves are willing to let go of what does not serve them.

Loving yourself, then, means to prioritize being happy. And as you just found out, a big component of being happy is letting go of the things that make you unhappy. Remember what makes you unhappy isn't what you are looking at. It isn't the people, circumstances, and events in your life. Instead, it's your thoughts *about* what you are looking at that make you unhappy. It bears repeating, as it's really important: It's your thoughts about the people, circumstances, and events in your life that make you unhappy.

Stop Resisting Your Good

One of our greatest sources of unhappiness is the belief that things *should* be different than how they are or were. This is a state of resistance to what is and what was. You cannot live a happy life and hold this state of resistance at the same time. To love yourself, you have to be willing to stop resisting what was and what is, and extract the value out of the moment you are in.

One of the best ways to begin doing this is to step way outside the box and take the thoughts that cause you pain and reverse them. Here's an example: First, I reverse a thought that I know is true, like, *I am Teal Swan,* and I change it to its opposite, *I am not Teal Swan.* Then I come up with every possible way that I can to make this reverse statement true.

You can reverse a thought in multiple ways. You can reverse a thought to its logical opposite; you can reverse a thought so that the nouns or verbs are flipped or changed to their opposites; or you can reverse a thought back onto yourself.

For example, the thought *She hates me* can be reversed to its logical opposite, which is *She loves me.* The nouns can be flipped to *I hate her.* Or the thought can be reversed back onto yourself by changing the thought to *I hate me.*

So an example you can use would be to reverse the thought *My husband should love me* to *I should love me.* Then come up with every possible way that you could make that alternate or reverse statement true. If I were to come up with three ways that *I should love me* is true, I might say, "Living in my body, as myself and hating myself, is no way to live." And "I have no control over whether other people show me love, but I do have control over whether I show love to myself." And "I am here on earth; I have been created, and so I must serve some purpose and be of some value—otherwise, I wouldn't have been created in the first place."

You can do this reversal process with every single thought in existence. This exercise helps to expand your perspective so you can see that alternatives to the thought you are thinking might be even *truer* than the one you are currently thinking. The thing that is causing you the most pain is that you believe that the painful thoughts you are thinking are absolutely true.

Using Your Brain to Maximum Benefit

One of the most important steps to changing our beliefs is to discover what we actually believe. We have many thoughts that are conscious and others that are subconscious. But because they are subconscious doesn't mean we can't control them. It just means that we have thought a thought so often, usually beginning in childhood, that our brain did its job and took responsibility for that thought. Our brain created a neural pathway that is now in charge of communicating that particular thought to the rest of our body without any effort on our part, without requiring any conscious awareness anymore.

This means that the more you think a thought, the more the neural pathway, which is responsible for the conversion of that thought, is reinforced and the less effort you have to exert to think that thought in the future. When this process has become as efficient as it can get, we can think thoughts, which the brain then converts so quickly into physical reality for us, that we have no awareness of having thought at all. We call this kind of thought "subconscious."

We can celebrate the incredible efficiency of the human brain when it comes to something like swimming or making coffee in the morning. It's wonderful that the brain can enable us to do a backstroke without wasting any effort of having to think about doing the backstroke while we're doing it. But that same highly efficient brain is superbly detrimental when it comes to something like poor self-worth. We can sabotage ourselves without ever noticing the thoughts that went into that split-second decision to take the action of sabotaging ourselves.

The best way to make sure that our brain is *only* telling the rest of us to perform actions that serve us is to feed it *only* thoughts that benefit us. This means we have to be very deliberate about our thoughts. We have to discover and replace the subconscious thoughts, which are self-sabotaging. We also call these *negative core beliefs*.

The Path to Better Beliefs

When you are in a situation that is causing you to experience strong negative emotion, you have the absolute perfect opportunity to find your negative core beliefs. You can do this by chasing every statement you have with two questions:

Why would that be a bad thing?

What would it mean if that were true?

Here's how it works. Say you are in a situation in which you are afraid, such as being very afraid of failing at something. The statement "I am afraid I will fail" is not the core belief; it is an emotional reaction to the actual core belief. You can drill down and find the core belief by asking, *Why would that (failing) be a bad thing?* The answer may be, "I will look stupid." You then ask yourself, *Why would that (looking stupid) be a bad thing?* The answer may be, "Other people will think I'm stupid."

Then ask yourself, *Why would that (other people thinking I'm stupid) be a bad thing?* The answer may be, "I will be rejected." Then ask, *What would that (being rejected) mean to me if that were true?* The answer may be, "I will feel worthless and be alone." Then ask, *Why would that (feeling worthless and being alone) be a bad thing?* The answer may be, "I will never be happy if I am alone."

That's it. The negative core belief in this case is "I will never be happy if I am alone." You have chased down the root of why you are afraid of failing. Often there is more than one layer to a core belief, and it is different for different people. So another person might have the same fear of failing, but they might hold a very different core belief behind it.

When you find a core belief within yourself, the belief itself may often sound totally illogical to you. It may even seem ridiculous to your logical mind. It's good when you have this reaction to a core belief because it means that it will be easier to start to think thoughts that are the opposite of that belief. It's easier to talk yourself out of a belief that seems ridiculous than it is to talk yourself out of one that makes sense. Even so, you must realize that even though it seems ridiculous, it *has* been a belief of yours. It's a belief that has rendered physical manifestations to match it; so it's a core belief that is affecting you greatly and preventing you from your bliss.

What's Holding Up Your Negative Beliefs?

Uncovering your core beliefs is a process that takes some time and practice. It's not easy to get past the surface layer of our thoughts, feelings, and reactions to find the beliefs that are beneath them, but it's a highly beneficial exercise. Once you identify your self-limiting core beliefs, you can look at them and decide what you would *rather* believe. You can work on changing them one by one.

Before you begin to do this, I want to give you an analogy that will help you understand how beliefs work. I want you to imagine a table. The top of the table represents the belief itself. The legs of the table represent the evidence that you are using to support that belief. Now picture that there is superglue that secures the table legs to the floor and that the superglue represents the emotional payoff for keeping the belief.

In order to replace that belief, you will have to do the following:

1. Decide if the emotional payoff makes keeping the belief worth the harm that the belief causes. If you decide that the emotional payoff of keeping that core belief isn't worth it and that you are ready and wanting to replace it with a different belief, that decision "dissolves" the old belief from sticking to you in the same way that you would dissolve superglue, which keeps the legs of the table stuck to the floor.

2. Next you have to knock the legs of that old belief out from under the table. You can do this by shooting holes in the evidence that you are using to support your old belief and do it to such a degree that the evidence no longer holds true. When you have done this, the top of the table (which is the belief itself) will fall because it will no longer have any legs to stand on.

3. Now you get to decide on a new tabletop you like better, and you do this by picking a belief you would rather believe.

4. Then you have to build new legs under the new belief to support the tabletop; meaning, you have to go looking for new evidence to support your new belief.

5. Finally, you have to add superglue that will secure that new table to the floor by finding the emotional payoff for your new belief. Hey, your job is done. You get to start enjoying the fruits of your labor, and you get to start enjoying the payoffs of your new belief.

If this sounds complicated, fear not. Here is an example of how this process works, and you can apply these same steps to any negative core beliefs you want to dissolve and replace.

HOW TO DEAL WITH THE BELIEF *"I AM STUPID."*

Step 1. Determine the emotional payoff of keeping that belief and whether that payoff is worth the pain it causes. Here is an example of this thinking process for a man who is convinced that he is stupid: *If I believe that I am stupid, I always have an excuse when I do fail. It makes it so that other people don't expect much of me. It gives me the excuse not to have to try. Thinking I'm stupid also makes it so that I will never know what I really am capable of.*

Step 2. Seek out alternative evidence and alternative explanations that undermine the validity of your detrimental belief. Replace the evidence you've been using to back up and support your detrimental belief with all the evidence you can think of that undermines it. Follow the threads below to see how this works. This would be the same example of a man who thinks he is stupid and has three beliefs: A, B, and C. Then when you look further at each of these, you can see how alternative evidence and explanations can help him undermine the original detrimental belief.

A. *I got terrible grades in school.*

B. *My mother always told me that men are stupid.*

C. *I am dyslexic.*

Looking further at A. I don't actually agree with the way that school is taught in general. Everyone has a different way of learning. I'm a "hands-on learner" and that doesn't make me stupid; it just means my interest doesn't get piqued when I'm listening to a teacher talk all day. My terrible grades came because I didn't care what I was learning about. When I care about something, I excel at it because I love learning about it. I was miserable when I was in school because my parents had just gotten a divorce, and expecting any kid to get good grades when their home life is falling apart is ridiculous. I asked questions like, *What is the meaning of life?* I am pretty sure that if I were really stupid, it wouldn't occur to me to ask those questions.

Looking further at B. My mother said that only when my father did something she didn't think was right. But my father always had good reasons for why he did things the way he did them. My mother grew up in a time when there was a lot of gender inequality, so some part of her always felt powerless to men, and I noticed that thinking women are smarter than men made her feel as if she got at least some power back. It seemed to be the only way she felt better about herself, but it doesn't mean all men are stupid. Looking at the huge list of men who have won Nobel Peace Prizes, I can see that being a man doesn't automatically guarantee that I am stupid.

Looking further at C. Dyslexia has nothing to do with how smart I am. It's nothing more than a symptom of a brain that organizes information differently. Just because reading and writing are hard for me doesn't mean other things are hard for me. Einstein was dyslexic.

Step 3. Figure out what belief you would rather believe. The man in this case decided that he liked this new belief: *I am uniquely intelligent.*

Step 4. Look for evidence and proof to back up the new, more beneficial belief, the one you would rather believe. Here is some of the evidence you might come up with. "You know what? I could solve a Rubik's Cube by the time I was ten! I can look at things one time and understand how they are put together. I am incredibly artistic. I am street smart. I can figure out how other people are feeling without them saying anything to me. I built my own car engine. When I'm interested in something, I learn about it so quickly that people are often dumbfounded at my progress. I can usually figure out how to do something without being told how to do it."

Step 5. Look for the emotional payoff of the new belief. Here are some payoff statements that you might consider. "I will have more confidence. I will try some of the things I've always wanted to try instead of feeling unfulfilled. I'll be more attractive to women. I may be able to find a job doing something I'm really good at and really love. I may just start my own business, which would feel really good. I will feel better about myself, and that will make me much happier. I would probably stop trying to conform to other people's ideas about intelligence, so I would feel free to live my own life. I could help other children who are dyslexic, so they don't grow up feeling insecure and stupid like I did."

You Are Worth the Effort

Now, you can see that changing a belief requires that you first sit down and put some time into the process of really examining it, questioning it, and replacing it. But this is time well spent, and you are worth it. Look at it this way: You can either sit down now for an hour and begin this process of deliberately changing your belief, or you can keep being frustrated by the effects that your old belief has on you while you continue to berate yourself about having no time to change it.

Truly, this is your happiness we are talking about. It's your life and your reality that are at stake, so we're talking about pretty high stakes. Love yourself enough to know it's worth an hour or two of your time now to do the work to replace a belief that needs to go. The old payoff just isn't worth it any longer.

That being said, recognizing and replacing beliefs is a gradual process. Don't be surprised if you fall back into old beliefs sometimes, as we all fall back into negative thoughts at certain times because we forget that we have control of them. The good news is that the more you commit to your new belief and begin to think thoughts that feel good to think, the more neural pathways your brain will assign to those new, positive thoughts.

Eventually, it will become easier to think the new, positive thoughts rather than the old negative ones. You will starve your negative beliefs by not feeding them those old negative thoughts that used to support them. Instead, you will be fueling your positive beliefs by feeding them the positive thoughts that support them.

TOOL #7

GRAND CANYON
OF AFFIRMATIONS

Proceed with Caution

Every thought we think, every word we speak, and every action we take is an affirmation to ourselves. An affirmation is a declaration of truth. Affirmations either benefit us or they don't. They can be positive or negative. People who love themselves take great care to affirm only what benefits them to affirm. In other words, people who love themselves take great care to make sure that what they affirm to themselves on a daily basis through their thoughts, words, and actions is *positive*.

From here on out, when I refer to an affirmation, what I'm referring to is a declaration of something positive that either *is* currently true or that you *want to be* true. If you begin to deliberately use affirmations, what you want to be true for you will eventually become true. It will become true because whenever you deliberately think a thought consistently enough, it *will* manifest.

But here's the caution: The reason why so many people find that affirmations don't work for them is that they aren't picking the right affirmations for themselves. All too often, affirmations become a way for us to escape where we currently are in our lives and are just a means of denying the way we feel or of lying to ourselves. If you have tried using affirmations and the process backfired or didn't work at all, you were likely not using the process correctly. You might be trying to deny reality, or leap too far ahead too quickly and ended up just feeling more defeated, particularly if you are coming from a place of self-loathing.

In order to begin showing yourself love through the process of affirmations, you're going to have to play the game of affirmations a little differently from how you've previously been taught. Don't get into a situation where you have to argue with your sense of intelligence. Instead of repeating thoughts that you don't yet believe in, try to approach affirmations in increments.

Cross Each Bridge as You Come to It

Instead of using an affirmation that makes you feel the full awareness of the current absence of what you want to be true, you can start first with an affirmation that *already* feels true. So if you currently don't love yourself and you find that saying "I love myself" is just too painful, don't use that one. It likely feels painful because it feels like you are lying to yourself and whitewashing over the parts of you that feel unlovable and it pulls you into the awareness of the severe lack of love you have for yourself.

Instead of that, I suggest you use a bridge statement that does feel good, which is on the way to self-love. An example of a bridge affirmation is *I am excited for the day that I will wake up and feel love for myself,* or *I love that I care enough about the quality of my life that I'm taking the time to do affirmations,* or *I love the color of my eyes.* These are still affirmations and if you say them enough, then you will eventually find that affirming the statement "I love myself" will no longer be a statement of denial. It will no longer carry with it the acute feeling of a lack of self-love. Instead, it will carry love.

If you love yourself, you can't ask yourself to jump the Grand Canyon. When we choose affirmations that feel completely untrue and out of reach for us as individuals, we are resisting the reality of what is and we are asking ourselves to jump the Grand Canyon. But if you choose affirmations that you *actually do believe* and that are closer to the affirmation that you *want to believe,* you will find that the jump from the place you are now to the place where that affirmation is true is not that far. It will feel good to you. The better your affirmations feel to you, the more effective they are.

Remember, you always want to make sure that your affirmations are in the present tense such as *I am* or *I have* or *I look forward to.* If you make your affirmations in the future tense, such as *I want* or *I will,* you are telling the universe and yourself to keep what you're asking for out of reach and always in the future instead of now.

You can keep an affirmation journal in which you practice writing daily lists of any affirming statements that make you feel good. Perhaps one of the best applications for affirmations is to record yourself saying your affirmations and then fall asleep listening to them through headphones as you lie in bed at night.

The art and practice of affirmations is meant to teach you that you can shift the angles by which you perceive something, and in doing so you can create and maintain your own happiness. The sky is the limit when it comes to affirmations. There is no end to the positive things you can start telling yourself. Trust your emotions to tell you which ones are the right ones for you to use, and remember you can always use the bridging technique if you find that some statements are too difficult for you at this point.

TOOL #8

RELEASING YOURSELF FROM GUILT

What Good Is Guilt?

Guilt is a major roadblock that stands in the way of self-love. Guilt stems from the same process of socialization that we spoke about in the introduction to this Tool Kit. You'll recall that the way most of us were socialized as children led us to reach a pivotal conclusion about ourselves, namely the realization *I am not good enough.* As a child, you then made an assumption based on the limited understanding you had when your caregivers punished you. Specifically, you assumed that you must *deserve* it; otherwise, it wouldn't be happening to you. Even though the assumption you made was incorrect, this assumption was the beginning of guilt in your life.

Because of our socialization and the misguided assumptions that we picked up, just about all of us carry several core beliefs that are at the heart of all guilt. They are:

1. *I deserve punishment.*

2. One step deeper than that, *I deserve to suffer.*

3. *I don't deserve to be happy.*

4. And worst of all, *I don't deserve to be loved.*

To begin with, please understand that guilt is an emotion. It's an indicator that tells you that you have done something that you don't want to repeat, something that was out of line with your idea of what is right and good. We often call this internal knowing that is indicated by the emotion of guilt our *conscience*. The guilt that our conscience experiences can bring your attention to ways in which you are out of line with your integrity. It can make you aware if you are doing something that is hurtful to yourself or others. It tells you when you are not honoring yourself or the universe at large.

When I refer to guilt throughout this chapter, however, I'm not referring to the momentary indicator emotion of guilt as it applies to conscience. I'm referring instead to guilt as a system of self-regulation, self-abuse, and self-blame that keeps us imprisoned in the emotion called *guilt*, which makes the whole thing a permanent fixture instead of a temporary situation.

Getting Out from under Guilt

Guilt, then, is not something you can release; rather, it's something from which you have to release yourself. If you feel guilty, it means you crossed a line inside yourself. You have violated a rule you have set up for yourself, such as, "Don't hurt other people." We make so many internal rules for ourselves that we end up living inside a maze of them. We can't go right or left without running into a barrier. We have accumulated so many rules that it's hard to live our lives without crossing them. So the key to releasing guilt is to change the internal rules that you have set up. We can do this by examining our beliefs.

Let's pretend you are in a building and guilt is like tear gas that has just been released throughout the building. Given how painful it is, all you want to do is run out the door and go somewhere else. Regret is how you know that self-blame and self-punishment have stepped in the door to keep you stuck in that building, drowning in that tear gas. Regret keeps you stuck in the emotion of guilt for things that have happened in the past, which you have already acknowledged are not things that you want to repeat.

Once you've acknowledged that you don't want to repeat something you have done, there is personally and universally *no* need to continue dwelling on it or feeling guilty about it. It serves no purpose whatsoever and does not move anything toward a positive change. It only keeps you in the place of guilt.

Here's why this is such an important topic for you to understand. You cannot hope to move in the direction of the future you want if you are still holding on to the past. You will simply stay where you are. If you want to love yourself, one of the first steps to take is the step of letting go. If you are struggling with self-hate, the chances are overwhelming that there are parts of you that are begging to be released from guilt. You need to give yourself permission to do that, find a way to do that, and only then will you be able to move forward.

11 Steps to Release Yourself from Guilt

Here are the basic steps you can take to release yourself from guilt.

1. **Realize the Truth about Guilt.** In order to change something, you must have understanding of it. So the first step to releasing yourself from guilt is to realize where guilt begins, what purpose it serves, and ultimately that it does not serve your highest good or the highest good of others. Guilt is, in fact, self-abuse. Realize that guilt and shame are negative emotions surrounded by negative thoughts that continue to feed your ego in a negative way instead of a positive way. What internal rule did you violate? Is that rule true 100 percent of the time? Does it serve you? How could you think differently about that rule or about that circumstance in a way that would decrease the feeling of guilt?

2. **Make a Decision.** Decide that you are ready, willing, and wanting to let go of guilt.

3. **Adopt New Thoughts.** Replace the beliefs that you deserve punishment and that you deserve to suffer and that you don't deserve happiness or love, with the belief that you do deserve to be happy and to be loved.

4. **Take Responsibility.** Take responsibility *only* for your part in a situation. Realize that taking responsibility is not the same as admitting shame;

it's simply acknowledgment of understanding. Responsibility is not about owning the blame for what happened, but rather owning up to the responsibility to choose to create repair to what you have done and/or to think or say or do something different in the future.

5. **Be Realistic about Your Past.** Take off the rose-colored glasses when you are looking for ways that the past could have been different. Guilt is fueled by looking back on a situation and seeing options that either weren't there or to which we had no access at the time.

6. **Apologize.** Apologize to anyone whom you perceive you have hurt, even if this is *yourself*. It's hard to let go of the guilt if someone else is still hurting. Offer a sincere apology, most important explaining the understanding that you now have of the whole situation. If the person or animal on the receiving end of the hurt is not around to apologize to, or if you simply don't feel ready to address them, write it on a piece of paper like a letter and then burn it. As you watch the paper burn, you can affirm the following: *I am ready to stop punishing myself; and instead, with my new understanding, I [state your new intention].*

7. **Plan for a New Future.** Make a plan for how you will do things differently in the future. The emotion of guilt exists to let us know that we don't want to repeat something we've done. So make this a conscious process by really looking for the lesson hidden in the experience. What are you going to do differently in the future? Without having a new way

to approach your life, you'll continue to do things for which you feel guilty. The point of freeing yourself from guilt is not to accumulate more guilt, but to start fresh with a new intention.

8. **Accept That Mistakes Are Only Lessons.** Recognize the value in mistakes. Without them, you could not learn. Without knowing what you don't like and want, you could not know what you do like and want. Don't let your mistakes turn into suffering, and don't allow shame and self-punishment into the equation. Instead, understand that your mistakes are only lessons.

9. **Release Judgments.** Uncover all the judgments you are making about yourself based on what you feel guilty about. The deep suffering you feel is not actually caused by the guilt itself. It is caused by the judgments you make about yourself based on what you feel guilty about. An example of this is *I feel guilty because I've stolen money from someone. People who steal money are no good; therefore, I'm no good,* or *I'm a bad person,* or *I'm a screwup,* or *I deserve to be punished.* You did things that were not in line with your true self, you vowed not to repeat them, but doing them does not mean that you are bad. Release your judgments, and replace the beliefs and assumptions, based on your new knowledge.

10. **Replace Guilt with Love.** Counter the guilt by showing yourself love. Remember, guilt is actually self-abuse. What's more, guilt makes us a match to more people and circumstances that reinforce guilt within us. So what is the best thing you can do when your

self-abusive ego is running the show with guilt? Show yourself love and care, and discover how to be your own friend. Look inward and see that you are in need of loving kindness yourself. Counter self-hate with self-love in whatever ways you can, such as taking a bath, writing affirmations, doing mirror work, watching a movie that makes you feel good about yourself, or doing a self-love visualization.

11. **Forgive Yourself.** Understand that every person on this earth always makes the best decision they can, given the perspective, information, and knowledge they have from where they are. Everyone does what they think is right in the very moment. Because of the way we are taught to punish ourselves, we develop guilt for not choosing options that, in all honesty, simply weren't there at the time. You shouldn't judge your past self by using today's expanded perspective.

TOOL #9

EXPRESSING YOURSELF

Expressing the Complete Truth

Learning to love yourself is a process of healing your thoughts and emotions. But the only thoughts and emotions you can heal are the ones you let yourself feel and express. Whenever problems or conflicts arise in your life, especially in your relationships, there is more to the story than meets the eye.

We will only ever get to the root of the problem or conflict if we discover and admit the complete truth to ourselves. We will only have harmonious lives if we learn to *express* the complete truth to ourselves. And people who love themselves want harmonious lives for themselves.

There are five basic parts that make up the complete truth when we are expressing ourselves:

1. Anger

2. Pain

3. Fear

4. Understanding

5. Love

Most of the time, we allow ourselves to be aware of, and express, only one part of the truth. For example, if we go out in our car and get rear-ended, we may immediately become really, really angry and blame the person who crashed into us. We may let ourselves and others become aware of *only* the anger part of the truth about how we feel about getting rear-ended, when really, the complete truth is much more complex and involves thoughts that correspond to all the emotions listed above.

In other cases, we may let ourselves be aware that we are hurt or afraid due to a specific conflict but *never* let ourselves or others become aware of the anger we feel. It's a natural defense. It's actually a common behavior that we learn in our formative years, where we allow ourselves to explore and express only certain aspects of the complete truth and not others. But healing and self-love come from knowing and expressing all of it.

Learning How to Express Your Truth

The following exercise will help you express yourself. Use a piece of paper to do it, or sit in front of a mirror. Pick something from your life or from a relationship that is really bothering you. I want you to express each part of the complete truth relative to that thing by answering the questions below in the exact order they are listed.

If you are using paper, you can write down the answers. If you are using a mirror, speak them out loud to yourself. Don't move on from one part (such as anger) to the next part (such as pain) until you feel that you have expressed and exhausted all thoughts and emotions that correspond to the current part. Don't suppress any emotions that come up. Emotions are healthy. Let yourself get really mad; let yourself cry; let yourself feel hope. Let yourself fully experience whatever emotions come to the surface, without judgment.

1. Anger

What am I angry about?

What/Whom do I blame and why?

Whom/What do I feel resentment for and why?

It makes me so mad when . . .

I'm completely fed up with . . .

I hate . . .

2. Pain

What about this makes me so sad?

I am so hurt by . . .

I feel so disappointed that . . .

3. Fear

What about this makes me so afraid?

I'm scared that . . .

It scares me when . . .

Why does it scare me?

What about this makes me feel insecure?

What is the deep wound hiding underneath the anger and sadness?

What painful thing does this situation remind me of?

4. Understanding

I regret . . .

I'm sorry that . . .

What part of this situation do I take responsibility for?

I didn't mean to . . .

I understand that . . .

I know sometimes I . . .

What do I want forgiveness for?

5. Love

Deep down I have the purest of intentions, and they are . . .

Deep down, in my heart, I want . . .

I promise to . . .

What solutions to this situation can I think of?

I hope that . . .

I feel gratitude for . . .

I forgive . . .

Processing the Truth about "The Accident"

Here is an example of someone using this process to tell the complete truth about the scenario we posed earlier: "I just got rear-ended in traffic."

1. **Anger:** "I can't believe that I just got run into; this day could not get any worse! I hate that idiot. I hate people. I'm completely fed up with how stupid people are. It makes me so mad when I don't do anything wrong, and I still suffer the consequences. This is so unfair. I feel like killing him."

2. **Pain:** "It makes me sad that people get hurt in this world when they don't deserve it. I am so hurt by the fact that it feels like other people have things go right for them, but nothing goes right for me. I'm

sad that this car I love is damaged and that I have to drive around embarrassed because it is dented. I'm so disappointed that this night, which I thought was going to go so well, has gone terribly. That just hurts. It hurts really, really bad."

3. **Fear:** "I'm so afraid that life isn't meant to be happy. I'm afraid that life is supposed to be about suffering. I'm afraid that I'm just here to suffer until I die. I'm afraid that if I find out that life is about suffering, I will fall into a deep depression and probably commit suicide. That's really the wound that is underneath it all: I feel powerless to other people just like I did when my father came home drunk and beat me up. One second I'd be watching TV and everything would be fine, and the next, for no reason, he'd come in and start beating on me. I was so little . . . I couldn't do anything about it."

4. **Understanding:** "I understand that I have no idea whether it's true that life means suffering. It's possible that I feel that way only because of my early experiences with my father. It's possible that I think that way so often that I only make myself a match to seeing more and more proof of the fact that life means suffering. I regret that I got angry at the man driving that car. He's probably having a terrible day, too. I didn't mean to take out all this fear, which has to do with my childhood, on a total stranger. I want forgiveness for the fact that I added to the problem instead of helping to solve it."

5. **Love:** "Deep down, my intention is to help everyone, including myself, feel better. Deep down, my intention is to heal the part of me that feels like a victim and feels like this world is a scary, bad place, so that I can find happiness. Deep down, my intention is not to feel like I have to control everyone and everything, but that I can trust myself to create only good things for myself. I hope that the man who ran into me is not unhappy all day. I hope that he lets himself off the hook, because everyone makes mistakes. I forgive him for making a mistake. Honestly, I love other people, and I want them to be happy. I want this world to be a happy place where we can make mistakes and learn from them, without being rejected or getting punished."

Let Healthy Expression Rule!

There is not a single situation that can't be addressed by using this process. It's profoundly liberating and self-loving. You will find that along with the fact that you've discovered the root of the conflict, which is always about suppressed fear and deep wounds, the emotional purge you experience will help you feel a profound sensation of relief.

The next time you feel a negative emotion, tune in to the feeling of sadness in your body. Close your eyes, and spend time really experiencing all the sensations. When you think you have a clear sense of the feeling that you're experiencing, love it directly. Visualize projecting love into (and around) the emotion that you are feeling. Project love directly *to* your sadness, your anger, your fear, or your guilt. Love it in the same way you would love a small, crying child.

If it helps, you can visualize hugging yourself and comforting yourself when you are feeling that emotion, as if you are embracing the emotion and yourself. Allow it and yourself to be cradled by you in your mind. Maintain this focus for as long as you feel the need to. Make sure you do it for at least two minutes.

To love yourself means to compassionately hear your true, innermost feelings instead of stifling them. When you practice expressing your authentic feelings to yourself in this way, it will become easier to express them to other people. Your relationships will become more harmonious, and you will have learned to honor how you feel and honor yourself exactly as you are instead of keeping yourself in the prison of how you *should feel* and how you *should be*.

TOOL #10

COMMITTING TO COMPASSION

A Moment-by-Moment Decision

Most of us are familiar with compassion to some degree. We remember the way we feel for someone we love when they tell us that something has happened that has caused them to suffer. To have compassion is to have sympathetic consciousness of another being's distress, coupled with a desire to alleviate it. In other words, to have compassion for someone is to be aware of, understand, be sensitive to, and care for the feelings, thoughts, and experiences of another being.

Unfortunately, most of us were also raised with the faulty belief that having compassion for ourselves is the same thing as pitying ourselves and that self-pity is a selfish, pathetic state of mind. So in accordance with this misconception, we throw out the baby with the bathwater. We do what we were taught *good* people do; we ignore, suppress, and push through our own pain. Because of this, we do not feel or show ourselves the same compassion that we were taught to feel and give to others.

Today you can view this in a new light: Compassion for yourself is really a choice that you can and should make. It's the choice to treat yourself *well* instead of treating yourself *badly* in the moment you are in. It's the choice to *give* to yourself instead of *denying* yourself in the moment you are in. It's the choice to focus *positively* on yourself instead of focusing *negatively* on yourself in the moment you are in. In this way, compassion is a moment-by-moment decision you make to go either in the direction of self-love or in the direction of self-hate.

Many of us fear being *nice* to ourselves when we have made a mistake or are suffering. We are deeply afraid that if we are self-compassionate, we are condoning our mistakes and will eventually end up being a *bad* person. The punishment-and-reward system that we were raised with certainly tells us that this is the case. We've been taught that if we punish people who make mistakes, they will stop making mistakes. So we are taught that when we show ourselves compassion for our mistakes, we are condoning the mistakes we made, and will therefore continue to make them.

Opening Your Heart to Yourself

Self-punishment, in all its various forms, is not helpful. It solves nothing, and, in fact, it only makes things worse. If you think about it for a minute, you will realize that you are not making yourself a better person by beating yourself up for your mistakes and by pushing through your pain. Instead, *all* you are doing is causing yourself to feel inadequate and insecure.

What's more, we have the tendency that when we make ourselves suffer, we take out our frustrations on the people who are the closest to us.

Something that most people don't know is that self-hate, and the self-punishment that goes with it, is in fact a coping mechanism. Coping mechanisms are strategies and behaviors that are carried out to mitigate, manage, or adapt to anything that causes distress. At first glance it may be hard to see how self-hate could possibly be a coping mechanism. After all, self-hate can't possibly decrease a person's distress, can it? The answer is yes it can. Whenever someone turns against something about us, it is perceived as rejection, which is intensely painful and also threatening to our sense of survival. When we are put in this position, we push that part of ourselves away. In doing this, we automatically create an internal antagonist. This internal antagonist takes over the job of constantly shaming and criticizing the parts within you that are seen as wrong and bad by others. This makes the hurt not only controllable, but predictable. We believe that by doing this, we might just be able to change the things that are so detestable about us. In this way, we become our own abuser and hater first, so that other people are never given the occasion or opportunity to do it to us. And if other people see us doing this, they tend to react lovingly towards us. For example, they see us insult ourselves and so they give us a compliment instead. In this way, self-hate becomes a strategy to avoid pain. This positive payoff is why self-hate is so hard to un-root.

Self-compassion doesn't depend on being special, being above average, or meeting goals, although these are the conditions that we have been taught are necessary in order to deserve love. Self-compassion depends only on the decision we make to show ourselves kindness, care, and love exactly as we are, right here, in this very moment. It depends only on opening your heart to yourself.

When something happens to us that causes us to suffer, a door to our heart opens, ready for us to enter and really *be* with ourselves and *be* with that pain in order to heal and become more whole. All too often, however, because of conditioning, we ignore this open door and instead distract ourselves from it in some way. We run in the opposite direction of our pain. The last thing we want to do is be with it, much less show it compassionate kindness. But this is what we must do if we want to love ourselves.

Part of compassion is the desire to alleviate pain. That is not the same thing as trying to *fix* it. Showing compassion to ourselves is being willing to see and feel the reality of our pain *without* covering it up or trying to fix it. When we try to fix our pain, all we are doing is resisting our pain, and whatever we resist tends to persist. When we think we need to fix pain, we are of the opinion that there is something wrong with pain, and there isn't. Pain always has something to teach us.

When something happens to someone else that causes them to suffer, we cannot love them and run away from them at the same time. We can't really love them and try to fix their pain for them at the same time, either. If you try to fix someone's pain, they will resist you immediately because they can feel through your actions that you must be thinking, *It's not okay for you to feel how you feel.* Instead, showing love means being with them and showing them compassionate kindness while you allow them to be with and process their own pain.

It works the same way when *we* are in pain. We can't love ourselves and run away from ourselves at the same time. And we can't love ourselves and try to resist our pain by trying to fix it at the same time. Instead, showing love to ourselves means being with ourselves when we are in pain, allowing ourselves to feel it, and showing both ourselves and our pain compassionate kindness. Doing so reveals the action steps we need to take in order to feel better. This is what ultimately heals us. This is the only way to move from a state of pain to a state of joy.

Practicing Self-Compassion

Self-compassion is not self-pity. Self-compassion is the willingness to be with yourself as a loving companion when you are in pain. It's a state of deep connection with yourself. You can practice self-compassion whenever you feel negative emotion. The next time you feel negative emotion, try the following exercise.

Stop doing whatever you are doing and sit down. Close your eyes and take five deep, slow breaths in a row. When you breathe in, fill your lungs to their full capacity, and then hold the breath for seven seconds. When you release your breath, do so slowly.

Fully own what you are feeling, as well as everything that you thought, said, and did. Then fully admit to the truth of the circumstances that happened. Don't rehash it in your mind. Don't focus on wishing it hadn't happened. Don't focus on thinking that it *shouldn't* have happened, and don't resist the fact that it *did* happen. Resisting is a waste of your energy. Own the fact that you are where you are and that whatever happened, *happened*.

Next, turn your focus inward toward the feeling. When you do this, name the emotions, sensations, images, sounds, and impressions associated with the feeling. Experience the feeling as if you are exploring a *thing* rather than a state of being. These sensations are meant to be acknowledged. What's more, they *must* be acknowledged in order to be processed.

Ask the feeling what it needs you to know. Look deeply into the experience of the pain for what it's trying to tell you. For example, your pain may say to you, "You're ignoring me. I don't want to do what you're trying to make me do. Why are you forcing yourself to do something that doesn't feel good?" Acknowledge that you hear the message, and what's more than that, have gratitude for its expression.

Condense the feeling into a single image. For example, this image could be a chasm in a snowfield or a small child crying on a park bench. Allow yourself to bring that image to resolution. This is an intuitive exercise. There is no right or wrong image. So let your mind tell you what image represents the feeling, and let yourself be inspired to work with that image in any way that causes you to feel better emotionally.

So, for example, if the image of the feeling you're experiencing is a chasm in a snowfield, you may feel inspired to mentally visualize filling up that chasm with something. If the image of the feeling is a small child crying on a park bench, you may feel inspired to mentally visualize walking over and holding that child in your arms and speaking calming words to the child. You may visualize giving the small child a warm home with a family that loves this child. Follow the visualization all the way until you feel a deep sensation of relief.

Then take a deep breath, wiggle your toes and fingers, and bring your attention back into the room. Reflect upon what you have just experienced. Did this process generate any insights for you? Look at what the feeling was trying to tell you and what it needed you to know. Are there any changes that you see are necessary to make in your life? Having done this exercise, how could you show love to yourself right now?

One of the most powerful demonstrations of self-love is to step into a state of compassion toward yourself. Show yourself compassion whenever you feel negative emotion, regardless of what that negative emotion is. Doing so enables you to be present with yourself and your truth. It enables you to find healing not by resisting your pain, but by allowing and transforming it.

TOOL #11

THE LOVE LETTER

Signed, Sealed, Delivered

When we take the time to write our thoughts down, we make the thoughts more real. A love letter is a classic, timeless expression of love. Writing a love letter means expressing your love in written form. It gives you time to get in touch with your deepest feelings and then decide which words will best express them.

Whether we have never received a love letter from someone else or receive a hundred a day from other people, the most important person to receive a love letter from is *you*. So, as you have probably guessed, the next step toward loving yourself is to write yourself a love letter.

To write this letter, pick a time when you're not going to be interrupted. It may help to play some music that puts you in an expressive mood. Pull out a pen and some paper. And begin the letter with "Dearest (your name)." Date the letter.

Then let the rest of the letter flow from your heart through your fingertips. Express your appreciation for yourself. This is your opportunity to say anything loving that you have ever wanted to say to yourself but haven't. This is your opportunity to express forgiveness, understanding, and compassion for yourself. And this is your opportunity to express your intentions for yourself.

Every love letter is unique. There is no right or wrong way to write one. When you have finished the letter, sign it however you feel compelled to sign it and put it in a sealed envelope. Put your address on the letter and put a stamp on it. Once you have done this, you can do one of two things: Either you can drop it off later that day so it will be mailed to you, or you can give it to someone you have faith in and tell the person to put it in the mail sometime in the next year, whenever he or she feels compelled to do so.

When you receive this love letter that you've written to yourself, save it for a time when you can sit down undisturbed, and then read the letter slowly. Focus on opening yourself up to let every word seep into you. Integrate the message into your soul. Then keep the letter somewhere where you can reread it if you ever want to reaffirm love to yourself.

Dearest Teal

So you can see an example of what a love letter to yourself might look like, here is the first love letter I wrote to myself when I was 21 years old:

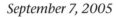

September 7, 2005

Dearest Teal,

You have not heard from me in years. But that is not because I don't care about you. I have simply been waiting for you to open the door and let me in. I am your real self. This morning, you decided that you are willing to live out of the sheer curiosity of seeing if this life could be better for you than it is now. You do not know yet if it can or can't. But I do.

I am writing you this letter to tell you that one day, you will be so happy that at first you may not trust it. One day, you will have found such joy that your heart will open wide enough to encompass this world. You will be an international symbol of forgiveness and freedom. I am here to tell you that it will all make sense. Everything happened for a reason. And you will come to know that reason, and set other people free with it.

The universe is watching you go from flame to ashes to freedom. And even though you haven't tasted the fruits of that journey yet, you will and you will read this letter and smile. You do not know how much I love you, but I do. I am here to tell you that it's all over. All of your suffering and struggle is over. You do not have to be so strong anymore.

No one saved you—you saved yourself, and it's not some lucky circumstance that kept you from going back . . . it's you. You say all the time that Doc's first mistake was the mistake that he made the night you escaped. But this was not his first mistake. His first mistake was picking you. He picked a child whose goodness could not be erased. He picked a child whose soul was untouchable. And all those things he did to hurt you will be turned around and used for good. It's the ultimate sabotage, in the form of the ultimate gift. You have stopped the chain of abuse. You have decided that it all stops with you.

You are wonderful. You are a force of nature. Your physical beauty is just a reflection of the magnificence of what it contains underneath. I will never abandon you. I will always be here for you. Now that you have decided that you want me, I will be here to love you in all the ways you have always wanted to be loved. You could never do anything to make me go away.

You are lovable with every perfection and imperfection that makes you who you are. Without them, you would not be so unique, and it's your uniqueness that makes you perfect just the way you are. You would not believe what is to become of your life if I told you. But it's nothing short of legend. Now, doesn't that sound like you? Anything less would not be befitting of who you really are, and you know it.

I will teach you how to love yourself. And, in turn, one day you will teach others how to love themselves. I will show you how to do it step-by-step. Let this letter be the very first step. When you read it and reread it, let these words sink into your soul. They are the truest words you have ever spoken to yourself.

You are wonderful just the way you are. Every self "improvement" you make is not an improvement, but rather just a step toward discovering who you already truly are. You may have covered your worth over in ashes and soot, but what was covered once will be uncovered soon, and how sweet your life will look then. We all wait with bated breath for that day. It's approaching faster than you could ever know.

And for all the days between then and now, know that there is nothing you need forgiveness for. The life you are about to lead is all the rectification you could ever want.

For all the days between then and now, know that you are a priceless piece of this universe. There has never been a moment when you have not been cherished and loved by me. There will not be a moment which could ever come that you will not be cherished and loved by me.

Whether or not I love you was never really your business anyway; it's my business, and I am telling you now that there is nothing you could ever do to make me not love you completely. Now it's time that you felt that love that I have held for you for so long. And how sweet a life it will be.

With love always,
You

Feeling the Love

When I wrote this letter to myself, I was truly weaving the fabric of what was to become my future. It's still the best letter I've ever received.

The reason is simple: No one can ever write me a better letter than one I send to myself because no one knows what I want to hear better than I do. Plus, of course, there is no one on this earth I want love from more than myself.

This letter does not have to be the only love letter you ever write to yourself. This exercise is so powerful, in fact, that I suggest writing one to yourself every year. But writing yourself this first love letter will be one of the most profound actions that you can take.

TOOL #12

Loving Your Body

Moving Beyond Body Image

You are currently living in a society that is composed of people who don't know how to love themselves. The result is that our society still operates under the misconception that in order to be wanted and loved, we must strive for perfection.

The first step we must take to move beyond the unrealistic standards we set for our bodies is to question them. We must think critically about the images we see every day instead of passively accepting them. The images we associate with the standard of desirability for both men and women have been airbrushed, retouched, and lightened. The alteration process would not need to occur if perfection truly did exist.

Ask yourself, *What does physical perfection mean to me? Should women, men, boys, and girls alter their appearance to fit the current beauty ideals? How far is too far? Is it healthy that we live in a world with so many different body types but where only one or two are considered attractive? What is the perfect body anyway? Is my idea of the perfect body my own idea, or has it been formed by what other people say the perfect body is?*

No matter how close your body is to the current ideal of physical perfection, chances are high that there is something you would change if you could. Even models and celebrities, who are considered to have bodies that are as close to perfection as bodies can get, have parts that they dislike. And the most prevalent source of suffering in current society is one's weight. For any given individual, fat may be an *actual* health problem that comes from a negative mental state, or it could potentially not be a health problem at all.

Living with the Enemy

When you hate your body, even in a small way, it's like living with the enemy. You can't escape your body, so hating even one aspect of your physical self guarantees that you will find something to be unhappy about every day. This is guaranteed suffering. Even if you succumb to plastic surgery, you cannot completely escape your body. Your body hears everything you think.

The moral of the story is this: If you want to live a completely happy life, you've got to find a way to start loving your body *exactly* as it is. Here are some suggestions for how to go about doing that:

1. Start to pay attention to and identify where you're picking up negative messages about your body. Do the magazines in the grocery-store aisles make you feel better or worse about yourself? Did you pick up some of your self-hate from your mother or father? Did either of them make you feel as if your body was not okay unless it looked the way that they thought it should look? It might not automatically make you feel better about yourself when you do wake up and consciously smell the roses about how you got to the point where you hate your body, but at least you will come out of the spell of blaming yourself for the way you feel about yourself. Feel free to disown any and all of the ideas that aren't actually your own original ideas about your body. This is the foundation for developing a positive body image.

2. Focus on what you *do* like about your body. Whether you are focusing on what you *want* or focusing on what you *don't want*, whatever you are focusing on, you will see more of. If you are constantly focusing on your flaws, you will create and see more flaws. This is the downward spiral of negative body image. If you focus on one flaw, you will notice more flaws, and as you focus on those flaws, you'll see even more flaws. Pretty soon your entire concept about your body is nothing but flawed. You begin to feel badly about yourself, and your self-worth goes down the toilet. What I'm proposing is a deliberate shift in focus.

Start by looking at yourself in the mirror, or look at a picture of yourself, and instead of looking for what you don't like about your body, look for what you do like about your body. Do you like your hair color? Do you like the slope of your shoulders? Do you like the even tone of your skin? Do you like your bone structure? Do you like the color of your skin? Force yourself to go on a mental scavenger hunt for what you *do* like about yourself.

3. Work with what you have instead of being upset about what you don't have. Show yourself love by finding some clothes that you feel confident in, that you love wearing, and that work for the body you have right now. Even if you have to buy something in a bigger or smaller size than you want to buy, there is nothing that self-hate likes more than the guarantee that you are going to feel bad later because you bought something today that does not fit you well and thus makes you more aware of your flaws.

4. Change only what you can change lovingly and only for the right reasons. Consider in depth what your true motivation is for wanting to change your body. Is it a healthy or an unhealthy motivation? Do you want to change something that you can actually change? Can you make this change in a way that is kind to yourself? Or is the only way to make this change to be unkind to yourself? You also can't make a change for anyone but yourself. Do you really want this change for yourself? Or have other people led you to the belief that you have to change something about yourself in order to be desired and loved? There is no such thing as right or wrong when it comes to body alteration. It's an individual decision. What message are you sending yourself when you're making changes to your body? Make sure that the message is: "I love you and I am doing this for you," not "I don't love you the way you are."

5. Create a gratitude list about your body and what it lets you do. Gratitude is the vibration of pure appreciation. It's the opposite of hate. We live inside our own skin every day, and so we take our body for granted. Pretend you are a space alien who is trying out your body for the first time. What would you marvel at? Do you appreciate the ability to express your emotions physically (such as when dancing)? Do you appreciate the ability to touch the one you love and express your love physically? Do you love the way that eyes can be like doorways to the soul? Try to compile a whole list of things about your body that cause you to feel appreciation for it. When you feel as if you have run out of things to appreciate, look up facts about the human body on a computer. You are sure to find a bunch more things to appreciate that you probably never even realized before. Then express your gratitude toward your body often, at least once a day. Every evening, before you go to bed, mentally thank your body for everything it has allowed you to do throughout the day.

6. Find a method of exercise that you are excited to do, and do it out of love. Forcing yourself to do something that you don't like to do is not self-loving. This is why it's so important to get your exercise by doing something that you love to do. Never do exercise to fight your body. You may hate running, but you may like to speed walk. You may hate contact sports, but you may love swimming. Contrary to popular belief, there's no such thing as an activity you *should* do to stay healthy and in shape. Exercise can really lead to self-love. It prevents and combats disease. It helps regulate your sleep patterns. It improves your sex life. It increases your energy levels. Exercise delivers oxygen and nutrients to your tissues and helps your cardiovascular system work more efficiently. When your heart and lungs work more efficiently, you have more energy to go about your day.

If you don't know what kind of exercise you'd like to do, just start trying things out. Use this time to experiment. If you try something you don't like, you never have to do it again. But if you find something you like, you've just added to your health and happiness. Pay attention to how you feel. Your body is wired to avoid pain. If something you are doing is causing you enough pain that you are developing an aversion to it, continuing with that activity can be considered self-abuse. So really take time to try new things and find the activities you like doing so much that you don't have to extrinsically motivate yourself to do them.

7. Allow yourself to sleep. Sleep provides an opportunity for the body to repair, rebalance, and rejuvenate itself. Sleep also helps you retain and process new things you've learned. Part of loving yourself is creating health. Give your body the quality sleep it needs and let it reset itself. Trust yourself to know how much sleep you need every night, and trust yourself to know what your own circadian rhythm is. Your body will tell you when it needs sleep. And if it feels better to you to have a sleeping schedule, then let yourself create one. The worst thing you can do is to ignore your body's clues.

8. Eat a self-loving diet. I could write an entire book on this one subject alone. What you put in your mouth eventually is converted into the body that you experience your life through. So if you are what you eat, it's easy to see how it would be so very important to be deliberate about what you choose to eat. Eat foods that support life and that are full of vital energy. Foods that are dead, genetically modified, preserved, and full of pesticides do not support life—they destroy it.

This may surprise you, but there is no such thing as a perfect diet that suits all people. While it's true that there is a long list of things whose energetic vibrations are incompatible with the energetic vibration of that which is "human"—such as foods with pesticides, sucralose, MSG, refined flours, and processed sugars—still a body's perfect diet varies from person to person.

The one universal truth is that *thought* is the trump card in this universe. You'll remember that earlier we discussed how our universe is being managed by the law of mirroring (often called the law of attraction). This law dictates that only like vibrations can match up and share reality in the physical dimension. The reason this applies to diet is because *you can only be attracted to foods that match your own vibration.* This is why when you are sad, you might gravitate toward ice cream, which is not the healthiest choice. When you are happy, the foods you gravitate toward are those foods that match and therefore reinforce happiness.

It can be highly self-loving to take the action of physically altering your diet so it consists of things that you know are healthy for you. But the best way to choose foods that match a state of self-love (and therefore, health) is to first get into a state of self-love and let yourself be naturally drawn toward the foods that are a match to self-love for you. Listen to your body and allow *it* to tell you how often it wants to eat and drink. The natural state of your body is health. You are not working against your body. It knows what it's doing and what it needs and how to tell you what it needs. This is also the best way to go about choosing a diet because you will notice that no one can reach a state of consensus about what foods are unanimously healthy and what foods are unanimously unhealthy for all people to eat.

You can't eat things you *believe* will make you fat and be skinny. You can't eat foods you *believe* are unhealthy and be healthy. You intuitively know what foods are right for you, but be open to that changing, because it will, especially the more you begin to love yourself and awaken spiritually. In fact, the more self-loving you become, the more sensitivities you will develop to certain foods. Suddenly, things you have eaten for years won't agree with your body because they are no longer a vibrational match to you.

9. Accept your body. Acceptance is a subject we're going to cover in a later chapter, but acceptance relative to your body is very important. Accepting your body is the opposite of resisting it. Resistance creates every single unwanted physical state within the body, all the way from painful menstrual cycles to cancer. It's easy to see, then, why acceptance is so vital. We live in a society that propagates nonacceptance. It has been going on for centuries and centuries. Shame and nonacceptance of our bodies is the opposite of loving our bodies. Defecating and urinating are part of being human. It's a process that enables us to stay in balance. It's a guaranteed part of life. For women, menstruation is a natural, guaranteed part of life. Until we can accept these widely resisted aspects of our bodies (along with all other aspects of our bodies), we will still be living according to self-hate.

Releasing Resistance

Take some time to ask yourself what aspects of your body you are resistant to. Is it the shape of your nose? Is it those few extra pounds that you think shouldn't be there? Is it the size of your breasts or your penis? Is it using the bathroom? Maybe it's a whole list of things. You are not alone. Almost everyone has some kind of resistance to his or her body. Whatever it is, it's time to accept it.

To accept something is not to be "ok with" or to "like" something. It is to swallow the reality of something. It is to recognize the truth or validity of something. The good news is that once you accept something, your focus eventually shifts to what to do with the reality you find yourself in. Your initial defense mechanisms against that thing begin to diminish. And you will spend less and less time and energy pushing against what is, and more time thinking about what to do from wherever you are.

One of the most powerful methods for getting into a state of acceptance is to find approval for something, so as to receive it openly, instead of resisting it. You can do this by changing the way you think. Pick something you are resistant to about your body and write it on the top of a page of paper. Then find as many facts and ideas as possible that make a case for approval of the thing you have written at the top of the paper.

This exercise is not about trying to lie to yourself that you like something that you don't like. It's about releasing your resistance to your body and embracing it instead. Here's an example of this technique in action. For this example, the subject we have picked is, *I have cellulite on my thighs*.

RESULTS OF THE EXERCISE TO RELEASE ONE'S RESISTANCE TO CELLULITE

Who decided that cellulite was unattractive in the first place? I think it's only because I've been taught that it is by society. When I look it up, I see that cellulite is caused by the herniation of subcutaneous fat within fibrous connective tissue. Cellulite doesn't mean that I'm too fat. Everyone has a layer of fat under their skin; cellulite just means that my skin allows the layer of fat underneath it to show.

About 80 to 90 percent of women have cellulite, and medical professionals consider it to be a normal condition of many postpubescent women worldwide, not a "problem." Stress causes an increase in the level of catecholamines, which have been linked to the development of cellulite. So, it's a good excuse to relax and try to eliminate stress from my life.

Companies are the ones that keep selling me the idea that cellulite is bad, but they're doing it so I will spend money on their products. If they convince me that cellulite is ugly, I'll be ten times more likely to buy their crappy product. I don't like that. They are taking advantage of people by decreasing their self-worth in order to get them to buy things. I don't want to buy into it anymore.

Besides, cellulite is responsible for me taking time to question my own thoughts and learn how to love my body. I know my life will get better as a result, so in a roundabout way, cellulite is responsible for improving my life.

Some men prefer the grainy texture of cellulite to the alternative. They say they don't feel as if they are with an actual woman unless she has it. Cellulite can't be considered a flaw if someone *likes* it, and some people really do like it. I've even heard that there are people who find cellulite to be a turn-on.

I don't want to play into society's expectation for a woman to be flawless. That kind of thinking does some real damage, so when I resist my own cellulite, I'm validating society's damaging ideals. Now that I think about it, cellulite is making me realize how much I care what other people think. That doesn't feel good to me. It's time to increase my own self-esteem and become surer of myself. My cellulite is responsible for this realization. Thank you, cellulite!

You know what? I want someone who will love me for me anyway, not love someone that I have to diet or exercise to become. So in a way, my cellulite is a "test" that will allow me to weed out people who aren't worth being with from those who are worth being with.

The more facts and new ways of looking at this that you can come up with, the better! It may take some time, but if we question our beliefs about what we are not accepting, and try to find new ways of looking at it, our lives will get a lot better, and our bodies will be a lot healthier because of it.

Feeling, Seeing, and Believing

Another activity that is helpful is a self-love visualization:

Picture yourself in your mind's eye. With this image in your mind, identify the parts about yourself that you don't approve of. In other words, identify the parts of you that you feel are not lovable. These parts could be personality traits, feelings, thoughts, or, more commonly, parts of your body that you feel are unlovable aspects of you.

Pick one of these parts to focus on. Now think of something that you love more than anything else. When that emotion is built up and intense, visualize permeating and surrounding that unlovable part that you chose with that feeling of intense love. You may want to visualize that love as a light that fully bathes the unlovable part of you in its essence to such a degree that the part of yourself that you chose is transformed.

When you feel as if the process is complete, mentally say to the part, "I love you so much, and I fully approve of you."

Repeat this process with each part of you that you feel is unlovable. This visualization will help you release resistance to yourself. Remember, any disapproval you hold toward an aspect of yourself is resistance, and resistance to yourself is the opposite of self-love.

This process is powerful because believing is being. Your mind and your thoughts form a bridge between your spirit and your body. You find harmony with your spirit through your thoughts, and you use thoughts to create harmony in your body. Your entire body originated as a thought. When you are thinking negative thoughts, it's the same as if you are rewriting the blueprint of your body. Doing this ensures that eventually, disease must manifest.

However, if there is no weakness present in the premanifested vibrations of thought, then there is nowhere for illness to occur. There is no way for a virus or bacteria to affect you, and your genetic predispositions toward a particular disease will be *dormant*. At first glance, you may be taken aback by this concept. After all, we are taught that the world exists outside of us and that we have no control over things outside ourselves. You have probably grown up thinking that if a virus is seeking a host cell, and finds one, you will get sick whether you want to or not.

But if you were not practicing thoughts that made your body open to weakness, you could not be the "victim" of a virus or bacteria of any kind. Viruses and bacteria are opportunistic. You would not experience a system-wide takeover by them if your body did not already have enough weakness present within it that the opportunity existed for the virus or bacteria to take over.

It's very easy to fall into the path of shortsightedness and say that an illness comes from a specific virus and that you know this because you can see it hacking into cells with a microscope. But this is the same as believing that the light that illuminates a room comes from a lightbulb. The story of where light itself *actually* comes from can be traced much further than that. It's a much longer story, just as the story of an illness is much longer than what is obvious and visible; and it goes back, then, to what you think of as the *cause*.

When you trace illness back further than the thing you call the obvious cause, you will find that painful thought is the root of all illness. Painful thoughts prevent the natural flow of the stream of energy, which your eternal consciousness is focusing through you at all times. In the absence of this energy flow, the body begins to deteriorate and becomes weak and vulnerable.

So when it comes to your body, it's a two-way street. The loving things you do to your body and with your body reinforce self-love. In this way, those self-loving thoughts not only improve your body image, but those thoughts also manifest in your body as vibrant health.

TOOL #13

THE TROJAN HORSE

Swallowing Self-Love

When we have spent many years in the landscapes of lack of self-love, even the idea of extending love toward ourselves causes us to feel uneasy. I remember that when I first set out to discover how to love myself, when I would say affirmations to myself that were in any way positive, I'd get a queasy feeling in my stomach like I was going to throw up. I figured that this reaction was just a by-product of the extreme abuse I suffered as a child. But since that time, I have discovered that everyone who really makes a practice and lifestyle out of self-hate has the very same reaction.

I also discovered that those of us who make a practice and lifestyle out of self-hate can't believe or receive anything positive that comes our way. When we say or think loving things toward ourselves, we feel as if we are lying to ourselves. When other people say and do loving things toward us, we don't believe what they say, and we distrust their motives.

Have you ever seen those movies where an army is attacking a castle head-on, and they aren't making any headway whatsoever because the castle walls are too high and thick? In all those movies, the way the army eventually wins is by devising a sneaky entrance into the castle after discovering a different way to get in. Empires are so often destroyed in this way. They come up through the dungeon drainage systems, they give the gift of a Trojan horse to the opposing side with warriors hiding inside, they use long-forgotten underground tunnels, or they disguise themselves as some kind of friends— anything to get inside.

No matter what the strategy is, they all have one thing in common: Instead of trying to bust down the front door, they eventually win by "going through the back door." Self-hate has made sure to secure every defense so that love can't ever enter the front of the castle. But we have learned from all these movies that there is a solution: Why not introduce self-love through a back door?

Self-hate is really good at "keeping our cup empty" by allowing us to give love to others but never receive it ourselves. So we have to be very strategic to beat this enemy, and I am proposing a most unusual way. We can allow self-hate to think that we are busy depleting ourselves by focusing our miniscule supplies of love on someone else, and instead, turn it inward on ourselves. Self-hate has no defense for this strategy.

SIPPING A LITTLE LOVE

To employ this technique, you need a glass of water. Sit down with the glass of water in front of you, and think of someone or something that you really love. Focus on that person or thing, and imagine it in any way that causes you to feel intense positive emotion (love) toward that person or thing.

Then imagine sending or focusing all that positive emotion and love into the water that is in the glass. Maintain this focus for about five minutes. If you need to, you can use a picture of that person or thing to help you intensify the emotion. Music also works quite well to help intensify the feeling. If you have trouble thinking of anything specific that you love, you can choose to focus on the water itself and project love for and to that water. Once you have done this, drink the water.

By drinking water into which you have focused love toward another person or thing, you are forcing your body to accept love. Once you swallow that water, your being has only one option: To accept that love. It doesn't take any effort on your part, either. The strong, high-frequency energy of the love you have focused into the water causes the low-frequency energy in your body to change. You can think of it like music. Drinking the love-infused water forces the low-frequency tone of self-hate that you have inside you to come into alignment and resonate with the new high-frequency tone of self-love.

This technique is not just about the mental metaphor of drinking love. Focusing love onto water actually affects the water itself. In the recent past, a debate has raged between scientists on this matter. There are some who set out to prove that thoughts can change the structure of water molecules, and there are those who set out to prove that the entire idea that thought affects water is "quackery." The scientists in the latter category are mostly those who either still subscribe to a Newtonian model of a mechanical universe or those who comprehend only a portion of the implications that quantum physics is pointing toward. In short, what science has not yet fully accepted is that *our reality is not fixed.*

Like any aspect of physical reality, water reflects thought. But it does this unlike any other substance known to man. Water behaves as if it is a living thing, in and of itself. Water has memory, and its surroundings affect it. And nothing affects the frequency and subsequent structure of the water itself more than thought.

Being an extrasensory since birth, I can visually see the affect that thought has on water. This is ultimately what caused me to conduct the water experiment on myself that you read about in Chapter 3 of this book. When water is subjected to thought, the water retains the frequency of that thought. Water *adopts* the frequency of any thought that is focused toward it. So drinking water that has adopted the frequency of love causes the water in your body to entrain with and resonate at the same frequency as love. This is even more incredibly powerful when we stop to acknowledge that about two-thirds of the weight of an adult human consists entirely of water.

TOOL #14

THE MAGIC OF
MIRROR WORK

Discovering Your True Reflection

When it comes to self-love, few techniques are more pivotal than mirror work. Mirror work has been the staple of self-concept improvement for years, and for good reason: It works! At first, doing mirror work can feel awkward and uncomfortable. You may find that you feel embarrassed or ridiculous. But if you are committed enough to continue despite this feeling, you will discover that on the other side of that resistance is a wonderful payoff.

Mirror work is relatively simple. It's the act of doing any positive process in front of a mirror so you can *interact* with yourself. It can be used in so many ways. We can use it to reinforce affirmations. We can use it to ask ourselves (and reveal to ourselves) the honest truth. We can use it to get in touch with what our heart wants us to know. We can use it to get in touch with our true selves and to discover our true feelings, which are so often suppressed and unrecognized. We can also use it to overcome self-critical, perfectionist attitudes toward ourselves.

You will be surprised by how much the following exercise increases your self-esteem and confidence. It will help you feel comfortable in your own skin because thinking different thoughts toward yourself not only changes you, but it also changes the world around you. The more loving focus you have toward yourself, the more loving the outside world will become toward you.

When you begin to deliberately focus love toward yourself in this way, you are in essence affecting the projector, which is your mind. By doing so, you are affecting what it is projecting out to the world. Because of this, your reality will become a much more compassionate, loving, and accepting place toward you.

Making the Mirror Work for You

Mirror work can be done anytime you feel you need to do it. But to begin with, especially until you become comfortable with it, it's important to make it a part of your routine. Every night before you go to bed, you want to take every measure to ensure that you are in your most raw form. This means removing your makeup if you're wearing any, washing your face, brushing your teeth, and getting naked. If you feel too uncomfortable to be naked at first, that's okay. You can set it as a goal and remove your clothes to do this exercise only when you feel ready.

Find a mirror in your home that you can stand in front of alone and *undisturbed* for at least ten minutes. Remember there is no right or wrong way to do mirror work. Trust your feelings. To begin with, use *any* mirror that you feel comfortable using. Eventually, you can graduate to a full-length mirror so you can see *all* of yourself in the reflection. For the first couple of minutes, just stand there and really look at yourself. Look as deeply as you can into the reflection of your own eyes.

Chances are if you've never done this before, it will probably feel very uncomfortable or awkward, and you may find yourself wanting to turn away from the mirror. This is a completely normal reaction. Simply direct your attention back to the reflection of your eyes and really look at yourself.

Don't judge yourself. Instead, you want to just perceive yourself. If you hear thoughts creep up like, *I have such wrinkly eyelids*, or *I'm kind of scary looking*, or *This is ridiculous*, don't feel discouraged or resist the thoughts. Rather, just notice them and let them go by like clouds in the sky.

After you have stared into your own eyes, simply take in your whole image. Notice your skin, your cheeks, your forehead, your nose, and so on. If you're standing in front of a full-length mirror, look at each part of your full body, head to toe without judgment. After you've really looked at yourself, say gently and out loud to yourself, "I love you, [your first name]."

While continuing to look at yourself in the mirror, begin to deliberately project love and compassion toward yourself from your mind. Imagine sending it into the reflection, into your own heart. Imagine seeing your heart take that love and compassion and pump it through your arteries and veins throughout your entire body. Send that love and compassion anywhere you feel your reflection needs it. Can you feel how much your reflection wants and needs that love?

When it feels as if you have soaked in enough love to continue with the exercise, begin to use the mirror to look for things that you like about yourself and then acknowledge those qualities out loud. For example: "I love that you care." "I love the unique, cobalt color of your eyes." "I love that you are brave enough to do this exercise." "I love how loyal you are." "I love how artistic you are." You can focus on anything about yourself that feels good to focus on, whether that is a physical characteristic or a personality trait. The key is to find things that you can truly love and appreciate about yourself as well as acknowledge yourself for.

Once you are done with that part of the exercise, reflect over your day, and think of things that you are proud of yourself for accomplishing. Acknowledge yourself for anything and everything, no matter how big or small. Try to find at the very minimum ten things that you did during the day that you can appreciate yourself for, and say them out loud to yourself.

Here are some examples: "I'm so grateful to you because you were faced with the choice between doing what you *should* do and doing what you *wanted* to do today, and you chose to do what you wanted to do." "I'm so proud of you for eating a healthy dinner." There is no limit to what you can recognize and appreciate yourself for. This is your chance to stop taking yourself for granted and instead acknowledge yourself the way you have always wanted to be acknowledged.

To finish this exercise, look deeply into the reflection of your eyes again and tell yourself whatever positive messages you feel like you need to hear at that time.

These messages can be affirmations that you've chosen for yourself, or spur-of-the-moment messages that you feel that the "you" in the mirror needs to hear. Say these out loud to yourself.

You could say things like these: "I'm here for you, and I will never abandon you because I love you unconditionally." "It's okay not to be strong anymore." "I want to know everything about you."

Look at yourself in the eyes one last time and again say, "I love you, [your first name]." Allow yourself to feel any feelings that come up, no matter if they are positive or negative, and just let them be there. Loving yourself means loving all that you are, and this includes feelings. When you feel that you are ready to be done with this exercise, take a deep breath, hold it for the count of six, and release the breath. Then go to bed.

Commit to doing this exercise every night for a month. Ideally after you do it for a month, it will become a habit or at least serve to cure you of your mirror work jitters, so you can use mirror work sporadically when you feel that you need it. Also any time you pass a mirror throughout the day, make it a habit to simply glance at yourself and say, "I love you," either out loud or internally.

TOOL #15

PRACTITIONER OF PLAY

The Power of Play

When we are children, we know how to have fun. We don't have to be coerced into play. We don't need a reward to give us incentive to play. Play is just a natural, intrinsic function of being human or of being any animal, actually. Naturally, we relish the experience of our senses, and we understand that enjoyment is all the motivation that we need to create anything we wish. We also understand that enjoyment is the only way to lead a healthy life.

Loving ourselves means stepping outside of rigid social controls and removing the shackles of, "There are more important things to do." When you play, your brain releases endorphins into your bloodstream. Endorphins are natural feel-good chemicals. Playing also helps you heal faster and can help prevent certain medical conditions.

But what exactly is play? Play is defined as engagement in an activity for enjoyment and recreation rather than for a serious or practical purpose. This is where we have to stop and think. In the very definition of the word *play,* we find the dysfunction of the society we have co-created. We have all grown up thinking that play is not synonymous with any purpose.

Then we grow up and wonder why we aren't happy without realizing that it is because we don't take the straight path to happiness by prioritizing enjoyment. Rather, we spend our lives beating around the bush, hoping that our happiness will come as the end result of other priorities like keeping a reliable job or reaching our goals.

Instead, let's consider that enjoyment has a serious, practical purpose. In fact, enjoyment is really the only aspect of our lives with any ultimate value. All other values, are values people hold because they perceive that those values are the key to their enjoyment. For example, a person whose top value in life is honor believes the only way they can enjoy life is if they have honor and if other people have honor. Also, consider happiness within the framework of good and evil. Then consider happiness within the framework of right and wrong. What you will find is that what is considered "evil" or "wrong" is only called that because it's not desired. It's not desired because it diminishes the happiness of an individual or a group.

What Do You Value?

Likewise, those things that we consider "good" or "right" are called those words only because they are desired. They are desired because those actions and things increase the happiness of an individual or a group. Value, then, means nothing more than someone or something's utility in terms of facilitating happiness. Some of us value justice, while others value knowledge, beauty, love, health, achievements, peace, or money. What we miss is that the only reason we value any of them is because we think they are ultimately a means of facilitating happiness.

Unhappiness is what creates all manner of atrocities from wars and terrorism to crimes and illness. Alternately, when we become happier, we become better, healthier people. We become more financially successful, more compassionate, more philanthropic, more energetic, more creative, and even more emotionally and physically healthy. Basically we become more of everything we want to become.

When we become happier, we become more of who we truly are. Happiness is both our highest goal and the most effective means of achieving our other goals. Given this understanding, enjoyment and play seem to serve a pretty serious, practical purpose, don't they?

People who love themselves make the decision that the most important priority in their lives is how they feel. One of the key aspects of happiness, which is often overlooked, is play, and childhood is not the only time we need play. We need it just as much when we are adults, but we tend to get worse and worse at it. Most of us haven't played for so long that we've forgotten how to do it.

There is no right or wrong way to play. It can take the form of a game like poker. It could be playing a sport like volleyball. It can take the form of a leisure activity like taking a bath or be some kind of totally spontaneous action like climbing a tree. No matter what it is, the only criterion that the activity (or nonactivity) must meet is that you are doing it for one reason and one reason only: to enjoy yourself.

Having fun isn't just about the big "fun" things like skydiving—it's also about the small things, like giving yourself permission to take a leisurely walk along a beach, go on a date, or even get totally wet instead of covering up when it rains one day.

Rediscovering Your Playful Self

When we're getting back in touch with play, it's important that you identify what you enjoy. Start by making a list of things that you do simply because you enjoy doing them. If you are having trouble coming up with ideas, it's time to try new things. Just start trying out things that you know other people enjoy doing to see if you enjoy them also. If you do not like something you try, you never have to do it again. If you do, you've just added to your quality of life.

Every time you find something new that you enjoy doing, add it to the list of things you already know you love to do. Commit to doing at least one of the things you have on your enjoyment list every day. Once this becomes easy, you can dedicate a weekend to doing nothing but play. That is, set aside at least two days where you don't do anything unless you enjoy it. Pay attention to how well your body and mind start to feel when you allow them to act according to their own enjoyment.

Once you're putting more stock in your own enjoyment, it's time to develop your awareness of the "spontaneous play impulse." As we've discussed, the most natural state of your being is enjoyment. Because of this, your soul does not have to be coerced into playing. But in the same way that someone might have to tune in to and recognize his or her emotions, you have to tune in to and recognize your play impulse.

For example, when you are walking on a beach, you may have the spontaneous inspiration to run into the surf regardless of whether you are wearing pants or shorts. A sensible person who has trained themselves to ignore and defy their play impulse would choose not to heed that inspiration to play and instead would immediately argue with the impulse by justifying why it's a bad decision.

Maybe they'd think about getting their pants wet and then getting their car seat wet and then having to do laundry. Whatever the case may be, they would not allow themselves to play. They may defy their play impulse so often that they no longer recognize the impulse at all. A person who has recognized the value in enjoyment, on the other hand, would recognize the impulse to play and heed that inspiration by running out into the surf immediately. This isn't an irresponsible action—it's taking full responsibility for one's own happiness. A person who runs out into the surf in this scenario would most likely value the enjoyment of that moment over the *need* to have dry pants or a clean car.

Set a conscious intention to pay attention to your impulses. You get them all day, every day. You may be aware of your impulses to hit someone when you're angry or hug someone when you're excited. Now it's time to recognize your impulse to play. It may take a good deal of bravery, but when that impulse comes up, let yourself act on the impulse to play. Let yourself climb that tree if you suddenly get the impulse to climb it. Let yourself buy the finger paints you pass in the grocery-store aisle and paint with them. Give yourself permission to roll down a grassy hill in the park even if you're wearing a skirt or a suit and tie. Sign up for scuba-diving lessons if you've always wanted to try it. What you came into this life to do was play. So do it!

Combining Work and Play

This brings me to my next point: If your job doesn't fit the definition of play, you have not yet lined up with what you are meant to be doing here on this planet. A person who loves him-

or herself chooses a career that is not just a job, but something that is enjoyable for them, something they can be passionate about every day.

When you have lost touch with your true self, your joy and purpose are lost to you as well. To recover them, you must be willing to take a risk and place value on your own joy. When you take this kind of risk, you're committing to the willingness for your entire life to change. You are committing to your direction changing perhaps several times over the course of your life.

But it's only by making this commitment that it becomes possible to be truly happy. So it's time to prioritize play, not just in your personal time, but also in your choice of career. Your profession is meant to be an activity where enjoyment, in and of itself, is the practical purpose of engaging in the activity, and the money you make doing it is meant merely as a bonus. That being said, some people may find that making money in and of itself is what they consider to be "fun" and for them, it is therefore in alignment to prioritize that directly.

TOOL #16

NO MORE TRIPS TO THE HARDWARE STORE

Searching Endlessly

While sitting in the common area of the university in 2006, I ended up across from an older gentleman who was reading a newspaper. Being the curious person that I am, I did what I usually do when I find myself sitting in that awkward silence between "strangers" who are right near each other: I struck up a conversation with him. It was during this conversation that this man told me something I will never forget. This was one of those triggered realizations you find afterward that you can't keep living your life the same way you used to.

As we chatted casually and I responded to his questions, I found myself detailing to him the complicated romantic, familial, and friendship relationships I was maintaining at the time. He listened and then said to me in a quiet sort of way, "It seems to me like you're going to the hardware store for milk."

Our conversation ended with hugs a short time after that, but I remained in an introspective mood for a good hour after the interaction. I still don't know the name of the man I met that day, but what he told me with that one sentence has become a hallmark of my teachings on self-love. Up to that point, I never gave much thought to hardware stores, but I do now.

You see, when we don't love ourselves, we don't allow ourselves to look for the things we need and want in the places where we can *actually* find them. Instead, we keep trying to make the current people, places, and things in our lives give us what we want. The trouble is that they're never going to do it. It's as if we are walking into a hardware store and asking them to give us milk, and every day the clerk tells us that they don't carry milk. Every day we leave the store sad and deprived of milk . . . but we still return the next day.

We tend to stay stuck in this pattern until we realize the hardware store is never going to carry milk. It's only when we realize and accept this fact that we *allow* ourselves to go find a store that does sell milk.

As you can tell, the milk in this analogy represents love. When we do not love ourselves, we continually try to get our current relationships to give us the love we need and want, but they never will. This is because our current relationships are just projections of the internal relationship we have with ourselves. They are projections of our current *nonloving* state.

For the people around us to reflect love when we are not in a loving state ourselves defies the laws of this universe. Our current negative-feeling relationships might lack love, but they serve as an important contrast because they show us what we *do truly want*—and that is love. However, all too often, once we know that we want love, we then turn around and expect the contrast in our lives, the nonloving relationships, to magically transform from lack into love.

We are meant to allow ourselves to go get that love from someone who actually offers love, but we have to realize where to look and how to go about it properly. It is not selfish to seek love; we all crave it and need it.

In fact, the act of allowing yourself to go find love from people who are actually offering love is a self-loving act. Once you come to this realization, you will really benefit from this self-loving act. It changes your relationship with yourself, and, in turn, you will find that you actually *will* connect with people who can offer you love.

Hardware Stores Only Sell Hammers

To take this analogy to the next level, you will find that going to the hardware store for milk is what we are doing any time we are looking in the wrong places for the things we need. We are going to the hardware store for milk if we hate our job, but keep trying to get our boss to change things at the office so we will like it better. We are going to the hardware store for milk when we repeatedly try to fix an item that isn't fixable instead of buying something new. We are going to the hardware store for milk when we keep trying to rely on friends who have demonstrated again and again that they are flaky, but we still become disappointed when they continue to be flaky.

It happens at home, too. You might find yourself going to the hardware store for milk if you are homosexual and keep trying to get your family to accept you when they won't. You might keep trying to get your mother or father to understand that you hold a specific important belief, but they just don't get it. And if you are a woman, you are going to the hardware store for milk when you stay in an abusive relationship with a man, hoping that one day he will miraculously decide *not* to hit you anymore. It's the same for abusive partners of any kind.

So how do you break out of this endless search? Start by examining your life. Are there ways in which you expect other people, things, or circumstances to change into what you want them to be, instead of just allowing yourself to go find other people, things, and circumstances that already *are* what you want them to be? Try to be as honest with yourself as possible and identify the ways that you tend to go to the wrong places to meet your needs.

Ask yourself where you really should be looking instead, and then go to the right place. Let yourself go find milk where milk is sold. Let yourself find a new job that you love. Let yourself gain a network of friends who are like family to you and who fully accept you for being gay. Let yourself retire that old item you've been trying to fix, and buy a new one. And, most important, give yourself the love that you have wanted so badly to receive from others.

Human Needs

When it comes to giving ourselves the love that we want so badly to receive from others, nothing is more important than learning the right ways to meet our needs. No matter what race, sex, or religion we are, no matter where we are born or how we are raised, as we all have needs. And people who love themselves don't fight against their own needs. They meet them!

No matter how much you may want it to be different, you have needs. A need is something that is required in order to live, succeed or be happy. Here is a very short list of examples of needs: Love, contribution, understanding, consideration, intimacy, certainty, security, enjoyment, variety, purpose, connection, honesty, autonomy, meaning, health, stability, support, trust, warmth, acceptance, improvement, expansion, significance, affection, appreciation, belonging, cooperation, communication, closeness, inclusion, respect, play, touch, food, air, water, movement, rest, choice etc. Naturally, we feel much more confident about meeting some needs than others.

When it comes to needs it is important to know that you cannot un-require something that is required. You cannot argue your way into seeing that it isn't necessary. You have one option when it comes to your needs and that is to meet them. I'm going to repeat what I just said so it sinks in . . . Your one option when it comes to needs is to meet them.

Why is this your one option? Because if you do not meet those needs consciously, you will meet them subconsciously. This is what manipulation is. Manipulation carries a big stigma and makes it sound as if someone is malevolently controlling someone else. In reality, it is highly subconscious and also quite innocent. Manipulation is what we do when we feel we cannot meet out needs directly, so instead we try to meet them in round about ways. We try to influence others to do what we want them to do so our needs are met. For example, a person who needs to feel safe but who cannot ask directly to be protected, may create a situation where they have to be rescued by someone else or paint the false picture that they are in danger so other people will step up and offer their protection. Or, a person who needs help or needs to feel supported, but who cannot ask directly for help or support, may develop an illness that makes it so people have to help or support them. Or a person who needs to feel accepted, but who can't seek that out directly, will become a chameleon to try to influence people to accept him or her.

Every one of us manipulates. The question is to what degree are we conscious of that manipulation? Some common ways of manipulating people are lying, dropping hints, guilting others, self-sacrificing, being passive aggressive or using emotional punishment against them, flattering people insincerely, being a chameleon, being seductive, making false promises, doing favors, making yourself out to be the victim and making threats etc. Keep in mind that we all use what we have, so we will usually manipulate people with whatever is currently working to our advantage. For example, a spiritual medium may use their abilities to "divine" messages for you from God simply to keep you dependent on them and thus guarantee that you will never leave them.

Manipulation doesn't make you a bad person, but dare to take a look at your life and ask yourself, how do I manipulate? In what ways do I ensure that I will get the reaction I want from others instead of just asking for what I want upfront? In what ways do I think I can meet other people's needs just so that they can meet mine?

Manipulation will always feel out of alignment with your own sense of integrity because if you are manipulating, you are not being authentic. So, a good question to ask yourself might be . . . What things cause me pain or make me feel ashamed of myself that I cannot give up or get over or stop doing? For example, a person might find that even though it causes them pain to cut themselves, they cannot give it up because when they cut, they get people to stop what they are doing and attend to them with concern. Therefore, the cutting is a way of meeting their need to be seen and understood. Also, take a look at what was not ok to need or want in your family. We tend to manipulate to get the needs met which we feel are not ok to have, especially emotional needs. And once you find those needs, ask yourself one by one, how do I go about getting this need in my life currently?

Stopping ourselves from manipulating is difficult for one major reason...it requires us to be brave enough to be vulnerable. We have to be willing to admit to needs that we feel are not ok. Once we become conscious of our manipulation, it no longer feels good to do the manipulative thing that we were doing and we will naturally find ways to replace our way of meeting that need. When we catch ourselves in the act of manipulating, we can ask ourselves, "What is it that I am trying to get by doing this?" And then we can express that need directly or meet that need directly in another way.

Get in touch with what you want and what you need. You've got to take the time or take pauses over the course of the day to ask yourself what you really need or really want. If you need help, look on the Internet for a list of needs. Physical, mental and emotional needs. And from those lists, make a list of your individual needs. Then, when you feel negatively, go to the list and identify the need you have and find ways to fulfill that need or express it to others. In my community, sometimes we bring these sheets of needs to someone in the community and ask them to point to the one they need.

Another good exercise to do throughout the day is to ask the inner child what it needs. Inner children are better at picking out the need they have from a list than they are at verbally expressing it. With each and every need, you can then brainstorm ways to meet the need yourself and have the need met by others. Involve other people in this brainstorming task if you get stuck. If you are truly clueless about your needs and wants, take a look at what you know that you don't want. To the other side of those aversions, are preferences.

You may have heard of the hungry ghost, which represents greed . . . the concept that if you begin to give into your needs, they never stop and you just keep wanting more and more. This couldn't be any further from the truth. Imagine for once that a need that is met is a need that is met and that if you meet a need, you will feel satiated. As we covered in a previous chapter, greed is not a natural state . . . because starvation is not a natural state. If one's needs were met consistently, one would not become concerned with the self-centered desire to hoard resources. Hoarding only occurs in the presence of the fear of scarcity. So not meeting your needs is a great way to become greedy.

No need is too childish . . . It's tempting to see needs like being held or like being comforted as childish needs. But these needs often exist because they were not met within us in childhood. If a need isn't met in childhood, we never actually mature past that point. And it may be tempting to think that if we start to meet the needs of the inner child as an adult, that the inner child will never be satiated. But it will and the result of satiating the inner child's needs is that the inner child grows up. In other words, if needs were not met in childhood, they must be met FOR us to grow up. And as a side note, they will be met by us in round about ways whether we like it or not, in fact most of the sexual fetishes in the world are actually about unfulfilled childhood needs. I'll tell you a personal story. I was not protected as a child and some time ago, I realized that I needed to feel safe and didn't especially when I was sleeping at night. So I directly asked one of my housemates to sleep next to me. I found that the next day, I felt much more secure in the world. Now let me ask you a question, would it have been better to deny this need because it was childish? Would that have made me a "better person?"

You may think you are needless, want less or anti-dependent. You may think you don't need anything from anyone. But in this world, you are dependent on other people. You need them and they need you. This doesn't mean you are powerless. When you are in the space of thinking you don't need anything from anyone, you are too afraid to be vulnerable and so you don't ask for what you need and so your subconscious runs the show, getting you what you need in all kinds of roundabout and highly manipulative ways that you may not even recognize.

The reality is it's scary to acknowledge your needs to others, after all someone might say NO to your needs. But I want you to think about it this way . . . If you were honest about your needs from the get go, people who could not meet those needs would gravitate away and people who could meet those needs would gravitate to you and your life would look a lot different than it does currently. And guess what? It makes us happy to meet each other's needs. And meeting someone's needs, might just meet your own simultaneously. For example, one of us might feel happy when we are meeting someone's need for comfort. Meeting their need for comfort may in fact meet our need for connection. On the flip side, another of us might feel like meeting someone's need for comfort is as pleasurable as getting our teeth pulled, meeting their need for comfort may in fact conflict with our need for autonomous achievement. So we simply need to allow ourselves to line up with and select people whose needs are met by meeting our needs. You might just be surprised . . . the people around you might just be relieved to know what your needs are and to be able to meet them. A good question to ask yourself is, what needs make me happy to meet?

And for those of you who are wondering, what if the person you have chosen for a partner doesn't want to meet your needs, here's your answer . . . Ideally, your needs would be met through various people, not just one. Powerless dependence happens most often when one person is your sole resource for your needs getting met. But you have to be very honest with yourself about what needs you specifically want to have met through a partner and which ones you are ok with getting through someone else. This is an individual preference. And if you find that the needs you specifically want to have met by a partner cannot be met through your partner, let yourself find another partner. Honoring a person when they say No to meeting your needs is a very important thing because it means you can put them in the proper place in your life. For example, if one of your needs in a partnership is emotional availability and your partner can't be emotionally available, you can now choose to take them out of the role of partner and place them in a friendship role in your life or you can choose to alter your expectation of a partner if that is possible or you can choose to be unfulfilled in that partnership. In my opinion, it's better to not make each other miserable, resenting each other for things you aren't providing for each other.

The word *desire* means something that is wanted but something that we can do without. But in truth, we cannot do without our desires either, so our desires are also needs. Our happiness depends on our ability to meet our needs and get those needs met in healthy ways. Our perceived powerlessness to meet those needs in healthy ways is what creates the kind of love that we call "painful attachment." It's what prevents us from developing a truer form of love, which is unconditional and is free from painful attachment. You can think of resistance as a component of that painful attachment.

The Who and How of Meeting Your Needs

Everything you ever do, whether it's ultimately beneficial or detrimental, you do for only one reason and that is because you think it will meet one or more of your needs. Meeting these needs is what gives rise to the sensation of happiness. That's why we can also say that the only reason *anyone* does *anything* is because they think it will add to their happiness.

It's crucial to our happiness that we meet our needs. Contrary to popular opinion, the goal is not to rid ourselves of these needs, but rather it is to find out how to get those needs met. Providing those needs for ourselves also entails finding people whose joy is genuinely satisfied by providing us with those needs that we can't or don't want to meet for ourselves.

It's a travesty that humans try to force themselves to not need what they need. Indeed the basis of many world religions is the individual quest to reach a state where we no longer have desires or needs. We come up with this idea that desires and needs are the root of suffering only when we feel incapable of meeting those desires and needs.

The world is moving on a continuum, away from utter powerlessness at one end, progressing to independence, and beyond that to interdependence. We are constantly told by advocates of "independent self-sufficiency" that it's not appropriate to try to fulfill ourselves through other people, that it's not okay to try to use people to fill the void within ourselves. This group feels that every need should be filled by one's self and only by one's self. The people who resonate with teachings of personal empowerment that inspire independent, self-sufficient reality creation are those who have felt powerless to others, especially to other people who could or would not meet their needs. Those people had no choice but to turn to themselves and to "God" or "The Universe." But this perspective they hold is based on the assumption that other people are separate from you, this is not true. We are all one, so in fact everyone around you is part of you. Therefore, if you use others to fill the void within you, you are in fact using part of yourself to fill the void within you.

Let's pretend that you needed your loved one in order to feel comforted. One could argue that you are powerless because they could die and you'd be left at the mercy of that experience, which is torture. So, the only lasting peace is to find wholeness and comfort in and of yourself alone. But this is merely an attempt to avoid interpersonal pain. And to believe this, you would have to assume that you are in fact at the mercy of *their* presence, and could not manifest someone or something else to feel comforted by. It's the disbelief in your ability to create or find what you need that is actually hurting you in this scenario, not the fact that you are dependent in general on something or someone other than yourself.

In a world that is one, you can only ever be dependent on that which is you. And in a world that is one, you are dependent on everyone else, and they are dependent on you. This does not mean that you are powerless. We sometimes mistake dependence for powerlessness, most especially the powerlessness to create. But they are not the same thing.

You cannot really become independent. To do so would be to separate yourself from the rest of the universe. Empowerment is about meeting your needs, including those needs that require the participation of another person. You are not an island. No person is. Stop trying to be one. People who love themselves actively embrace interdependence.

In summary then, it's not your job to deny yourself of your needs. Even the most enlightened being in existence has these same needs. The enlightened being has simply perfected the art of meeting those needs in healthy ways. Now it's your turn to determine how you are currently meeting those needs. It's your turn to replace the unhealthy ways with healthy ways that accomplish the same end: your needs being met. When you do this, you will no longer feel a sense of lack, and your relationships will be a source of joy instead of pain.

And in your quest, remember that you cannot keep taking trips to the hardware store for milk. It's a self-created hell to try to make things change that will not change or to keep searching in the totally wrong places for the things you need. We cannot deprive ourselves and love ourselves at the same time, so make the choice to love yourself and acknowledge that you deserve to get whatever it is that you are wanting. Then let yourself go find it in the places where *it can be found.*

TOOL #17

Learning to Say *No*

Selfishness or Self-Love?

The definition of self-love sounds pretty straightforward. To include all parts of yourself as you . . . Not to push them away or exclude them. When you practice self-love, you practice the art of seeing, hearing, feeling, understanding, valuing, considering and caretaking all the parts of yourself. You practice a deep devotion and affection for yourself. These things are what we hope for in a marriage, and we feel those things toward the individual we stand in front of at the altar when we say "until death do us part."

But what about doing these things for the person you committed to first? What about the person who is going to be with you until the end of your life beyond a shadow of a doubt? What about *you*? You committed to your own identity upon coming into this life. The person who you can absolutely guarantee will *always* be there with you in this life is *you*. So *you* should be your number one priority. You are the love of your life even if sometimes you don't know it yet.

Now let's contrast that self-love to selfishness because the two words are often used in the same discussion. Selfishness is defined as concern only for one's own welfare, benefit, and interests regardless of the impact on others. Selfishness is not a natural state. It only occurs when a person is convinced that no one will caretake *their* best interests, so they must fight against the best interests of others, for their own best interests. We often confuse self-love and selfishness, but there is a big difference between the two. Selfishness is created when those who have not experienced love, and therefore trust, feel a sense of internal deprivation and then spend their lives trying to fight for their own personal best interests, despite other people's best interests.

People who are considered selfish and people who are considered selfless are both coming from the same mentality of *lack and narcissism*. That is why they seem to always find each other—they are a perfect vibrational match. They see the energy in the world, especially love, as a finite resource that can be used up. They don't recognize it for the eternal stream of energy that is infinite and always flowing. And they believe that no one will act in their best interests, so they must act in their own best interests. And they find many overt and covert strategies for doing so.

Selfless people feel as if they must surrender love and other resources because of the belief that giving it to themselves means they are depriving someone else of that love and those resources. As if there is only so much to go around! Selfish people also think that there is only so much to go around. They think they must take love and other resources; otherwise, they will not have enough to survive.

But what if I told you there is no such thing as selflessness? Most of us have grown up believing that our only hope of being loved is to be good. We are taught that being selfless is what good people do, and so to be loved, we must be selfless. Therefore, it's very common that the motivation behind being selfless is to in fact *get* from others. Selflessness is therefore backed by a self-centered motive.

Most people who are seen as selfless are in fact those who have spent their lives meeting their own needs in a manipulative manner. For example, they sacrifice themselves in order to get approval. Or to make it so they can guilt someone later into doing what they want them to do. Or for a sense of self-esteem, because they can see themselves and be seen as right and good.

Learn to Say No

When we have deprived ourselves of self-love in the attempt to avoid being selfish, we often develop the inability to say no. We set ourselves up for failure by never saying no, because we commit ourselves to a life lived for other people and not for ourselves. This isn't sustainable, because it takes a toll on our energy, body, and relationships. This is also a big ruse because living a life that is "for others" is really at its root, a roundabout way of trying to meet our own needs.

When we say yes to others whenever we are asked to do something and whether we actually want to or not, we might not mean it, because deep down we feel resentful even though it was our decision in the first place. We suppress those feelings of resentment, but emotions like resentment are energy, and energy has to go somewhere. So it does. Those negative feelings express themselves through your body and begin to corrode the bond between you and the people in your life.

While it can be uncomfortable to think about saying no, it's important to remember that every time you say yes to someone or something else when you don't really want to, you are saying no to yourself and to your priorities. It's also important to remember that the reason we can't stand saying no is because it makes us feel selfish. But the very reason we are saying yes is the result of a self-concerned desire: such as the desire to be loved or to be seen as good or to avoid conflict etc. We are really saying yes to others for ourselves and not for them!

The problem is that it doesn't work well, because yet again we are not in control of how much of any need we will actually get from others when we say yes to them. We keep extending energy toward things when we have no energy to keep extending. This is a recipe for burnout.

If you want to learn how to say no, begin by figuring out what your priorities are. You will not know what to say no to until you figure out what you actually want to say yes to. Make a list of priorities. Think about what makes you the happiest and what you want to give your attention to in your life right now. Some examples that could go on this list are my health, spirituality, my marriage, my children, earning money, making time for myself every week, exercise, going to school, home repairs, and so on.

Once you've compiled this list, pick your top three priorities. On top of that list, in the number one spot, write "Take care of myself and allow myself to be happy." No matter what you picked, you will not be able to do any of it if you do not take care of yourself first. You can't take care of other people or perform tasks if you burn out. As you review the list, can you see how your life may need to be reorganized? For the next week, make a commitment to *not* say yes, or commit yourself, to anything that isn't on your priority list.

Once you've compiled a priority list, make a list of everything you would like to say no to. Compiling this list may cause you to feel guilty. But this is your time to be totally honest with yourself about what you really want to do in your heart and what your heart is telling you that you don't want to do.

If you could say no to someone or something with absolute surety that there would be no negative consequences, who or what would you say no to? Is there a commitment you've made that you want to cancel? Is there a project you want to give up? Is there a relationship you want to end? Pick the most important thing on this list that you really want to say no to and say no to it. That means that if it's a date, cancel it. If it's a project, give it up. Take that step to free yourself from burden.

Think about how you could go about saying no that would be easiest. Maybe it's talking to someone face-to-face or maybe it's making a phone call. Maybe it's an e-mail or a letter. Let yourself take the path of least resistance. Don't expect yourself to do it the hard way; it's already hard enough to say no.

Once you have said no, give yourself some time to see how much better it feels to be free of that commitment; and if you're ready, say no to the rest of the things you wrote down on this list. This is a practice exercise, and if you do it often enough, it will get easier and easier to stick with your current priorities and not let them slip. It will get easier to stay true to yourself and what makes you happy.

"Let Me Get Back to You"

One of the best ways to learn to stay true to yourself is to delay answering people right away. It's really hard when you've been practicing saying yes for a lifetime to suddenly feel good about saying no up front, the minute you are asked. But if you're really deliberate about it, you can catch yourself before the word *yes* leaves your lips. Practice this simple statement: "Let me get back to you." In this way, you've deflected the pressure of having to answer and you've given yourself the time to go home and be really honest with yourself about whether the answer is yes or no.

Saying no does not only apply to saying no to other people. It also applies to saying no to ideas that originate from self-hate. When we are operating from self-hate, we feel the need to *do* something to deserve the love and relationships in our lives. We feel the need to justify why someone is or should remain in a relationship with us. It's as if doing things for other people becomes our insurance policy for love. Because of this, we develop a habit of self-sacrifice.

Often no one in our lives is even asking us to sacrifice ourselves. We simply volunteer to do it. We fall into the role of martyr by committing to things that we know in our heart we don't actually want to do, without even being asked to do them. For example, we know we don't have time to add one more project to our already full schedule, but we offer to do the project anyway. Or we know it doesn't feel good to offer someone the opportunity to live with us, but we offer the person a place to stay anyway even though they did not expect or even ask to stay with us.

When we do this, we feel the temporary high of self-esteem because we feel like we are a good person. But this feeling quickly gives way to a feeling of dread. We feel put-upon by the person when they didn't even put anything upon us. We did it to ourselves. We threw ourselves under the bus, so to speak.

Why would we sabotage ourselves in this way? We do it for several reasons. The first reason is that we want people to feel a certain way towards us and we don't think we can say no without them having a negative opinion of us. And we feel that this has negative consequences that we can't face. Another reason is to prevent ourselves from experiencing the pain of watching other people experience pain. Another reason is that we want to do what we believe is right and good. Another reason is to avoid feeling guilty or selfish. And another reason is to maintain a connection with other people to prevent them from abandoning us.

But ultimately what we are doing is meeting the needs of others at the expense of our own needs. On the surface, we often appear content to self-sacrifice, when underneath we feel a deep sense of emotional deprivation, which leads to anger and resentment toward the object of our sacrifice.

It's important for those of us who self-sacrifice to accept that there really is no such thing as self-sacrifice. Every self-sacrificing behavior is done with a self-centered motive in mind! It's important that we learn to take an active role in meeting our own unmet needs *directly* instead of trying to use our self-sacrificing behavior as an attempt to gain worth, seek approval and recognition, or prevent people from leaving us in a backdoor manner.

Ending the cycle of self-sacrifice can be hard to do, especially given the fact that we live in a society that places high cultural and religious value on self-sacrifice. But it's doable, and it begins with the realization that our self-sacrifice does not originate from the pure joy we experience when helping someone. Instead, it's a by-product of our own internal deprivation.

If we can set an intention to wait when we feel the immediate, momentary urge to offer help, the mud of our schemata will settle. We can say no to our momentary urge to self-sacrifice. Then, from a space of clarity we can ask ourselves whether what we are about to do is self-sacrificing or something we genuinely *want* to do because it makes us happy to do it. We can ask ourselves what we feel needy of.

Ask yourself, *What is it that I was trying to get as a result of the self-sacrifice I was about to commit?* When you find the answer, you can ask yourself the more important questions: *How can I get that more directly? And/or how might I give that to myself?*

TOOL #18

Victim to Victor!

Who Is the Real Victim?

Part of loving ourselves is stepping out of the role of the victim. Before we continue, I must make something crystal clear. People in the world find themselves in positions where by human definition, they are absolutely victims. In the spiritual and self-help field, this is often denied, giving rise to a movement of victim shaming; as if it is always wrong to feel like a victim or to perceive yourself as one no matter the circumstance you find yourself in. This is not what I am saying at all. There is a big difference between the very real experience of being a victim (including the thoughts and emotions that come with the healing from that experience) and victim mentality in and of itself.

Many of us think we do not have a victim mentality when in fact we do. There are varying extremes of victim mentality. It can manifest when we have a handicap and pity ourselves for an accident that we can't change and that has now caused us to feel as if we are incapable. It can also manifest when we have a job we hate but are convinced we *have* to keep.

In fact, we are in the role of the victim any time we feel powerless to something else, whether we feel powerless to a self-limiting belief, a person, a government, or a circumstance. It's easy to slip into the belief that we aren't in control of our own lives, but whenever we don't see that we are in control of our own lives, we get stuck in the role of the victim.

Being a victim does have some nice perks though. First of all, it allows us not to have to take on responsibility, which can feel like a burden and can get very, very heavy when we are adding blame on top of that responsibility. Interestingly, the universe does not recognize blame. Blame is something that originates from the human psyche.

Yet another perk of being a victim is that you don't have to take responsibility for your future. It's hard to realize that no one is going to save you from your situation. One of the most painful realizations you can have is the realization that no one can rescue you from yourself.

When you feel powerless already, the awareness that there is no one to help you but *you* is enough to push you right over the edge. Many people commit suicide when they come to this realization. I almost did myself. Those of us who feel the most powerless are faced with the decision either to commit to life and do what we can, with what we have, from where we are, or to commit in the other direction and choose death.

Taking responsibility for our future means we have to drop the thoughts, words, and actions that aren't getting us anywhere. It means we have to change, and change is scary. It's scary to hold the weight of your own life in your hands. But our lives will only become lives of joy, freedom, and peace when we can own the responsibility not only for what was, but also for what is and what is to come.

Another perk of being in the victim role is that we get attention and validation for it. We mistake the concern and pity we get from others for love. It begins to become the only way we feel love. We become very scared that if we gain autonomy or our problems go away, we will be all alone. People get tired of giving us attention and validation for our pain after a while. They begin to gravitate away from us and we feel abandoned. Our only hope is to find someone new to validate and pity us.

Owning Your Own Life

So it's understandable that we would seek out a role as victim when we have not learned how to love ourselves yet, because all that is left (without pity and attention) is deprivation. This pseudolove we are filling ourselves up with is never enough, though, because it's a poor substitute for real love. Although it feels temporarily good, it ultimately handicaps us.

When we play the role of the victim, we get to be right and everyone is on our side. But feeling righteous is a temporary high. Being the victim feels completely powerless, so feeling right feels a little bit more powerful than that. Besides, other people join our side, and we feel loved when they agree with us and defend us. We feel safer when others are on our side, which also feels better than being a defenseless victim.

Regretfully this is not real love, and this is not real safety. It's pseudolove and pseudosafety. People may defend us and agree with us that we are the innocent ones while someone or something else is the bad guy, but no matter what other people say, we are still victims. We are just pitied, nonresponsible, validated, righteous, and defended victims.

The truth is, we are all just the victim of victims. So the question is, where does it end? Living a good life begins with the decision to be the true "owner" of your own life.

Learning Gratitude and Forgiveness

As you now know, I was severely abused in childhood. And standing here today, I have completely forgiven the man who abused me as a child. So when it comes to forgiveness, I am overqualified not just as a teacher of universal truth, but also as a personal survivor, to share with you the truths and myths about forgiveness.

One thing people cannot seem to agree upon is what it means to forgive someone. To forgive someone is to give up feeling resentment, anger or the need for requital that you hold relative to someone or something that you feel has hurt you. It is experienced as a deep relief. A deep relief of tension occurs in forgiveness because you are no longer stuck on a hook of not being able to move forward in life because of what happened. You are no longer on the hook to need something like retaliation or compensation from them in order to move forward. You are no longer plagued by painful feelings of resentment or anger or resistance towards them.

Let's begin by making a statement that I never want you to forget about forgiveness. It is going to set the stage for your understanding of forgiveness, and here it is: *You Cannot Force Forgiveness*. You cannot TRY to forgive. You cannot force forgiveness no matter how much you want to. The greatest misconception relative to forgiveness is that you can simply choose to forgive. People approach forgiveness as if it is a red button that you can just push and that if you haven't pushed it yet, you must be either intellectually challenged or enjoy stubbornly refusing to get over something.

People want you to forgive for two reasons. The first is that it is natural to want people to feel good instead of bad. The second is that it makes them feel uncomfortable feelings for us to have negative feelings, especially if those feelings are about a specific person. And most especially if those feelings are about they, themselves. In other words, they want us to change the way we feel because *they* are not ok with feeling their own negative emotion. To tell someone that they have to forgive is emotional abuse. It is to tell someone they shouldn't feel how they feel and therefore to stop feeling how they feel. It is to shame them if they can't just decide to feel differently. And if you are telling someone to forgive someone specifically, you just became a pardoner of the other person's offense. You told the person who feels deeply hurt by someone to just take it. This makes you worse than a bystander. It makes you an enabler.

You want to forgive for two reasons. The first is that it is natural to want to feel good and if you feel like you can't get over something, like you are resentful and angry and need requital, you aren't feeling good. The second is that forgiveness is considered to be so virtuous and non-forgiveness so bad that you cannot be in a state of non-forgiveness and feel like you are a good person. You feel like you have to forgive in order to maintain a positive self-concept. Except there is one scenario where this is flipped and that is with regards to forgiving ourselves. Subconsciously we feel that forgiving ourselves makes us bad. That we must never forgive ourselves for the way we have hurt ourselves or others because if we do let ourselves off of the hook, we run the risk of causing harm again. This is our engrained sense of penance.

The main reason you can't force forgiveness is that a lack of forgiveness is about painful emotions. You cannot just choose not to feel a certain way, as if hitting a red button with your free will. Emotions do not work like this. Your feelings never ever lie. They never lie because they are always a perfectly accurate reflection of a perception that you hold. *In order to feel differently therefore, you have to change your perspective entirely.* And unfortunately, changing your perception is also not something that you can just choose to do as if pushing a red button. For example, if a drunk driver hit someone and they ended up paralyzed, it takes a hell of a lot more than just deciding to see it as a good thing in order to consider it a blessing to have been paralyzed instead of feel like it is a curse every time you have to hoist yourself onto your wheelchair.

I cannot tell you how many people I have shaken hands with who tell me that they have forgiven someone and it is total and complete malarkey. What it is, is bypassing and suppression. Spiritual bypassing is the cancer of the spiritual world. It is a disease that has run rampant in both religious and non-religious circles. Spiritual bypassing (or whitewashing) is the act of using spiritual beliefs to avoid facing or healing one's painful feelings, unresolved wounds and unmet needs. It is a state of avoidance. Because it is a state of avoidance, it is a state of resistance. I personally, consider Spiritual bypassing to be the shadow side of spirituality. Spiritual beliefs of any spiritual tradition and even simply societal beliefs can provide ample justification for living in a state of *inauthenticity*. They can all provide justification for avoiding the unwanted aspects of one's own feelings and state of being in favor of what is considered to be "a more enlightened or virtuous state of being." In today's world, we have little tolerance for working through our pain. We much prefer instantaneous solutions that involve numbing out pain.

When we use spirituality to whitewash over our issues and try to avoid them, we use the goal of spiritual transcendence to try to rise above the raw and messy and real side of human life before we have fully faced and made peace with it. This can be seen as premature and false transcendence. And it is dangerous because it sets up a major division internally. It creates a definable split between where one really is and where one thinks they should be. It enables us to lie to ourselves and delude ourselves and live our lives through the projection of a *false self.*

When we have been hurt, we so often suppress, deny and disown the part of us that feels those raw unresolved feelings and identify with a coping part of ourselves that is "beyond it all." We cannot heal unless we are willing to admit to where we are and who we are. Bypassing is like breaking your leg, but being unwilling to admit to it, putting a band-aid over the compound fracture and trying to continue forward anyway.

It takes a very, very keen perception to discern whether someone has really forgiven or whether they have erected a false persona whilst suppressing the rest of themselves that happens to be beyond it all. I'll give you a tip. *If someone has truly reached a place of forgiveness, they will not ever tell you to forgive.* Also, if someone has bypassed instead of truly forgiven, their world is full of people who mirror the parts of themselves that they suppress. People who have not forgiven and whom are mad at them for their transcendent stance on issues.

When we turn away from our pain or away from "wherever we are," we abandon ourselves. We resist the very thing we are trying to avoid. But most terrifying of all (and this should come with a huge warning) we guarantee that it will come up in our realities again; only it will come back bigger next time. It is at this point that we eventually have to face whatever it is that we actually have to face and really integrate those painful emotional states and come up with a perception that changes the perspective of our most hurt aspects, not a perspective that enables us to suppress, deny and disown them. True forgiveness happens when all parts of us are able to move forward and feel good doing so, not just some parts of us.

How One Actually Gets to a Place of Forgiveness

1. When you or someone else is in a state of pain relative to feeling hurt by someone else, get the idea of forgiveness out of your head. Don't even bring it up. Get the idea of healing in your mind instead. Forgiveness implies profound healing must take place. And when you walk the path of healing, forgiveness is something that happens to you and often quite spontaneously. It is as if forgiveness falls in your lap as a result of taking previous and seemingly unrelated steps on the healing path. But what is healing?

At the most fundamental level, everything is energy. Energy is simply potential energy until different patterns arise within that energy. These patterns are what dictates whether energy ultimately becomes a toothbrush or an emotion or a tree. Patterns are like the blueprint of your physical existence. Because everything is a pattern, all forms of illness are also specific patterns. To heal something is to change that pattern. Therefore, the first layer to understand about healing is that to heal is to *change a pattern*. It is the opposite of repetition and redundancy. Now we must look at how to change a pattern.

When something is unhealed, it is exhibiting a pattern that we don't like. It is in a state that is unwanted. Therefore, *we can greatly simplify healing in that it is a change of a pattern that is unwanted into a pattern that is wanted.* This usually entails changing it into the opposite pattern. Therefore, the second layer to understand about healing is that healing is *to experience the opposite.*

If our leg is broken, to change that pattern of broken into its opposite is to put together/ mend it.

If we feel demeaned, to heal is to feel valued.

If we are abused to heal is to be treated lovingly.

If we feel powerless, to heal is to feel empowered.

If we are stuck, to heal is to be able to move.

Now that you understand that to heal is to change a pattern into the opposite, look at whatever situation you feel a lack of forgiveness about. Look at the pain you experienced. What would the opposite pattern be? Make that your aim, not forgiveness. Sometimes, the changing of a pattern like this (the move from powerless to empowered for example) happens with the changing of one single belief and takes no time at all. Other times, it is a process that involves the changing of several beliefs and the experiencing of several things and many layers until a person is truly experiencing the opposite and therefore has healed.

If you look at people who have truly forgiven, you will find that you are looking at someone who is already living out the healed state of being. For example, if your adult relationships are still painful as hell as a result of your childhood relationships with Mom and Dad, chances are you have not forgiven Mom and Dad. Every time a relationship proves to be a repeat of that original relationship programming, you hate them because you feel hurt by them and you feel you can't move forward because if it had only been different, you wouldn't be in these painful patterns today. When you find yourself in a truly good adult relationship, it is as if you have transformed the pattern that was caused by that original wounding and so, you do not need anything from them anymore in terms of requital. You already have what you need and what that situation caused you to want. More than that, you can see how that wounding may have been a pivotal part in even getting that.

2. You have got to stop resisting where you are, stop expecting yourself to feel better and expecting yourself to forgive. Instead, you have to admit to where you are. Accept that where you are, is the reality. It isn't about approving of where you are. It is about accepting the reality that where you are is where you are and how you feel is how you feel. And instead of running

from those very painful feelings and the part of yourself that feels them, be completely, unconditionally present with them. Listen for the very important personal truths being conveyed by each emotion. With each emotion that arises, you need to:

#1. To become aware of the emotion

#2. To care about the emotion by seeing it as valid and important

#3. To listen empathetically to the emotion in an attempt to understand the way you feel. This allows you to feel safe to be vulnerable without fear of judgment. Seek to understand, it isn't about whether all of you agrees or not.

#4. To acknowledge and validate your feelings. This may include finding words to label your emotion. To acknowledge and validate feelings, we do not need to validate that the thoughts we have about our emotions are correct, instead we need to know that it is a valid thing to feel the way that we feel. For example, if the thought behind your emotion is, "I feel useless," we do not validate ourselves by saying "I'm right I am useless." We could validate by saying "I can totally see how that would make me feel useless and anyone would feel the same way if they were me."

#5. To allow ourselves to feel how we feel and to experience our emotion fully before moving towards any kind of improvement in the way we feel. We need to give ourselves permission to dictate when we are ready to move up the vibrational scale and into a different emotion. This is the step where we practice unconditional presence and unconditional love. We are there with our emotions without trying to "fix" them.

#6. After and only after our feelings have been validated and acknowledged and fully felt, we can strategize ways to shift into a better feeling state. This is the step where you can find new ways of looking at a situation that may improve the way you are feeling.

Often times, when we are accepting a reality relative to something that has hurt us, we end up in grief. Grief is a process that we must allow ourselves to fully experience, not try to escape out of. There is often a perception of a loss in association with being hurt. For example, I perceived that I had lost my whole childhood and would never get it back due to my childhood abuser. In my case, in order to heal, I had to grieve for that lost childhood. Feelings of anger and revenge are a part of this process. The reason that we feel revengeful and anger is because it is an improvement upon the powerlessness that we feel when someone hurts us. If we spend our lives resisting what happened, which is what we are doing when we cannot accept the reality of what has happened, and the way it makes us feel, we are living our life pushing against what was instead of putting our energy towards what we want to create instead.

3. Forgiveness occurs when we find a perspective that truly changes the way our most hurt aspect views the situation. You can look literally anywhere for this. Perspectives are absolutely everywhere. I am a big fan of doing this in a way that does not suggest that we shouldn't be holding the perspective we are holding. For example, let's say you were hurt by your mother. If someone says, "Her childhood was even worse than yours she did the best that she could," this perspective will do nothing in terms of creating forgiveness, in fact it only makes the way you feel worse because it implies that because of that perspective, we shouldn't be holding our own. What we have to be doing is to be looking for a perspective that without invalidating our own, makes us change the way that we see the situation so that we feel genuine relief relative to anger and resentment and no desire for requital. The perspective that works is going to be unique for each person and unique to each situation.

For me, this happened quite spontaneously. After years of being on the healing path relative to my childhood, I was thinking about a memory that changed my perspective so drastically; it threw forgiveness in my lap entirely. I remembered that every time he would sodomize me, which happened any time I was with him when the wind was strong, he would stand up as if horrified and run away. I rarely saw any emotion from him. One day, he did this in a field where I saw where he went. I watched him on his hands and knees in the field crying and rocking. I realized that he was doing the same thing to me that was done to him all along. I realized that he had succeeded in pulling me into the hell he couldn't escape from and now, I was the person who understood his pain and trauma more than anyone else in the world. In that instant, I could no longer see him as a monster, but a desperate person who was so alone in his torment, he had pulled me into hell with him. Ironically, this was something I had said I felt like doing any time I saw people laughing and talking about their normal lives during the time I was trying to overcome all the scars my childhood left on me. I started crying like crazy that day and my anger evaporated. I did not want punishment for him any longer. I wanted healing. To bring that healing to people like him had become part of my mission on this planet. I needed nothing from him anymore. I could see in that second how everything that happened fit into my purpose here on the planet and how without those experiences, I'd be less than half as good at what I do today. I'd have lots of spiritual information but absolutely no clue how to bridge the gap between that information and the depths of hell that make that information sound like total BS. And here's the thing, if you had suggested any of those perspectives before I was ready, it wouldn't have worked. It would have been like trying to force a paraplegic to get up and run a week after the accident.

4. Compassion and empathy. This step should never be done prematurely. If you try to get someone who was hurt to find compassion for the person who they feel hurt by, it is abusive. It is to ask a person to open their heart to someone who is kicking it. This has to be something a person genuinely wants to look for, not so that they can feel like a good person or do what is "right," but because they are ready to stop the terrible feeling of tension that the resentment and need for requital creates. Compassion is a form of connectedness because it arises when we feel a sympathetic commonality with someone. In other words, we experience a *shared* felt experience of pain. There is a harmony inherent in shared feelings, as well as shared understanding. When we feel compassion, we feel sorrow and understanding and concern for the suffering of someone or something else. And having that shared commonality of pain and therefore sorrow and concern for them, then compels us to alter our perspective and feelings and actions towards that thing. Think back to a time when you were watching a movie or a show where a character experienced something that caused them to suffer and instantly you got a physiological sensation of connection with that character. You instantly related to that person and understood them as well as what they need. This is compassion. Compassion immediately arises when someone experiences pain that we relate to. Compassion naturally arises as a result of relating to someone's suffering. Therefore, all we must do in order to feel compassion and know what action to take towards that thing is to deliberately look for how you relate to their pain.

5. Gratitude or appreciation. One of the best ways to step out of a victim mentality is to develop gratitude. Gratitude is simply appreciative notice and conscious acknowledgment of what brings you joy to focus on in the present moment. Focusing on gratitude shifts you out of self-pity. You can't think

the thought *poor me* and be grateful for something in your life at the same time. It allows you to ask yourself the question, *What is the hidden blessing or opportunity within this situation?* When you recognize the answer to that question, it's impossible to feel like a victim.

Just like I said with the step of compassion, this step should never be done prematurely. If you try to get someone who was hurt to find gratitude or appreciation for the way they were hurt, it is abusive. It is to ask someone to kiss the hand that slaps them. Often this happens naturally and on its own as a result of living into the state of healing. This is the step where a person is ready to open to the perspective that contains the gift of the experience. This is where you can see how the painful experience or painful person added positively to your life in some way.

6. Face the step of forgiveness called the refusal to forgive. Resentment is a huge part of forgiveness. We can't be fully conscious about resentment without being conscious about the subconscious positive intention below it. It is a refusal to forgive. Letting go or forgiving gives most people the feeling that they simultaneously have to let go of the unmet need to be treated fairly and justly in a way that creates trust. It feels like self-betrayal. And so, in order to *honor their pain as well as honor their need* to have just and fair treatment, they will not forgive. Resentment essentially can be like a wall that a person uses to protect themselves and try to get their needs met.

A person may keep resentment as both a boundary and a personal reminder as if to say "No one will ever do this to me again." Also, the sense of self, also called the ego can feel a sense of itself being right and good when it is in the victim role (good and right) with someone else being in the perpetrator role (bad and wrong). Often, especially in close relationships, being the one who was wronged puts the other person in a role where they have to "make it up to you." This is a less powerless role with more of a guarantee of fair treatment going forward. So it can be a way of using past wrong treatment as leverage to get what you want from someone and/or to stay safe.

If you distrust someone because they treated you unfairly, it is quite tempting to control them through guilt in this way. For this reason, it is beneficial to ask yourself honestly, *what bad thing am I afraid would happen if I were to forgive the person I feel resentment towards today or if I forgave myself for my role in the situation?* For example, perhaps my answer might be, if I forgive him or her, I make what they did to me ok and it isn't ok. Or if I forgive him or her, they will not get how much they hurt me, so they will do it to me again. Or if I forgive him or her, I'm being like a human punching bag or doormat, which is pathetic. Or if I forgive him or her, I'll never receive the justice and fair treatment I need. Then question this perspective. The anger and resentment and expectation for compensation that you feel is so, so natural. You are right to feel that way. But that doesn't change the fact that it is a poison that eats you from within. Thinking that it will do something to the person who has hurt you is like drinking poison, thinking it will harm the other person.

You must know that all people are being intrinsically led in the direction of improvement and healing. You do not have to force them to heal any more than you have to go over to them and hold the two sides of their cut together in order for it to heal. It does not feel good for people to be in a place of anger and resentment and needing requital. And so, all people are being intrinsically led to forgiveness.

But you can ask yourself "What do I need in order to let go of this situation or what do I need in order to forgive in this situation?" What can I do with what I have, from where I am? When you forgive someone, it's as if you are setting a prisoner free only to discover that you were the prisoner all along. Happiness and internal freedom is found in the alteration of the point of view you are holding about a subject. If you remove yourself far enough from the limited point of view of pain, you will see that we are all nothing but the victims of victims. But you cannot force forgiveness because you cannot force the process of healing.

Forgiving is not forgetting. You cannot lie to yourself forever that you are where you aren't. You can't will yourself into forgiving just because you know it would be such a better place to be. Forgiveness is healing the state of pain in your own life. You have not fully forgiven something until you are able to find genuine approval for it having happened to the degree that there is nothing left to forgive. And this perspective is one that all people have the capacity to reach if we will only have the love in us enough to let the process of getting to this perspective unfold within them.

We don't even need the other person present in order to forgive them, or to forgive ourselves. The healing takes place within us and for us alone. Forgiveness is not about taking anything back. Instead, it's about releasing ourselves so that we can go *forward*. If we have any pain present within us at all, it means we have something to forgive.

Forgiveness Exercise

There are thousands of self-help techniques and meditations aimed at forgiveness. Some of them may not work well for you, while others you will find truly transformational. I am going to introduce you to one that I've had great success with myself and that I've heard was life changing for others.

Sit alone, as if in meditation, and focus on your breathing for a time. Then set a timer for two minutes. In those two min-

utes, think of something that someone else said or did that made you feel very hurt and you are still holding on to the memory of. Remember how it felt, where you were, and what you were thinking. Allow yourself to be taken back completely into this space of pain.

When the timer goes off, set it for five minutes. During these five minutes, visualize yourself walking up to that person and saying, "I forgive you." Tell him or her any healing thing you can think of that lets them know that you understand the painful emotions they were feeling that allowed them to act the way they acted or say the things they said.

Imagine this person fully accepting your forgiveness. Imagine them wanting it and just being afraid to ask for it. Imagine yourself embracing them. Stay with this feeling, creating the thought of this reconciliation, until the timer goes off.

Then set the timer for two minutes. During the two minutes, recall a time that you did or said something you regret doing. Let this be the memory of something you still carry the pain of having done. Recall the way it felt when you did it, where you were, who was there, and the pain on that person's face. Allow yourself to be taken back into that space of pain.

When the timer goes off, set it for five minutes, and for those five minutes imagine asking forgiveness from whomever you hurt. Imagine wanting it. Imagine the person giving it to you freely. Imagine him or her feeling joy in giving forgiveness to you. Imagine the pain going away completely as you create and allow the reconciliation, knowing it's all okay now. It's over. You are forgiven.

This time, when the timer goes off, without setting it again, imagine you forgiving yourself for this same action or the thing you said. You can say to yourself, "I forgive you," "I know you are a loving person," or "I know you never meant *to hurt anyone." Say anything to yourself that you need to hear in order to free yourself from your feelings of guilt or disappointment. Imagine hugging yourself. Imagine telling yourself that you understand why you did it. Let yourself know how much you believe in yourself.*

Maintain this visualization for as long as it takes for you to begin to feel a sense of peace, release, and even hopefulness. When you feel ready, open your eyes.

Some people find it easier to do this visualization with someone else instead of alone. If you want, you can ask another person to be the one to watch the time for you and verbally guide you through the different sections of this process that you may be afraid to initiate alone.

Be aware that this process can be very difficult. It can be like uncorking a dam that has been building up pressure for years. It can make you aware of your deep wounds and vulnerability. It can even make you break down. Just remember that breaking down is better than the pressure you were living with, because what you are in fact breaking down is everything that is preventing you from loving yourself.

Words of Forgiveness

Another way to find forgiveness is to write a letter (no matter if the person is alive or dead) either offering someone forgiveness or asking for it from him or her. You can send this letter if you want to, or you can partake in a very cleansing practice of going somewhere, where there is no risk of anything catching fire, and burning the letter. You can watch the fire consume the words you have written, knowing everything you have said is being absorbed by the universe. Let the fire pull away the pain in you as it pulls the words and the paper into itself.

It's very profound to write yourself a letter asking for your own forgiveness or giving yourself forgiveness, and then burning it. Give yourself permission to experience the very strong emotional release that often accompanies this process. You can follow the intense release of such a practice by making use of the fertile ground of nonresistance that is present afterward and focus strongly on something positive. For example, take the time after the burning ritual to write affirmations or write lists of positive aspects about your life right now.

We are not really free if we are still angry. We are not really free if we are still sad. We are not really free if we still yearn for justice.

Negative emotion is your indication that you are still feeling like a victim. I'm not saying that to forgive something means that you resign yourself to something that is negative, although that is what it has been bastardized into. Instead, forgiveness in this sense is letting go of what is holding you back so you can turn in the direction of happiness and stop carrying your past into your present.

Every piece of happiness is found in the alteration of the point of view you are holding about a subject. If you remove yourself far enough from the limited point of view of pain, you will see that we are all nothing but the victims of victims. Remove yourself even further than that, and you will see that there is no such thing as a victim. Victimhood is a prison, and forgiveness is the way out of it.

When we allow ourselves to be victims, we are letting the people and circumstances in our lives dictate how we will feel, and ultimately, who we will be. We feel powerless to own our own lives, and we waste our time asking, "Why me?" instead of doing what we can, with what we have, from where we are.

When we have the bravery to take control of our own lives and look at life's challenges as opportunities for us to become more and to grow and expand into more genuine expressions of ourselves, a whole new set of possibilities arises from every experience we have. Even in the midst of the most terrible experiences, we always have the power to choose our thoughts about the experiences and our responses to the circumstances. We are always responsible for who we're being in relationship to the experience.

The choice between staying a victim to your own life and becoming the victor of your own life is always available to you right now. Your life does not belong to anyone else. It's *your* life.

It's my promise that if you choose to move forward, and become the champion of your own life, you will come out the other side. The other side is beautiful, and on the way here, you will find yourself. You will discover just how capable and powerful you are.

Look at your life and ask yourself this question: *If I were to take full responsibility for my life, and really own my own life, what would I do differently today?* Then when you are ready, go for it. You do not have to improve all aspects of your life at once; just take the next logical step from wherever you are. Once you are done with that step, take the next one. Simply keep taking the step that is right in front of you—and one day, you will be living the kind of life that you do *want* to own.

TOOL #19

CHOOSING HAPPINESS

Make Happiness Your Intention

By now you have probably figured out that self-love and happiness are synonymous. It is a recurring theme throughout this book because the first loving action we can take toward ourselves is to orient ourselves toward happiness. When we are approaching ourselves from an attitude of self-hate, our last priority is happiness because self-hate wants you to think that happiness is superficial and selfish.

But to love yourself means to deliberately choose and create happiness regardless of the people, events, and circumstances that are external to you. Happiness is not something you are either born with or not born with. *Happiness is the result of a series of ongoing choices.* You may have been born wealthy or impoverished, you may have been sick or well, or you may have been treated well or abused; regardless of your background, happiness is a personal choice.

Making happiness our intention means making the fully conscious decision to prioritize happiness and make it our goal. Happiness becomes our modus operandi. But unless we intend to be happy, we will not have the motivation to actually create happiness for ourselves. Until we *consciously* make it our intention to be happy, we will continue to try to get happiness subconsciously, going about it the hard way, and we will always be at the mercy of limiting beliefs.

One way to formally make an intention to be happy is to create a list of your most important intentions. Think about your priorities when you're compiling this list. Some examples of intentions might be "I intend to landscape my house," "I intend to be a good parent," "I intend to get a college degree," or "I intend to reach enlightenment." Make it as long as you want. Look over your list and eliminate any intentions that are not so much things you *want* to do as they are things that you think you *should* do or *need* to do.

With the rest of your list, finish each intention with this statement: "And I intend to feel happiness while I'm doing it." So, the first intention above would read, "I intend to landscape my house, and I intend to feel happiness while I'm doing it." When you look back over each intention, now that you've modified them by adding the intention of happiness, does it seem as if the intention of happiness has factored into your intentions before?

In other words, you may have intended to landscape, but did you intend to be happy while you were doing it, or were you approaching it more like a chore or something you just had to get through? Do these revised intentions generate any insights about the way you have been living your life up to now or about things you may want to do differently?

This is a good time to ask yourself the following questions:

Does happiness factor into my decisions and goals?

Why haven't I had the intention to be happy?

What is the benefit of being unhappy?

Did I grow up in a family where I got attention for being unhappy?

What am I afraid will happen if I become happy?

You will gain valuable insights by looking at things this way.

Become Accountable for Your Happiness

Choosing to center your life on happiness is arguably the most important choice when it comes to self-love. People who love themselves make happiness the number one goal of everything they are doing. They don't put off things that bring them joy as if joy were a future reward to reach for. They don't spend their lives working hard so they can have a nice, happy life of retirement later.

Choose to make the things that bring you the greatest joy the central concern in your life. Choose to live every day to its fullest, spending each day doing the things you love to do. These choices enable you to express yourself fully. They will allow you to come into your unique individuality and be authentic to what brings you happiness.

Don't let people undermine your focus on happiness. Realize that if others resist your decision to make happiness the central focus of your life, it is not because they are right. It is because they are afraid for themselves, afraid for their own happiness, which they do not currently feel in control of.

As you stand up for yourself, be accountable and assume full responsibility for your own thoughts and actions. Take charge of your own happiness. Don't focus on problems or argue about any of your limitations or blame anyone else; rather, focus instead on finding solutions and the freedom you have to do so. Taking accountability for your happiness means figuring out where you want to go from here and initiating a way to get there step-by-step.

But just make sure it is your own vision of happiness that you are chasing. You are bombarded by other people's versions of happiness all day every day. As people, we are constantly trying to impose our own ideas of happiness on others because we want to be validated. We want people to agree with us. Your lover, your parents, and your friends tell you what you should be doing if you want to be happy. The media even tries to sell you on things that will make you happy.

Identifying what makes you happy gives you a lot of insight into who you really are. This process of personal inquiry as it applies to happiness is not just a process that applies to big things; it applies in every moment of your day-to-day life. It applies when choosing things like clothing, figuring out what to eat or not eat, and deciding what you want to do today.

The best way to integrate this choice into your life is to set an alarm to go off several times throughout the day. Every time the alarm goes off, ask yourself, *What would make me happy right now at this very minute?* When you get the answer, act on it. Implement your own vision of happiness.

Take Inventory

To start taking charge of your life, take a realistic inventory of what you can change. You can focus only on the part of any equation that you have total control of, and that is the part you play. Any time you find yourself in a less-than-desired circumstance, you can ask yourself these five magic questions below. I recommend these questions in different chapters; they help you understand the bigger picture when things go wrong. In this case, they will help you focus back on happiness after an upset or wrong turn.

1. *How did I make myself a match to this?* (This doesn't mean to look for ways to blame yourself for it; it means to look for the power you had in creating it.)

2. *What am I meant to learn from this?*

3. *What is this pain causing me to know that I want?*

4. *What is the positive that has come or could possibly come from this?*

5. *What can I do to change things for the better, right here and now?*

By answering these questions, not only do you gain incredible insight, but you also take control of your own destiny. It may seem counterintuitive to ask these questions when you are in the victim role with an obvious "bad guy" to blame for why you feel the way you feel. But this is the best way to be happy and keep your focus clearly on your own happiness, which as we know is the one thing that you can control.

An Exercise in Honesty with Yourself

Honesty goes hand in hand with the choice to discover and live according to your own version of happiness. It's a choice to be truthful with yourself and eventually the world. We tell ourselves lies all the time, and we lie to other people. Even those of us who pride ourselves on our honesty maintain illusions with others and with ourselves. We do it even when we think we are telling the truth.

Sometimes, instead of telling lies outright, we keep secrets from ourselves and other people. We tell lies and keep secrets because we are afraid that if we tell the truth, there will be consequences we feel we can't face. However, people who are happy choose to live according to their own personal truths. Honesty is a kind of freedom. We can't love ourselves and conceal ourselves at the same time.

To love ourselves and to be happy, we must be truthful about ourselves to ourselves and to others. We must confront our own myths and look at ourselves in an open and honest way so we can decide what is right for us to think and do individually, regardless of what other people around us think that we should think or do.

In this way, happy people live according to their own sense of internal integrity. They view happiness as a kind of internal contract with themselves. They use this internal contract as a guiding light to ensure that they can never lose track of their true selves. Being honest means bringing our subconscious into our conscious awareness. It means uncovering our deepest fears, insecurities, thoughts, feelings, and desires.

Until we bring these things into our awareness so we can understand them, they are running haywire and covertly controlling our lives. Until we fully understand the truth of ourselves, we will make all kinds of choices that make no

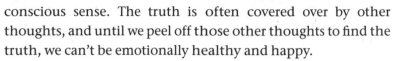

conscious sense. The truth is often covered over by other thoughts, and until we peel off those other thoughts to find the truth, we can't be emotionally healthy and happy.

A good way to admit to your own truths is to sit down with a piece of paper and write the following:

"I tell myself that _____, but the truth is _____."

Write this down several times on the paper and fill in the blanks. For example, "I tell myself that my dad will come back one day, but the truth is that he isn't coming back."

Then on a second piece of paper write:

"I tell other people _____, but the truth is _____."

Once again, write this several times on the paper and fill in the blanks. For example, "I tell other people that I got a degree from Harvard University, but the truth is I went there for only one semester."

Finally, on a third piece of paper write:

"I pretend that _____, but the truth is _____."

As before, write it out several times on the paper and fill in the blanks. For example, "I pretend that my family is close and down-to-earth, but the truth is that's how I want them to be. In reality, they are distant and cold, and none of us really gets along with each other."

Don't worry about not being able to come up with things to put in the blanks. Your deepest secrets and lies want to surface and *will* surface because your true self wants them to be seen and discarded.

Just remember that nearly everyone pretends something. Nearly everyone maintains a facade for themselves and for others. This does not make you a bad person, nor does it make you hopelessly messed up. It makes you normal. But behaving according to what is normal does not guarantee that you are behaving according to what will make you happy.

We need to be willing to be honest about our true thoughts, our true beliefs, our true needs, our true feelings, our true personalities, what really makes us happy, and our lies if we ever hope to be happy and love ourselves. We can't withhold the truth from ourselves or from others and be happy.

Truth is the key to finding inner harmony. It's as true now as it was when it was first said: *The truth shall set you free.* The way to be truthful with yourself is to question yourself. Introspection is a lifelong process, but it's a process that inevitably leads to happiness.

The Deliberate Pivot

Honor Your True Feelings

I once overheard a married couple fighting in a restaurant. The husband, who was clearly at a loss for what to say, was trying to help his wife feel better. He said to her in a loud enough voice that half the restaurant heard him, "You just have to turn the lemons into lemonade, you know." She was crying at this point, and she threw her hands up in the air and said, "Oh my God, I just want you to let me *taste* the lemons for once!"

It is true that people who are happy are those who make an absolute art form out of turning lemons into lemonade. But the part that we don't recognize is that happy people let themselves *taste* the lemons before they turn them into lemonade.

In a moment of desperation, that woman in the restaurant had exposed a little-known truth: Choosing to be happy is not about going into denial. It's not about avoiding all negativity or avoiding the way we feel. Repressing feelings is a recipe for misery or what's even worse, numbness. Negative emotions are not the cause of our unhappiness; it is our *resistance* to our negative emotions that causes us to be unhappy.

Choosing happiness is about allowing yourself to feel the way you feel first and then moving up the emotional scale by converting problems and tragedies into meaning, importance, and opportunity. You cannot tell yourself to "just get over it" when you are faced with struggle. That is the least self-loving thing you can say to yourself or anyone else. When you say that to yourself, you are invalidating the way you feel. You're saying it's wrong to feel the way you feel. It's a form of denial that does not lead to long-term happiness.

Denial assures you that whatever you are avoiding *will* catch up with you one day. We don't need to avoid the fact that sometimes pain is a part of life. But happiness depends on how we handle the experience of that pain. This may also seem counterintuitive, but choosing to be happy means to dive headfirst into the emotions you are feeling and listen to what your emotions are telling you.

If we don't honor our feelings, we are running away from them. It's only easier to avoid things in the short term. In the long run, anything that we avoid comes back even bigger, and we will find that avoidance the first time did not work. And by the way, there is no set amount of time for someone to be done fully tasting the lemons; in other words, it may take a short time or a long time before they are finished experiencing their full feelings about something negative that happened.

So if healing must occur on the emotional and feeling level of your life, you must address the emotions and feelings themselves. That is, you must address the causation of those emotions and feelings. Here's the catch. The minute you say, "I need to heal something," this implies that you have to change or fix something, which means that you disapprove of something. You will only damage yourself emotionally and continue feeding self-hate when you view yourself through the lens of "something needs to change."

Think about how painful it is to have someone tell you that you are not okay the way you are and that you have to *be different*. Feels awful, right? So if you approach your feelings and your body with the attitude of "I need to fix you," you've just taken a serrated knife to a wound. You haven't healed anything. And so what's the alternative? What's the solution here?

Be Completely Present with Your Emotions

The alternative to trying to fix or heal the emotions is to embrace the feelings and emotions entirely, no matter how painful they may be. Just be with the feelings and emotions instead of trying to change them. Listen to them and what they need you to know. Each emotion is a carrier of information. Each one conveys a message about your personal truth in a given situation. We can call this process of being present with and intentionally perceiving the message inherent in an emotion *integration*.

Every day for 20 minutes at least, as well as any time you have a particularly intense emotional reaction to something, find a quiet and comfortable place to be completely with how you feel. Observe the sensations, feelings, and emotions in your body. They will intensify as you focus on them. Breathe continuously without unnecessary pauses between breaths. Breathe in and out of your nose, and notice the way you feel.

Your entire goal is to be with your feelings, which is to be with yourself fully. If you like, you can repeat this one sentence to your emotions like a mantra: *I am completely here with you now.* Keep in mind that this process is not only for negative emotional states; it is also for positive emotional states. In fact, some people find that they are much more comfortable being with their negative emotional states than with their positive ones.

After you have been with the emotion completely, no matter how uncomfortable it is, and you feel like you want to know more about the causation of the emotion, ask yourself four questions:

1. *How do I feel?* This is your opportunity to bring the feelings to your conscious awareness and name what is occurring within you.

2. *What personal truth or message is this feeling trying to show or tell me about myself?*

3. *When did I last experience this exact same feeling?* Without looking for the answer, allow your being to offer one up, like a river washing something downstream to you.

4. *When did I first experience this same feeling in my life?* Again, without looking for the answer, allow your being to offer it up.

If nothing comes, be patient with that. Trust the process. Trust that you will receive the exact experience you need at this time. If you find yourself experiencing an emotionally traumatic memory, observe the memory and then mentally alter it in a way that feels emotionally positive. As I mentioned earlier, this is what they call *inner-child work*.

For example, if you are taken into a memory where your father left you, imagine the adult-you approaching the child-you, consoling the child and finding a way to meet the child's needs. You could become the stable parent for your inner child, or you could give the child a reliable father figure of his or her choice. Or you could explain the whole situation objectively and help the child-you to not take the action personally. Altering the memory in this way changes the causation of the trauma. This alteration ensures that all that has transpired as a result of that trauma is altered as well. You are affecting the very blueprint of your emotional life.

Offer Yourself Further Healing

Writing about your experience of "being with your feeling body" is a good idea because it will not only make you subconsciously feel as if you care about yourself, but it will also help you to understand and integrate the experience you've just had. Keep in mind that any trauma that took place before you developed the capacity for language is not likely to be something that you can verbalize. Just remember that you don't have to verbalize it or conceptualize it in order to integrate it.

When we have a strong emotional reaction to something, the strong reaction means that our past trauma has been triggered. This practice of being with the emotion allows us to take our attention off of the "messenger," which is the physical event, person, place, or thing that is triggering us. It allows us to step back from the story that is urging us to react so strongly and detach mentally from the trigger. It allows us to place our attention on how we are feeling so that we can recognize what deep, unresolved past wound is not yet healed within us and is thus continuing to mirror itself in our lives.

After we have completely been present with our emotions, we can either stay with the calmness of the present moment that arises when we are no longer running away from our emotion, or *we can pivot*. Some people will be ready to pivot after a few minutes, others might be ready after a few hours, and for some people, it can take years. This time also varies, depending on the circumstances.

For example, if you are dealing with having lost a loved one, it could potentially take you a longer time to experience your emotions fully before pivoting than it would take for someone who is dealing with an altercation with someone at work.

When we are ready to make the choice to create happiness, we take an internal vow to transform darkness into light. We convert suffering into joy, hatred into love, and powerlessness into limitless freedom. The way we do this is by transforming our negative feelings into positive feelings by opening our mind to insight about the situation. We shift our attention to the positive potential of what is and what could be (now that we are where we are) by asking ourselves, *What now?* Spend time searching for the meaning and the lesson that comes out of the negative experience. This is a *pivot*, where we search for the hidden opportunity and value of an event that seems only detrimental. When we *pivot* deliberately, instead of the experience being detrimental, it becomes beneficial to us. It becomes one of the necessary conditions for our growth.

Blessings in Disguise

If we want to be happy, we can begin by looking at the world through the lens of "everything comes to bless us." Even if we don't fully believe that statement yet, the possibility that everything does in fact come to bless us is profoundly beneficial.

It causes us to orient ourselves toward looking for the value in a negative situation.

The concept of the phoenix rising from the ashes in a rebirth is a story of pivoting. Pivoting causes transformation. It ensures that tragedy and problems will not hold us captive. There is a reason why most of the men and women we identify as truly great people in this world have come out of experiences of great pain. It's because pain has value. It causes us to ask the questions that lead to the most important answers—those that liberate the human soul. Pain is an opportunity to become *more*.

Without knowing what we don't want, we would not know what we do want. There would be no expansion in this universe without pain. Just as you cannot understand white without the reference point of black, without pain there would be nothing to compare joy to. We would not know joy if not for pain.

So after you've let yourself really taste the lemons by fully and deeply experiencing your emotions, you can begin to pivot by looking for the blessing in disguise. Begin looking for anything positive within the situation, and start turning your lemons into lemonade.

It is helpful to ask yourself these questions:

What have I learned about myself and what I want?

What can I do in my life right now to move in the direction of what I've discovered that I want?

Are there any positives that have come from this circumstance?

Are there any positives that I can see potentially coming in the future because of this situation?

What am I meant to learn from all of this?

How am I now better because of this?

I may not be grateful that it happened, but what is there to be grateful for about this situation?

What thoughts (that I actually believe) can I think about this situation that make me feel better?

What can I do right now to move in the direction of happiness?

Remember that pain tends to strip us of our illusions, like the layers of an onion being peeled away one by one. As these layers are removed, we get closer and closer to knowing our true selves. Once we are free of illusion, it is possible to touch greater and greater heights of happiness. Pivoting ensures that happiness is not only in our control, but that we can always regain it if we lose hold of it. Pivoting allows us to see the truth and realize that the mysteries of our deepest pain can be exposed as the seeds of our greatest joy.

TOOL #21

LOVE IS FOR GIVING

Who's in Charge of Happiness?

In our society, we often give things to other people and try to add to their happiness out of guilt. We try to erase our sense of guilt by giving and giving in the form of sacrificing ourselves. But when we give to others from this motivation, we resent giving and that form of giving doesn't add to happiness. What it really does is detract from it.

You cannot be happy and give anything to someone else that you don't honestly want to give. To add to someone else's happiness doesn't mean that you are taking responsibility for other people's happiness. It means you begin treating others the way you want to be treated.

But all this being said, giving is a choice that does lead to happiness—if your giving is entirely intrinsically motivated, coming from within you and not done with any expectation or desire to get something back. The choice to add to other people's happiness will not make us happy unless we expect no attention, no acknowledgment, no appreciation, and no reward for doing it. It's a choice to let our happiness overflow into the world because it feels so good to see others happy.

Unfortunately, the society we have co-created is rarely unified. We stand in elevators without saying hello to each other. We hide our problems from each other, becoming convinced that we are the only ones who feel the way we feel. Sometimes we have no idea who is living right next to us in our own neighborhoods. A lot of unhappiness comes from this separation, and yet, all too often we wait for someone else to change it.

We live in hope that someone else will suddenly show us love and add to our happiness one day. But what really happens is that everyone stands around waiting for someone else to do it, and we all remain stuck. It takes only one person to get the ball rolling, and that's you. Start to give from your heart and miraculous things will happen.

How Many Ways Can I Give?

As you've been learning in these chapters, when we accept that oneness is the truth of this universe, then we know that the way to love the world is to love ourselves. But a little known fact is that it also works in reverse: An excellent way to give love and happiness to yourself is to give love and happiness to others. Every kind gesture that you extend toward something else comes back to you in other forms of goodness, and that is why it can feel so good to give. We receive every time we do it. When we create a world of kindness for ourselves, we create a world of kindness for other people. When we nurture our own happiness, we nurture other people's happiness.

Extending kindness is not all about grand gestures. There are thousands of random acts of kindness you could do very simply, very inexpensively, every day. Remember, each time you give of yourself to others, in the long run you'll get back more than you give. Here are some ideas to jump-start your goodness:

Pay for someone behind you in a tollbooth.

Write anonymous positive notes on scraps of paper, and place them randomly on car windshields throughout the city you live in.

Donate things from your house to a charity or to a library.

Visit people in a seniors' home.

Throw someone a "just because I love you" surprise party.

Hold the door open for someone.

Give someone a genuine compliment instead of keeping the appreciative thought to yourself.

Mentor a child or teen who is at risk.

Donate blood.

Volunteer to walk and play with the animals at a pound or other pet adoption centers.

Pick up litter.

Let someone merge into traffic in front of you.

Adopt a soldier as a pen pal.

Call or visit someone who is sick, and bring soup.

Smile and converse with someone you wouldn't normally connect with, such as a store clerk.

Return lost belongings to the owner.

Send someone a "just because I love you" letter.

Rub a loved one's back.

Plant a tree.

Give a co-worker one of your vacation days.

Cook a meal for someone.

Help someone carry a heavy load.

Shovel snow or do some yard work for a neighbor.

Return a stray shopping cart to its rightful place.

Get as creative as you can. Random acts of kindness can be anything from smiling at a stranger all the way to paying off someone's college tuition. Every single act counts. Random acts of kindness don't have to add stress to your life, and doing them shouldn't make you feel as if you are sacrificing yourself and what little energy you have. You don't want to do things that take away from your own happiness. Do only what feels good to do. You can practice random acts of kindness whether you are a millionaire or you have only the clothes on your back to your name.

Attitudes about Gratitude

Any of you that are practicing conscious manifestation have been made aware of the power of gratitude. You have learned that the key to manifestation is having an "attitude of gratitude." Some of you have embraced this idea of living from a space of gratitude full heartedly. Others of you hear the word gratitude, much less the phrase "attitude of gratitude," and immediately cringe. The thing is, gratitude is where happiness begins. And gratitude genuinely *is* a priceless tool when it comes to conscious manifestation. Therefore, today I'm going to make a case for gratitude which will cause those of you who are gratitude resistant to release your resistance to gratitude; and which will cause those of you who have embraced gratitude to love it even more.

Let's start by addressing the resistance to gratitude. If you are someone that cringes when you hear the word gratitude, the reason you feel this way is because of pain. People who struggle with gratitude have had or are having a painful life experience. When this is the case, focusing on what they are grateful for often feels like self-betrayal. It can feel like you are kissing the foot that kicks you. It can also feel emotionally abusive because it can feel like you are invalidating, negating or denying the very real pain that you are in, pain that needs to be acknowledged and resolved instead. So, the things causing you pain will never be changed. And the parts of you that are in pain begin to feel like they are being whitewashed over or sugarcoated and therefore will never be helped, instead they are condemned to suffer forever and suffer alone.

On top of this, people who struggle with gratitude often have had painful experiences relative to gratitude itself in relationships. For example, chances are high that someone in your past was the kind of person where when you acknowledged something positive, it made it more likely that they would never acknowledge or change whatever it was that was causing you pain. And chances are super high that someone in your past (usually an authority and caregiver in your childhood) did things for you and gave things to you in an impure way. Often with hidden transactions and with strings attached. And gratitude became something that made you unsafe. For example, a parent may do something for a child not because of genuine love for the child, but because they want the child to be indebted to them and therefore to do exactly what they want. This becomes a manipulative power play whereby if the child does not do exactly what the parent wants, all the things that the parent did for the child will be held over the child's head. They will be called ungrateful.

Or for example, a child may start to complain about something in their life that is painful to them. And instead of that pain being seen, felt, heard and resolved, it is turned against. And the child is shamed for the way they feel, led to believe they shouldn't feel that way and that something is wrong with them because they do. An adult in their life (or many) might make it very clear that they should be grateful for what they have. They may follow this up by telling the child about someone else who has it so much worse than they do. Or they may follow this up by countering whatever the child is complaining about with something else in the child's life that is good and should therefore negate the painful thing. Such as: "You should be grateful for these hand me down shoes, don't you know some children in Africa and India don't even have any shoes?" Or imagine that the child gets upset because he or she doesn't see Daddy much anymore. An adult in the child's life might say "But look at the bright side, your best friend lives next door."

On top of this, people who struggle with gratitude often experience pain when they are around someone who is demonstratively in an attitude of gratitude, much less telling them that they *should* be too. Have you ever been in serious pain and been around someone who is in a happy little bubble, making you feel like something is wrong with you because you aren't too? Have you ever been in serious pain around someone who is willfully ignoring or who is in total denial of anything negative? It makes you feel worse and less grateful, not more grateful. People who understand the power of gratitude often seriously mess up with people who are in pain. They don't realize that they are making a person feel worse and taking them further away from a state of gratitude when they suggest that they should adopt an "attitude of gratitude." They are condemning the person to feeling in pain and like something is bad about them and wrong with them for feeling pain instead of just being able to shift their focus so that they feel good. And totally alone, in their own parallel reality, in that pain. They are condemning the person to a painful parallel reality. To understand more about this, you would benefit by watching my video titled: The Most Dangerous Parallel Reality. And when you are caused pain by these "attitude of gratitude" people who seem to deny and ignore anything negative in favor of only acknowledging what is positive and good, you associate gratitude with *them* . . . the person causing you pain. You don't want to be anything like the person who hurt you, so you throw out gratitude when you decide to be nothing like them.

Gratitude can become a tool of abuse. When these types of painful experiences happen with gratitude, an association begins to form within a person between gratitude and being shut down emotionally, gratitude and being minimized, gratitude and being invalidated, gratitude and being made to feel bad/wrong, gratitude and enmeshment, gratitude and being controlled, gratitude and being humbled, gratitude and being in debt to others, gratitude and being manipulated, gratitude and shame, gratitude and being obligated, gratitude and power struggle, gratitude and the people who hurt you, gratitude and putting up with what you have rather than what you want, gratitude and your pain never being resolved because people will simply think everything is ok, when it's not, etc. An association forms between *gratitude and pain.* No wonder you cringe at the idea of gratitude.

Anytime you have a painful association with something, the way out of it is to develop a new relationship and form new associations with it. For example, if you have had a terrible experience with a dog, what heals that is having a wonderful experience with a dog. If you hated Christmas, what heals that is to take charge of the holiday and fill Christmas time with the unique things you specifically want Christmas to be about; things you can look forward to all year long. Just because gratitude is something that may have brought you pain in the past, doesn't mean that it always will and doesn't mean that your trauma relative to gratitude can't be healed. Just because an "attitude of gratitude" can definitely be used as a tool of resistance and denial and therefore cause people pain, doesn't mean that it can't also be a very valuable tool to have in your own tool box . . . a tool that you can use for your own happiness and a tool that you can use to manifest what you want.

Making A Case for Gratitude

1. Gratitude does not negate anything negative or unwanted. Gratitude does not cancel pain out. Gratitude does not minimize anything painful. Anyone who is using Gratitude in this way, is in a state of resistance and is using gratitude as a tool of resistance. They are afraid of seeing and

acknowledging the painful, the unwanted and the negative. The truth of this universe is that polarity exists. In any moment, you have the negative and the positive; the wanted and the unwanted. To be in reality, is to clearly see both. *And Consciousness* is where we need to head if we want to truly become conscious. But chances are that if you are resistant to gratitude, you are resistant to acknowledging the positive. You are afraid of looking at the positive. Ask yourself why. Directly see, hear, feel and acknowledge your resistance to gratitude and work through it. When this is the case, you lack awareness of the positive and wanted side of the equation of life. And this means, in order to be conscious, you need to expand your awareness there! Know that gratitude does not and should not invalidate the things in your life that are painful, unwanted and negative. Gratitude is simply one of those powerful tools you have in your tool box.

2. Forget all that crap about being indebted or obligated or being expected to give thanks. To have gratitude for something is to have appreciation for that thing and to be conscious of the benefit you receive by having that thing. And to appreciate means to see the full worth of something. It is to see the positive about it. Gratitude implies that you acknowledge that you are pleased with something. Therefore, think of gratitude as notice, awareness and acknowledgement of what is positive about something. And therefore, acknowledgement of the worth and value of it.

3. On an energetic level, gratitude is actually no different than putting your order in with the universe

regarding your life experience. It calls the positive and the wanted to you. This is why it is such a powerful manifestation tool. When you are focusing on what you are grateful for, you are letting the universe know what you love. Vibrationally speaking, gratitude is a big "yes, I like this and I want more of this!" Gratitude is a state of receptivity to the positive. This is a pretty powerful state to be in vibrationally speaking. And this interests the universe because it tells the universe more about what it is and what to choose to become. This means, by focusing on what you are grateful for, you are assisting the goal of self-awareness that the universe at large has for itself.

Have you noticed that when someone seems to really be conscious of the full worth and value of something you are or you do, and indicate that they love it, you feel more and more compelled to be that way or do that thing for them? How do you feel when someone takes you and/or something you do for granted and doesn't really see its positivity, worth or value? One feels like an openness to you, the other, like a closedness to you. And the universe at large is a macrocosm. The universe at large responds the same way you do to appreciation. When you really appreciate something, you are opening up to receive from the universe. When you are only focusing on the negative and unwanted, naturally you are closing off and pushing things away from you. And in a universe based on the law of mirroring, this means the "other" closes off to you. Acknowledging and really feeling what you are grateful for is mirrored back to you as abundance. Only noticing and feeling what you don't have and what you don't like is mirrored back to you as lack.

4. Gratitude creates happiness in relationships and increases the strength of bonds in relationships. Let's look at gratitude as it exists only between two people. What happens to you and to how you feel towards the other person and to how you feel towards the relationship that you have with that person, when another person is only focused on what is displeasing, what is a problem, what is bad and wrong, what is negative, what is unwanted and what is a problem about you? What happens when they don't see or acknowledge your value and worth? Eventually, you feel like crap about yourself, you feel hurt by the other person and so, you might even start to see them as an adversary and start to hate them. You feel unhappy and the relationship feels painful and unhealthy. You may even want to leave the relationship. Having gratitude for other people and for the relationship you have with them and expressing that to them, functions the exact opposite way. It makes the other person feel good about themselves, feel positive towards you, feel happy and fulfilled in the relationship, feel closer to you and see you as an ally. And this in turn causes them to pull you closer, committing to you more.

5. Your emotional system is designed to reflect thoughts. You will not feel happy if you are thinking about what is negative, what you lack, what you don't want and what is bad and wrong. Those type of thoughts will reflect in your being as things like anxiety, fear, constriction, depression, sinking, darkness, soreness, heaviness, cold, pain etc. This does not mean that there isn't an important place and purpose for looking at those things. Don't take this to that place where

people in resistance take it when they say things like "the key to life is to focus only on the positive." All this means is that if you want to feel the sensations you judge as feeling good and that you associate with happiness, you can feel them by thinking about what is positive, what you have that you appreciate, what you want and what is good and right . . . Gratitude.

6. Gratitude can be compared to eating healthy food or exercising or bathing or making healthy lifestyle choices. It is a powerful element of self-care and health. Gratitude causes a cascade of physiological effects. It does the mind, emotions and body good. It causes you to feel optimism about the future. It improves your self-esteem. It rewires your brain for the better. It causes your tissues to relax. It causes you to breathe deeper. It causes your heart rate to slow down and to be coherent. It builds your resilience. It causes you to feel "up" instead of "down." It pulls you out of fight or flight mode. It increases dopamine in your brain. It dramatically reduces pain. It makes you more rational. It decreases inflammation in the body. It causes you to be open to life. It reduces your stress. It makes you better at communicating. It regulates your metabolism. It puts you in a state of receptivity to positive things, where you are a vibrational match to what you are wanting and what you like. It increases your immunity. It acts as a buffer against trauma as well as the development of PTSD as a result of that trauma. It decreases both envy and jealousy. It makes you kinder and more generous. It gives you better sleep. It creates stronger social bonds and improves your relationships.

Practicing gratitude does not have to be difficult, cheesy, pathetic, trite or painful in any way. And you can do it in "your" way.

WAYS TO PRACTICE GRATITUDE

1. You can start a gratitude journal where every day, you write down a list of anything from big things to very simple and small things that you are pleased with, that you like, that you are happy you got to experience, that you see the positive in, that you want more of, that you recognize the worth and value of and that you are thankful you have.

2. Any downside has an upside and any upside has a downside. See if you can increase your awareness by finding the upside to any downside. Relative to anything that you are displeased with, don't like and see as negative, can you find the hidden positives in those things? For example, potentially getting fired contains the positive of having time to focus on what really makes you passionate and you don't have to be around that colleague you don't like anymore and you are no longer tied down to living in this specific city or place and it's kind of exciting to think about what new life experiences and new people and what different chapter of your life might be coming next as a result.

3. You can choose someone specific and intentionally demonstrate gratitude for them in some specific way. For example, you can write a message of gratitude to someone. In this letter, you can write to them about the things about them that you like, that you see the

value and worth of, that you are pleased with and what about them you are thankful for. If you're not a big writer, you can speak it to them instead. This being said, keep in mind that people are often very limited in terms of how they recognize gratitude. Many people only think of gratitude in terms of words of affirmation. But any of the love languages, such as physical touch, words of affirmation, gifts, acts of service and quality time can be demonstrations of gratitude. Even things like someone defending you, asking for your opinion, showing you loyalty, committing to you, taking actions to change the things about themselves that cause you pain, staying in touch with you, keeping you in a certain place in their life or in their heart etc. can be a way that they show gratitude for you.

4. You can do an awareness meditation where you pretend to be someone who has much less than you have. For example, you could pretend to be someone who is very poor financially or who is less free than you are or who lacks resources regarding their emotional needs. And imagine going into their body and walking through your life, but as them. What might they appreciate about your life?

5. You can do a practice I call the "scavenger hunt for positives." To do this exercise, you simply look around you, taking notice of literally anything that is positive or that you like. And you mentally say what it is, in your own head. For example, say you are driving. You might take notice of a car whose color you like, you would mentally say to yourself "The color of that

car." And then if you saw a dad with his daughter on his shoulders, you would mentally say to yourself "The way that dad is being with his daughter." You might even say to yourself "That I am doing this focus exercise right now and am able to change the way I feel." And so on and so forth. It may help you to set a timer or to decide upon a block of time to be disciplined about this exercise. Just like meditation, if you feel your mind going back to problems or to what you don't like, don't fight that it happened, just re-direct your focus back to hunting for things you like.

To make a deliberate practice of gratitude is this simple: It is to make space for appreciation in your life. For most people, gratitude is not something that just happens to and for them. It isn't something you just feel. To feel gratitude, you have to do something actively to feel it. But doing something actively so as to feel it, is a very powerful tool. It can help you to bring about not only happiness, but also whatever it is that you are wanting.

TOOL #22

LETTING YOURSELF OFF THE HOOK OF PERFECTION

Perfectly Imperfect

I'm not going to feed you the cliché that says perfection doesn't exist. No one really knows if perfection exists or not. It may exist; it may not exist. That's not the point. The point is that if you want to love yourself, you can't keep measuring yourself against standards that were set by self-hate. Perfection is a standard set by self-hate, and we are all subject to its tyranny.

When we are little, we come to the conclusion that to be loved, we have to be good. Because we want so badly to be loved, we spend all our energy trying to be good, trying to earn approval, and trying to win other people's good opinions. In short, because we want love, we spend a lot of time trying to be *perfect*. We don't know how to do anything differently even though we know that all the efforts we're extending to gain love aren't working.

This is how, early on, we became caught on the hook of seeking perfection. The problem with perfection isn't the idea of perfection in and of itself; it's that we attached our self-worth to the achievement of our idea of perfection.

This just doesn't work because perfection was never meant to be something to measure ourselves against. Perfection isn't something we have seen with our own eyes; it's merely a symbolic idea that self-hate has fallen in love with. Self-hate has figured out that it can use the idea of perfection to keep us chasing a carrot that we can never catch. That is why self-hate is the one that sets the standard of perfection. The only way that it can stay in control and keep us chasing the carrot is if it convinces us that unless we catch that carrot, we are worthless and no one will love us.

If perfection is the standard by which you measure yourself, I can guarantee that you will never improve enough to meet your own standards. The solution is to ignore the idea of perfection and accept and embrace yourself exactly as you are, right here and now. I'm not talking about embracing your potential or what you *could* be. I'm talking about embracing and accepting all of you, as you are in this very moment.

Flaws and All

You've been taught that it is not okay to think how you think and feel how you feel, and that you should not have the "flaws" that you have. Basically, you have been taught that it is not okay to be how you are. So it's understandable why the idea of accepting yourself exactly as you are kind of makes you want to cringe. You've internalized what other people have taught you. Even if you didn't learn this pattern from your parents, human society tends to base value upon how much someone accomplishes or achieves.

As a result you have made other people's approval the basis by which you value and love yourself. When you base your self-concept on external standards, you are vulnerable to the opinions and especially the criticism of others. You have developed an attitude of nonacceptance toward yourself and now you live your life trying to change everything you don't approve of about yourself. But perfectionism is a self-defeating state of mind. To love yourself, you must stop trying to be who you wish you were, long enough to find out who you really are and allow your true self to exist in the world.

This brings us to the truth about *acceptance,* a word that holds different meanings for different people. Some of these meanings are beneficial; others are detrimental. On the positive side of this word, acceptance is the idea of making peace with what is instead of pushing against it. When you are fighting against something, thereby not accepting it, you are introducing friction into your life by trying to push against something you cannot get rid of. Any attention you pay to it just reinforces it instead of eradicating it. However, to accept is to let go of resistance, thereby allowing your focus to attend only to what you do want in your life experience.

True acceptance does not mean settling for, tolerating, enabling, or validating; it simply means releasing yourself from negative focus and discontinuing the combat against anything, which only keeps it in your life. It is of paramount importance to accept where you are and who you are. It is also of paramount importance to accept where other people are and who other people are.

Though it always feels fabulous to be accepted by others, this is not the key to happiness. This is why having a desire for acceptance from others means you are experiencing a lack of acceptance for yourself. When you do not accept yourself or others, you cannot experience other people accepting you. You are not a vibrational "match" to it. A key ingredient to self-love is healthy acceptance of yourself and others. If you have acceptance for yourself and others, you will not desire acceptance from anyone. You will not need it.

Personal Acceptance

To accept your acceptance of yourself, a powerful exercise is to receive yourself with an attitude of *approval*. If you have been living according to the standard of perfection, comparing yourself to people that you think are better than you, you have been approaching yourself up until now with an attitude of *disapproval*.

Developing an attitude of self-approval takes practice. You need to find ways to withdraw focus off of things that cause you to feel as if you are not good enough and place your focus on things that make you feel as if you are good enough.

You can start on this process today. Get out a piece of paper, and write this sentence down as many times as you can, filling in the blank:

I approve of _____ about myself.

When you read over your list of statements, did it teach you anything about yourself? How do you feel when you focus on what you approve of about yourself instead on what you don't approve of about yourself?

We can't be focused on what we don't approve of about someone and still love them at the same time. So of course we can't focus on what we don't approve of about ourselves and love ourselves at the same time.

But we can help ourselves to start off our day with an attitude of approval toward ourselves with this next exercise. Write down this sentence on a piece of paper, and post it near your bed in plain view:

I approve of _____.

Before you get out of bed in the morning, make yourself fill in that blank with something you approve of about yourself. For example, "I approve of my incredibly good sense of style." Imagine how good it would feel if you woke up in the morning and the first thing someone did was express their approval of you. Instead of waiting for the rest of your life for someone else to come along and do that, you're going to do it for yourself.

Overcoming the Pressure of Perfection

Those of us who are perfectionists are Olympic-caliber self-saboteurs. We like to set cruel goals for ourselves. We set goals where failure is inevitable, not because the goal is in and of itself impossible to reach, but because the way we go about trying to reach it and the standards and timelines we set for achieving it cause us to break down. Too often, we pick goals that require so much effort and are so difficult to achieve that our minds and bodies suffer breakdowns to try to prevent us from "killing" ourselves.

The constant pressure to achieve perfection reduces our productivity, and when we fail to meet our goals because they are ridiculous in the first place, we blame and criticize ourselves even more, and decide that we must be worthless. But really, there is nothing "wrong" with how our lives are unfolding, and we are certainly not worthless. In fact, there is nothing wrong with the world. This is difficult to understand when we get hung up on resistant ideas such as "people shouldn't be starving." But like the rest of us, the world is also engaged in a process of mastery.

But on your way to mastery, don't keep resisting the imperfections in yourself and others, because that is what is inspiring us all toward excellence. We can allow our vision to define what we want within ourselves and within the world, and then move toward that wider personal vision because of the sheer joy of experiencing advancement. This awareness is important for those of us who do have large visions, so that we don't continue to measure ourselves against impossible standards and a warped state of perfection. Our high ideals and visions can be like beacons that call us toward our desires, as long as they don't become the standards we judge ourselves by.

Perfectionism can be a form of self-abuse. When you are expecting perfection from yourself, you are applying incredible pressure to yourself. When you experience self-hate in the form of perfectionism, even the information in this book can be used to abuse yourself. For example, you may read this book and turn self-love into an ideal to measure yourself against. You may then proceed to get upset with yourself whenever you do something that is not self-loving.

Self-hate is yet another form of resistance. If we experience self-hate and resist that experience of self-hate, all we are doing is resisting our own resistance. All we are doing is saying, "I shouldn't be where I am," which as you know tends to keep you stuck where you are. In order to love yourself, you need to begin practicing a new mantra: *I am where I am.* Instead of resisting where you are, you embrace it. You own it. You just accept where you are and go in the direction you want to go in again.

This last concept is especially important when it comes to addiction relapses. Some of us may have developed addictions as a result of trying to escape ourselves and our current realities. If we shame ourselves for having a relapse, we have done nothing but dig ourselves deeper into a hole. If we have been doing something one way for a long time, expecting ourselves to do something else, and do it perfectly, is cruelty.

Self-love is not about expecting the idealized standard of perfection from yourself. It's about loving yourself in any way you can right now. When you do that, you start to recognize the perfection of the current you: the you who is always in the process of progression and mastery.

The sculptor not only loves the finished pot once it's thrown and fired. The sculptor loves the pot when the pot is still just a potential. The sculptor loves the pot when it is nothing more than cold, imbalanced clay against his or her hands. If you have practiced self-hate for many years, you have mastered it as your art form. It will obviously take step-by-step practice, and lots of it, to turn self-love into your art form instead.

Along the way you will have "mistakes." You will have moments and even days where you revert to the old, familiar self-hate. But those regressions aren't wrong. They are a necessary part of your process of learning to love yourself. Don't condemn them. Just find anything self-loving to think or do from wherever you are and get back on track.

Understanding the Layers of Love

Get out a piece of paper and draw a spiral. Now draw a horizontal line from the center of the spiral to its outer edge. You can see that if you trace the spiral from the inside out with your finger, you keep running into the same line every time you trace a full rotation. But you also notice that as the spiral gets bigger and bigger, it takes more time to get from the point where you hit that line to the next point when you hit the line.

Improvement always works in this way. As time goes by, you keep reaching new layers of improvement relative to a subject. You may have kept hitting the line when you traced that spiral with your finger, but the times when you hit that line became fewer and farther between the farther away you got from the epicenter of the spiral.

When you began reading this book, it was like you were in the epicenter of this spiral. As you began learning more about self-love and practicing it (tracing the spiral outward), you no doubt continued to run into some barricades of self-hate (the line). But as you progress, the time and space between each barricade also increases until one day, you will not experience them at all.

Don't think of these times where you experience another layer of self-hate as a regression. Even though that is what they feel like, it's not what they are. You are simply running into more expansive layers of self-hate that have to be healed. If you accept them as they come and move past them by taking the next logical step toward self-love, from wherever you are at that time, then you will experience a day when there are no more layers to run into.

I hope this example convinces you to give yourself a break. Any choice you make can be seen as a necessary part of your expansion, and the universe is in an eternal process of expansion. As part of this universe, this means that you, too, are in an eternal process of expansion, so you can't ever "get it all done."

When you realize these two things, life ceases to be about the goal and how fast you can reach that goal. It is then about the process of progression. Life is then about joy. So love yourself and let yourself off the hook of perfection. Let yourself enjoy whatever you can about the steps between the point where you are now and what you desire for your future. It will come to you in time once you truly embrace the process and journey toward self-love.

TOOL #23

EMBRACING MISTAKES

It's never pleasant to make a mistake, but we don't have to keep beating ourselves up endlessly the way many of us do. A mistake is basically any action that, upon reflection, we wish we had done differently. Mistakes and regret therefore go hand in hand, but they are not the end of the world. When we look at it, having made a mistake is usually the result of one or more of the following things: the failure to reach a goal, lack of information, lack of awareness, procrastination, impatience, overindulgence, emotional outbursts, misjudgments, misinterpretations, wasted effort, missed opportunities, absentmindedness, forgetfulness, or doing something that is out of line with one's own integrity. It sounds like a long list, but I think anyone can identify with times when one or more of these things contributed to a mistake in his or her life.

What we need to realize is that at the time that we make a mistake, we are convinced that we are in fact making the best decision. We are doing what makes sense and what seems reasonable to us at the time. We always choose the action that seems most likely to meet our needs in a given moment. It is only upon reflection when we can see that our decision may not have been the best one. This is why saying that something is a "mistake" is only something that we can do in retrospect.

We also make decisions based on our level of awareness. Since our level of awareness is subject to change, we can say that something is a mistake only after our awareness changes. Since we acted the best way we knew at the time, we should not focus on these things in terms of right or wrong. Instead, we should think of things in terms of beneficial or detrimental. We gain increased awareness about what is actually beneficial or what is detrimental by making mistakes in the first place.

Given these realities, it makes absolutely no sense whatsoever to let mistakes be the criteria for a decrease in our own self-worth. That is literally expecting ourselves to see what we did not see, know what we did not know, and do what we did not know we could do at the time.

If we judge ourselves and our worth based on that kind of retrospection, what we are doing is judging our past selves based on today's expanded perspective. How fair is it to expect yourself to know what you did not know at the time? Would you do that to a child? A child doesn't know that he will fall if he doesn't look where he is going. In fact, the way that he learns that he will fall if he doesn't look where he is going is by not looking where he is going and then, falling.

The only reason that you know the child will fall is because of your perspective. But that perspective doesn't belong to the child. So, if you judge the child for falling, you are making a judgment based on your perspective, which is highly unfair and highly unloving. The you who made that mistake is a *past* you. Even if you register something as a mistake one second after you do it, it is important to know that you were a different person one second ago than you are right now. Don't judge the *past you* based on the perspective that the *current you* now holds.

Instead of judging our past selves based on the mistakes they have made, we can feel gratitude for them. The gift of their mistakes is our current wisdom.

What's Your Motivation?

By now, you can probably imagine that your old friend "self-hate" loves to use the argument "But I knew better than to do that." We see this argument as a valid reason for why we should feel terrible about ourselves when it comes to mistakes. If you are beating yourself up for mistakes and basing it on this perspective, it is time to understand motivation.

Motivation is the direct result of a perceived need or desire. Often, we are caught between opposing needs. For example, we may have a desire to have a successful marriage. But in the moment, we may cheat on our spouse because our desire to feel wanted and loved is stronger than our desire to have a successful marriage. When this is the case, our awareness tells us that the best decision is to cheat on our spouse because our need and desire at the time tells us so.

Therefore, you can see that we might make the decision to cheat on our spouse from the perspective of our momentary, limited awareness. It may not be ultimately beneficial to us, and making the mistake may show us that the choice to cheat on our spouse is in fact detrimental, but it still doesn't change the fact that *in the moment* you still did what you thought was best at the time. If you didn't think it was the best at the time, you would not have done it. We make a lot of these choices that we think are best, but that turn out to be mistakes. But the truth still remains that we make mistakes only because we are not aware that they are mistakes at the time.

There is always a consequence when it comes to mistakes. The expanded awareness that one incurs when one has made a mistake is expanded awareness about the consequences of mistakes, too. Accepting and learning from these consequences allows us to make better choices in the future. But at no point does making a mistake make you a fundamentally bad person. At no point does it actually decrease your worth. You may have made choices from a very limited level of awareness that was unwise, ineffective, and detrimental. But your worth has nothing to do with your level of awareness. Your lovability and level of deserving also have nothing to do with your level of awareness.

Asking Yourself "Why?"

By asking ourselves some important questions, we can increase our level of awareness when we have to make a decision.

*Have I ever been in the same kind of situation before?
If so, what did I learn from it?*

*What potential short-term and long-term consequences
might come from either decision that I might make?*

Are these potential consequences worth it?

What do I want to get out of either option?

*What desire or need am I trying to meet by making
either decision?*

*Is there an alternative that would enable me to meet my desires
or needs and have fewer negative consequences?*

Which decision is in line with my highest good?

If we evaluate our decisions according to our answers
to these questions, we are making decisions from a higher
perspective with an increased level of awareness. It may not
prevent consequences from happening, but it at least enables us
to consciously and deliberately make the choice that we feel is
best in the moment.

Processing Mistakes in a Positive Way

Think of a mistake that you might have made in the past.
Close your eyes and mentally go back in time to relive the
mistake that you made. Try to remember the way you felt, the
thoughts you were thinking and what you were hoping for.
And ask yourself this question: *If I were to go back to that time, not
knowing what I know now, but instead knowing only what I knew
then, with the same needs, desires, perspectives, and lack of awareness
of the consequences, would I have done something different, or would
I have done the same thing?*

This is a way to help you realize that you were in fact
doing what you thought was the best thing to do at the time,
if you are to let yourself off the hook for past mistakes. The
key to loving yourself, even when you make a mistake, is to
change your perspective about the mistake—in other words,
to reframe the mistake.

To reframe a mistake, we must change our point of view
and therefore our interpretation of the mistake. It's within our
power to consciously and deliberately reframe our opinion

relative to anything. This reframing is the key to letting go of the thoughts that are not serving our highest good. In order to reframe a mistake, we have to look for the value hidden in the mistake and then find thoughts that enable us to let go of the self-blame, self-criticism, and self-condemnation that we feel for having made the mistake.

In other words, we have to metaphorically look through the bathwater for the baby, save the baby, and then throw out the bathwater. When you have made a mistake, the following questions will help you to reframe that mistake:

What valuable thing did this experience teach me that I would not have otherwise known about myself, another person, or the world?

What did this experience cause me to know that I want?

What am I going to do differently in the future?

How will this mistake help me to live a better life in the future?

Is there anything I can do to make reparations for the mistake I have made? If so, what are they?

How can I move forward from here?

When you are done answering these questions, make a list of all the positive aspects of having made the mistake that you made.

Better Choices for the Future

Some people worry that embracing their mistakes is like condoning the pain that they caused to themselves or to others. Others think that embracing their mistakes might cause them to make the same mistakes again. But neither of those things is true. Embracing a mistake is simply going to enable you to stop using that mistake as an excuse to hate yourself. Think about it. Beating yourself up for mistakes accomplishes nothing. All the condemnation and recrimination in the world won't make those mistakes go away. It does absolutely no good at all.

But when you can let yourself off the hook for the mistakes you've made, it becomes ten times easier to move forward, make reparations, and make different choices. It enables you to create a better life for yourself based on what you have learned from the mistake. There is no right or wrong way to reframe a mistake. Just remember that when you are reframing a mistake, you are looking to give the mistake a beneficial meaning instead of a detrimental one.

So indeed, every mistake tells you what you need to correct and therefore brings you closer to the likelihood of success. I have found that you can even apply this same principle to self-hate. You would have no desire or inspiration to know what self-love is if you never knew self-hate. So the self-hate you may now be experiencing is every bit as responsible for the self-love you will one day experience as the result of the skills that you're learning in order to develop that self-love.

TOOL #24

THE DANGER OF *SHOULDS*

Shoulds *Keep Dragging Us Down*

From time to time, we have all lived at the mercy of *shoulds*—the looming requirements that we place on ourselves because we were taught to place them on ourselves. *Shoulds* are the by-product of obligation, habit, and, worst of all, other people's expectations. A *should* is an ever-present requirement projected onto us by our families, friends, and communities. It is the projection that we should want what they want, do what they do, and believe what they believe.

In this way, a *should* is an external demand that we adopt and make our own. Many of these demands are a direct opposition to our own needs, our own personal truths, and who we really are; and that is why for so many of us they seem to always remain *shoulds*. We don't have the natural motivation to fulfill requirements that don't really originate from ourselves.

Most of us believe that *should*s are what keep us in line and motivate us to do and be our best. This couldn't be further from the truth. Being our best is the direct by-product of allowing who we really are to shine through our thoughts, words, and actions. In order to allow who we really are to shine through, we have to know who we are. *Should*s obscure who we really are because they do not reflect our true needs and desires. Instead, they reflect the color of other people's expectations.

Take a moment to inquire about the *should*s that are running your life. Write down all the things you think you *should* have done in the past. Then write down all the things you think you *should* be doing today and tomorrow. Then write down all the things you think you should be doing in a year and in ten years and by the end of your life.

Here are some examples: "I should lose weight." "I have done enough work on myself that I should be able to not get upset by trivial things by now." "I should have gone to college." "I should stop being so negative." "I should spend more time with my kids." "I should spend less time watching TV." You get the idea. Don't hold back, no matter how ridiculous you think these *should*s are. Notice that the things that will surface for you during this exercise have to surface because they are the expectations and requirements that are creating your unhappiness right now.

Take your list and address every single *should* by asking, "Why should I?" Write down the very first answer that comes to your mind for each *should* on your list. Take some time to reflect on the answers. By doing this exercise, you are consciously questioning your *should*s in order to see where these obligations really originate from.

Celebrating Your Individuality

*Should*s are excellent fodder for self-hate. You cannot love what is and be thinking that anything should be other than what it is. Replacing *should*s is an integral part of learning to love yourself. By letting go of them, you are demonstrating respect for your own wants and needs. By letting go of them, you are also being true to yourself.

It is a socially conditioned habit for most of us to say both "I have to" and "I should." So a great practice to get in the habit of is to replace "I should" and "I have to" with "I get to." For example, every time you catch yourself saying, "I have to go to work," replace it with "I get to go to work." Or every time you catch yourself saying, "I should go brush my teeth," replace it with "I get to go brush my teeth." This is a great practice to make a habit out of because it empowers you and causes you to become aware that every single thing you are doing is a choice.

When we live according to "I should" or "I have to," we are victims to expectation. We have no idea that we have a choice to live that way or not. So we believe in the illusion of being controlled. We are victims to a bad guy who doesn't actually exist. The expectations and standards that we hold ourselves to aren't objective. They're not real. Realize that we create them, and we are the only ones who are holding ourselves to them.

Never did a universal rule exist for how someone *should* or *shouldn't* be. People like to be validated. We substitute the individual, internal stability of self-esteem with the external stability of being validated by others. This is why we seek to get other people to agree with our point of view, and this is why we conform to each other.

Our minds want to quantify. Our brains are designed to rank and organize information, and we want to know where we fit into the scheme of things. Because of this, we tend to compare ourselves to others. But in order to be true to ourselves, we need to stop comparing ourselves to other people. It is not often that we compare ourselves with people who are less fortunate than we are and thus consider ourselves blessed.

More often, we compare ourselves with someone whom we perceive as being better than we are, having more than we have, or doing more than we feel we are capable of doing. This causes us to feel as if we are not good enough. It causes us to feel frustrated and jealous. Comparing yourself to others causes you to judge yourself negatively. That is one of the most painful things you can do to yourself.

People are destined to be different. We are here to experience and explore the individual perspective. No two of us are the same. We have different thoughts, we have different beliefs, we have different experiences, we interpret things differently, and we feel emotions differently. Even identical twins are completely different people. Given that we came here to experience the individual, unique perspective of our current self, comparing ourselves to others defies the purpose of being here. It is as useless as comparing an apple and an orange.

Besides, if you're always striving to be someone you're not, and living under the shadow of other people's *shoulds*, you'll never be able to love yourself. You were created with a unique set of gifts and abilities that will inevitably lead you to success. They will lead you to success the minute you become aware of what they are and find ways to develop and master them. You can change your current situation by changing your perspective and attitude. And no matter what anyone else is doing, you can always take action toward your true desires with whatever assets you do currently have from wherever you are right now.

Given that we are always improving, expanding, and in a state of creation, it is important to understand that "being yourself" does not mean picking a solid identity. Allow yourself to grow, to improve, and to change. The parts of your past that you aren't proud of don't define you. Those actions are not who you are. Replace your "shoulds" with "want tos."

TOOL #25

FACING DOWN THE
EIGHT FACES OF
SELF-SABOTAGE

There is No Such Thing as Self-Sabotage

So many of us struggle with behaviors that create problems in our lives and that interfere with our goals. Self-sabotage is a part of so many people's lives, is it not? The answer is no. The first thing we need to do is to look at some examples of self-sabotage. We have something to do, but we procrastinate it. We hold onto addictions like binge-eating or drinking. Consciously, we really want a relationship to work, but we keep pushing the other person away or doing and saying things to create conflict in the relationship. We consciously want a job, but we suddenly say things in the interview that makes the boss check us off his list of candidates.

Self-sabotage is essentially thoughts, words and actions (behaviors) that are self-defeating. They work AGAINST you when it comes to attaining something that you want. Clearly you can see that self-sabotage is a reality. But I'm here to tell you today that it is *not* a reality. How can that be?

Consciousness can and does split itself. This means that even though we call ourselves by one name and therefore identify ourselves as being one unified thing, the reality is that we are more of an amalgamation of fragmented parts or selves. We are more like a mosaic or a stained glass window. Our degree of internal suffering is about the degree of harmony (or lack there of) between these internal selves. If you are experiencing self-sabotage, it is because not all of your internal selves or parts agree with your conscious desires. One or more of them are resisting or opposing the parts that contain your conscious desires.

I am making a bold claim. I am telling you that there is no such thing as an internal saboteur and there is no such thing as an internal abuser. If any of your internal parts or selves are resisting or opposing your desires, or if any of them are hurting other parts of you in any way, it is because they think it is in your best interest for them to do so. In other words, they believe they are saving your life by *not* going along with the plan. For this reason, we cannot say that they are *against* you. They just don't agree with the rest of you about how to be FOR you.

Here are some examples:

1. We have something to do, but we procrastinate it.
    In this scenario, one fragment or part within us (the one we are consciously identified with) has made the decision to do something. The other part thinks that

doing that thing will lead to discomfort or some kind of pain. Therefore, it is trying to prevent you from experiencing that pain by keeping you from doing it.

2. We hold onto addictions like binge-eating or drinking. In this scenario, one part (the one we are consciously identified with) has decided it is committed to stopping the addiction. The other part believes that the life you want is not actually possible to achieve and so it thinks that letting go of the addiction will simply make it so you are in hell alone and now have to just sit in the agony of that misery permanently. It would rather you have the Novocain so to speak.

3. Consciously, we really want a relationship to work, but we keep pushing the other person away or doing and saying things to create conflict in the relationship. In this scenario, one fragment or part within us (the one we are consciously identified with) has made the decision to be in a relationship and make it work. Another part knows that relationships have been so painful in the past and that it has been abandoned, and therefore, thinks abandonment is inevitable. So it is trying to save you from the pain of getting attached to something you are inevitably going to lose.

4. You consciously want a job, but you suddenly say things in the interview that makes the boss check you off his list of candidates. In this scenario, one part of you has decided the best idea is to work at that job. The other part thinks that job is not what you should be doing. That it is in the opposite direction of your authentic essence. And therefore, life will be drudgery and will take effort if you accept that job.

5. Self hate. That's where you think you have me beat right? Obviously self-hate is the exception to the rule. Think again. When you discover the parts involved in self-hate what you find is that a person internalizes their external abuser. Essentially, one part feels that by hating and punishing and therefore trying to get another part to change, it is preventing them from getting that hate and disapproval and shaming and punishment from the outside, from another person. By doing so, it is trying to get the person the love they so desperately need from the outside.

Metaphorically speaking, what any form of self-sabotage always has in common is that one part thinks the answer to a good life and happiness is going left and the other part thinks that going left is literally the road to ruin. But what you must see is that both parts actually have your best interests at heart. We have to understand that no part within us is actually against us. We need to approach the issue with this understanding to create an alignment between these opposed parts.

There are limitless possibilities for why a part is opposed to our conscious desires. But in order to move beyond the behaviors we call self-sabotaging, we must see the self-preserving nature of them. We must empathize completely with the parts within us that think our salvation is in the opposite direction of our conscious desires.

One of the best methods for exploring this part is that you can close your eyes and ask to see this part that is doing the self-sabotaging behavior in your mind's eye – the one that is procrastinating or causing conflict in the relationship or is showing up to things late or is screwing up interviews. Let the image of that part appear however it appears. If it helps you,

you can see if this part within you has a name. You can begin to observe it and study its behaviors and perspectives and wants and needs and motivations. You can ask it questions. You can explore its relationship to other parts within you.

The goal is to seek to find a way for both of these opposed parts of you to agree upon a course of action. It is as if our objective mind acts as a benevolent mediator who can empathize with both sides and whose goal is to find a way for both sides to win or feel good with a course of action or decision. Be open to the idea that by exploring that part's perspective that you may change your mind about what you actually want or what is actually right for you to do.

You will see an end to the self-sabotage when you choose to resolve the pain contained in this part that is keeping it fragmented from the rest of you. You can meet its needs with your imagination and subsequently implement the changes this part of you needs in your day-to-day life. You can also improve the relationship that this part has with the part within you that it is opposed to. By doing this, you create internal peace and integration. You can restore yourself back to a state of internal peace.

If you experience self-sabotage, you fear yourself and you distrust yourself. But there is no reason to feel this way towards yourself. Even the parts within you that seem to be hurting you, are actually doing so because they think it is in your best interests. This means that even if they disagree on the general strategy for how to make you feel good and live the best life possible; this is what they all ultimately want. They want you to feel better. They want you to live the best life possible. And so, because of the purity of their intentions for you, it can be said that there is really no such thing as self-sabotage.

You can fit the many forms of what many people call "self-sabotage" into eight categories: self-criticism, self-doubt, self-blame, self-destruction, self-pity, self-deprivation, self-deprecation, and self-pride. I will speak to each of these in this chapter. Let me start with the most common one: self-criticism.

Self-Criticism, The First Face of Self-Sabotage.

Almost all of us have that little voice in our heads that spends its time judging and criticizing us. It is the one that tells us how we messed up, how we fall short, and what we did that was bad and wrong and what is not acceptable about us. Most people mistake this voice for all of themselves, as opposed to a part of the complex system of their psyche. Because the "self-critic" can cause so many problems and be so detrimental to our wellbeing, it is tempting to think of it as an enemy that constantly lives with you; and in your own skin. And because of this, the world is full of methods for standing up to your inner critic and fighting against your inner critic and ignoring your inner critic and negating and minimizing your inner critic. The problem is that these methods don't work. They will never work. They will never work because believe it or not, the inner critic is not against you. It is actually powerfully *for* you. It is trying its very best to protect you. And unless you understand this, you will add to your own suffering, increase your self-hate and intensify the internal war within yourself.

To understand the inner critic, you need to know that organisms that belong to the animal kingdom, including humans, find pain and stress that they cannot control and that are therefore unpredictable and out of their hands, so painful and terrorizing that they will often take their control back by being the one or by being the first to cause their own pain. You see this clearly with studies done relative to self-injury. When injury is inflicted on animals in a setting where there is no way to get away from that injury, such as electroshocks, they will often begin to self-injure. This restores a sense of control over pain. So, the principle is: self-inflicted pain is safer and more tolerable than pain inflicted by someone else, especially someone upon whom your life depends.

As a child, if you want your needs to be met, survive in society and have a chance at feeling things like love, belonging, contribution, and safety, you only have one option: To adopt the values, rules and standards of the family and society that you are born into. And hold yourself to them.

To understand this, I'll give you an example, let's say that when you were younger you got angry. And imagine that you were raised in a family that sees anger as bad and wrong. The adults in your environment would immediately react by turning against your anger. They would do this in order to discourage you from being angry. They might do something like send you to your room for a timeout or immediately become defensive and shame you for being angry or dole out a consequence like taking away one of your toys. The experience of disapproval is painful enough for a child, whose survival and every need they have is dependent on the adults in their life, that the child wants to avoid this experience in the future at all costs. In response, what you would do in order to be able to control avoiding it in the future is that you would adopt the social value of not getting angry and you would *make it your own standard* for yourself. You internalize societal values, rules and standards and begin to police yourself so that you stay in alignment with them. After that day, any time you feel anger creeping up, or if you get angry, you will begin to police yourself before anyone else has the chance to do so. You remind yourself of how bad and wrong your anger is. You remind yourself of how sub-par it makes you as a person. You beat other people to the punch and disapprove of yourself.

In the best-case scenario, you will either manage to do this quick enough so as to discourage yourself from doing whatever might cause you to meet with disapproval. In the worst-case scenario, you might do whatever causes you to meet with disapproval, but instead of meeting with the full force of their disapproval, you can decrease the consequences by demonstrating clearly that you don't stand by what you did and that you know it is bad and wrong and therefore won't happen again.

This part of you that takes on the role of this internal police officer that keeps you in line so that you don't align with anything that would lead to disapproval and the painful societal consequences of disapproval, is your inner critic. It is a part of you that is trying to protect you. And so, you could consider it your most inverted advocate.

The inner critic is a protector personality within the complex system of your psyche. It is actually trying to save your life, help you to avoid consequences and keep it so that you can get your needs met. Just like a police officer serves to keep people in alignment with human society, the inner critic is trying to keep you in alignment with other people. It is trying desperately to uphold your values and standards . . . Both those that are true to you and those that you adopted from other people in your social environment. The inner critic is the one that holds the truth of what matters most to you.

For example, perhaps what someone in your life rejected about you was that you were so sensitive. The self-critic will then constantly criticize and shame you for being sensitive. If you don't stop being so sensitive, it will escalate and its negative feedback will become more and more intense. It may even turn into shame, whereby you begin to triangulate yourself internally against the part of yourself that is sensitive. Your inner critic does this because it thinks that with enough disapproval of it, you will either stop being that way or be motivated to fix it. And this will get you the sense of belonging and safety that you want. In this example, the truth this self-critic aspect holds, is just how important belonging and safety are to you and how much you need those things.

It is tempting to think that the inner critic is self-sabotaging. In reality, there is no such thing as genuine self-sabotage. Any part of you that appears to be "sabotaging" you, is a part of you that thinks it is actually doing the best thing for you.

You will get nowhere when it comes to getting the inner critic to see that what it is doing doesn't work in your life today. And you will get nowhere when it comes to getting your inner critic to change the way it functions within you, unless you really, really put focus into *understanding* it. You must understand how and when it was created by you. How it being created was for your benefit at the time, what its motives are for saying what it says and what its intentions are for saying what it says. You also have to consciously examine your relationship to those values and standards and rules that the inner critic represents. As well as consciously examine the current reality of the consequences it is trying to help you avoid.

When you work directly with your inner critic, you will see just how benevolent and well intentioned this part of you is. You will also be able to show it how the way that it is going about protecting you may not be effective and might even be causing you worse pan than the consequence it is trying to police you into avoiding. You can end the adversarial relationship that you have with that little critical voice inside your own head. You can end the adversarial relationship that it has with any other parts of you that it thinks will lead to you getting disapproved of as well. The outcome of this allied relationship with your inner critic is the true inner peace you are looking for. A sense of internal support, alliance and self-esteem instead of internal war, judgement and criticism.

Your inner critic actually needs to be (and deserves to be) understood, respected, loved, recognized and valued for what it is trying to do for you. And this understanding, respect and positive recognition will be necessary in order to create any pliability within this part of you, regarding its willingness to change its perspective and methods. Whenever you are working with your inner critic, you need to figure out what valued and needed things that the self-critic is holding the truth of in any given situation where it is being noisy. As well as the truth of the consequences it is afraid of. Examine those values and needs consciously. If you consciously stand by them, get those things directly and from the people and in the places that you can actually get them from. Examine those consequences. Are they real or are they not real anymore? Given the answer you arrive at, how does that change things?

Do not ignore, stand up to, fight against, negate or minimize the voice of your inner critic. By doing so, you are turning against a protector within yourself. You are causing pain to a part of yourself that is fighting for your wellbeing. You are missing the opportunity to find out what value or standard or need your inner critic is fighting to keep you in alignment with. You are remaining ignorant of what consequence it is trying to help you to avoid. You are resisting a part of yourself, thereby creating rigidity instead of pliability within yourself. And you are treating this part of yourself as an enemy instead of as what it is . . . a friend.

Chipping Away at Self-Doubt

Doubt is just another kind of faith; it's faith in negative outcomes. You can think of self-doubt as self-hate preventing you from getting anywhere. It is the epitome of the belief, "I'm not good enough." If you struggle with self-doubt, bring it into the light by admitting to it. Recognize and acknowledge its existence. If you try to ignore or deny your self-doubt, it will operate covertly by imposing limits on your ability to act.

Spend some time trying to figure out what triggered the self-doubt and why. Can you trace it back to any early experiences? Ask yourself, *What am I so afraid of?* Then plan out a step-by-step strategy for transcending your doubt. Think about what small, manageable steps you could take that would cause you to feel more confident, and take the first step. When you're done, work on the next step and so on.

Another tool that is great to use for self-doubt is reversal. When you come up with a statement like, "I'm not pretty enough," reverse it to say, "I am pretty enough," and think of at least ten ways that the new statement is as true as or truer than the original statement. This technique requires some creative thinking. Consider it a mind game.

I find that it helps to pretend that you are a defense attorney in a courtroom and that your job depends on you searching for and presenting evidence that proves that the reverse statement is true. When you find yourself struggling with self-doubt, remember that it's not a giant monster preventing you from succeeding. It's just a speed bump you've encountered on your way to inevitable success. Nothing is impossible in a universe that is made up of infinite possibilities.

Realize that like all forms of self-sabotage, doubting yourself is a method you are using to try to keep yourself safe. For example, people tend to use self-doubt to keep themselves safe from taking risks and failing. Or they tend to use self-doubt as a way of keeping their social connections when they fear that succeeding would cause them to lose closeness with the people they love etc. How does doubting yourself keep you safer, despite the price you have to pay for it?

Don't Accept Self-Blame

Self-blame is the attitude that whatever has gone on is entirely your fault. When you engage in this form of self-sabotage, you take more responsibility than is actually yours. You take responsibility not only for your part in a situation, but also for other people's parts.

If you struggle with self-blame, realize that you are doing so because like all "self-sabotage" techniques, there is some positive payoff for doing so. Subconsciously, you feel that blaming yourself protects you in some way. For example, if you blame yourself, you don't have to feel powerless to what happened. Or if you blame yourself, you might feel that the pain of fault will keep you from ever making a mistake again etc.

If you are blaming yourself, ask yourself honestly, *What good is this doing? How is this keeping me safe? And what from? From there,* choose to make any amends that would cause you to feel better, such as saying you are sorry and or taking action to create resolve.

If you struggle with self-blame, the time has come to discover "what's yours" and "what's theirs" in any given situation. We tend to be hyper responsible if we suffer from this form of self-sabotage. This unhealthy form of responsibility causes us to become paralyzed under the weight of taking responsibility for everything. In any given negative situation, take out a sheet of paper and make two columns. Write your own name at the top of one of the columns and the other person's name at the top of the other. Under each, make a list of what is that person's responsibility is in the situation. Here is an example given to me by a woman who found herself in the middle of a divorce:

MINE

I was so desperate for belonging that it didn't matter what guy I was with. I had no discernment with men. I wasn't in love with him. I wanted to belong and I really wanted to belong with his family.

I married him one month after meeting him.

I was obsessed with pregnancy and whether I was pregnant or not and even lied to a few boyfriends that I was at that age because that = getting the belonging I was so desperate for.

I feel ashamed that I can't cope like "normal people."

I have toxic shame.

I believed naively that his family would love me even though we broke up.

I couldn't have a man that works and at the same time, I couldn't have a man that didn't work. This puts most men in a bind. I needed a "special circumstance" and couldn't wait around to find that because of my dependency/separation terror. My inability to be by myself made it so I went with the next guy instead of looking for a guy that was what I needed.

I didn't have the money for therapy at that time, so I didn't go to therapy.

I find it excruciating to admit to my limits because I'm so ashamed of them.

I need a man to take care of me.

I am actually very dependent in relationships and need
a man who is ok with that . . . My parents forced my
independence too early and I "false" advertise that I'm
strong and independent because of the protector selves
that buried my dependent selves. But they come out
in relationships with a vengeance and any time I need
someone and can't get them, I am shamed for my need.

My Husband's

He's pampered and his parents spoiled him and gave him
no taste of the world or of responsibility.
He was a child at the time and was not ready for marriage.
He doesn't want to be there for a woman, he told me so
last night.
He is condescending and thinks everyone is less than him,
especially intellectually.
He decided to marry me even when he knew I was bi polar
– assuming he wouldn't or shouldn't have to deal with
that in the marriage.
He "just gave up" with the pressure of taking care of me
and didn't even communicate about it or even put
effort into getting us help with it.
He is a horrible listener, who doesn't take anything you say
in, just looks for the next thing he can say.
He turned his family, who I really loved and wanted to
belong with against me so they'd save and protect him
from me.
He didn't try to remedy the marriage at all, just decided I
was the problem that he needed to run from.
He made it about me being too hard to handle instead
of also seeing that he was not able to provide what a
woman needs.

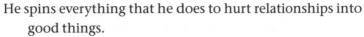

He spins everything that he does to hurt relationships into
good things.

He is not committed at all. The minute the going gets
tough, he gets going.

He wants an independent woman who does not depend
on him at all. He sees dependence as "sickness."
Therefore, he chose the wrong partner for himself
in choosing me.

Watch Out for Self-Destruction

Self-destruction is self-hate in proactive action. It can be
very hard to see how self-destruction can be something a person
does to keep themselves safe. But, self-destruction, like all
forms of self-sabotage, is something that a person does because
a part of them thinks it is in their best interests to do so. Self-
destruction is perhaps the most physical of all of the forms of
self-sabotage. When we are self-destructive, we put ourselves
smack-dab in the middle of circumstances whose outcomes are
the exact opposite of what we actually need and want.

If you struggle with self-destruction, identify how you are
abusing or undermining yourself. We have to admit that what
we are doing is destructive to us, if we ever hope to change.
We also have to want to change because without the desire,
there is nothing fueling the change and therefore no change
will take place.

The most important thing we can possibly do to heal self-
destructive habits is to figure out what's behind them. When
it seems like someone won't let go of something painful,
such as a behavior or a strategy or a belief or whatever it is
that is self-destructive, it is because that person believes that
regarding whatever situation they are in, they will be in MORE

pain without it. And they might be wrong about that, or they might in fact be right about that. Therefore, the painful thing is something that they perceive to be *decreasing* their pain and bringing relief and more self-preserving than the alternative, even if it comes at the price of self-destruction.

For example, Justine is 15 years old. She routinely engages in self-harm. Cutting and burning are the most typical forms of self-harm that she engages in. Her parents are absolutely perplexed about how someone could want to do things like that to themselves. They seek out counseling for Justine to figure out what is so wrong with their daughter that she likes and is addicted to pain. But the problem isn't that Justine likes pain. The problem is that in the household that Justine lives in, Justine is deeply unhappy. She feels like no one sees her, no one understands her needs and therefore, she will never have her needs met. She is alone even when her family members are in the room. She is not important and therefore, she has no reason to live. But on top of this, there is no tolerance in the household for negative thoughts or emotion. No matter what she may be acting like, her parents have a solid truth that they are good parents and that Justine has a good life. They have already decided that she should be happy and that if she isn't, something is wrong with *her*. This means that no matter what strategy Justine uses to try to get her parents to change something so that she feels better, they are both unresponsive. The *idea* that they want to maintain about themselves and about their life is more real and important to them than seeing the reality of their daughter is. Because of this, self-injury is not Justine's way of being in pain. It is her way of desperately trying to decrease her pain. Because her parents are so unresponsive to anything she does or says, self-injury is a way of escalating her message of desperation so they might just get that she needs something to change immediately. When she cuts, she feels relief because there is an alignment between how wounded she really is on the inside and what is happening on the outside. Her experience is therefore no longer a gaslight. And when she bleeds, she feels like the poison of the negative emotions that her parents won't tolerate her expressing, finally has an outlet to get out of her being. And the list goes on and on. Justine doesn't want to be in pain. She doesn't like it. And when people say she is attached to her pain, she's right back to that torment of not being seen or understood. The pain of being in emotional hell and alone, because her parents have already decided that the truth is that she isn't in hell, she's fine. What the pain of self-injury does, is it serves to decrease her pain and it serves as an attempt to try to self-preserve in an environment that is both dysfunctional and destructive.

Self-abusive behavior is often a form of escapism. This means it is important to dedicate time to working on whatever it is that you are trying to avoid. Observe your life and ask yourself, *What am I running away from? What are the issues I don't feel like I can deal with? What does this behavior accomplish?* What is the part of you that is engaging in self-destructive behavior trying to prevent? How is the behavior that you judge as self-destructive actually an attempt to self-preserve? And given the answer you arrive at, what is a different way that you can go about it? Your answers to these questions will make it apparent what you need to focus on. It's those things we are covering over with self-destruction that we need to focus on and begin to proactively heal.

The Truth about Self-Pity

Self-pity is the ultimate form of victimhood mentality. It's sabotage in the form of dishonoring yourself, ignoring your own potential, and not recognizing your own power. But, like all forms of self-sabotage, it is something that a person does because a part of them thinks it is in their best interests to do so. Self-pity has a positive payoff. If you struggle with self-pity, you are not alone. This is one of the most difficult forms of self-sabotage to deal with because the way our society views self-pity is detrimental to those healing from it. Society gives a mixed message in that society favors the underdog and it sees the victim as the one who is good and right. At the same time, we live in a "just get over it" society that sees self-pity as pathetic. Victims are glorified, but self-pity is seen as a selfish indulgence and is treated like an embarrassment.

If you struggle with self-pity, you don't have to feel guilty or beat yourself up about it. It doesn't make you pathetic or a bad person. It just means that you aren't giving yourself the love that you need. You are feeling powerless and incapable. You are viewing yourself as the underdog instead of focusing on your own power and worth, and that focus is keeping you from getting what you want.

The next time you notice that you're starting to feel sorry for yourself, allow yourself to admit that you deserve to feel sorry for yourself. Own up to the fact that you are justified in feeling that way. You don't need anyone else to validate this. Admit to yourself that you are where you are and then find a proactive thing to do that will cause you to come into your power instead.

If you are struggling with a situation that makes you feel sorry for yourself, instead of trying to self-preserve or to get your needs met through pity, take your power back instead.

Taking Your Power Back

Power is energy. It is the inherent capacity to create, direct, influence or do something so as to bring about what we want. Power in and of itself is wonderful. And it is something that all beings have. How that power is *used* is what matters most, because like anything, it can be used for harm and it can be used for good. We will all find ourselves in certain situations where we feel incapable of creating, directing, influencing or doing anything so as to bring about what we want. We feel out of control, disempowered and at the mercy of others. At times like this, it is super infuriating to hear people say, "you've given away too much of your power." It is an invalidation of the reality of the powerlessness inherent in situations where many of the elements involved *are* beyond your control. It also doesn't make immediate sense. You weren't aware of giving (and therefore didn't consciously choose to give) anything away. Which is why "taking your power back" is much more about becoming aware that you have power to begin with than it is about taking back something you gave away. So here is how to realize you have power and how to own it.

1. You have to get that free will is an absolute of your existence. No one can take that away. They cannot take away choice itself, only choices. All other people can do is to put intense amounts of pressure on you in the hopes that you will use your free will to choose to comply to what they are wanting. *They can't take your free will away, only put pressure on it.* You can't actually give your free will away even if you wanted to. Even if you comply, that is because you've decided to use your free will to choose in favor of what appears to be the lesser of consequences for you. This means, in every situation, you must challenge your assumptions about where you think the power lies.

    There may very well be situations where the pressure they use their power to put you under will cause you to use your free will to choose to comply with what they want you to choose. There are situations where no one can even fault you for making that choice because anyone would. You have every right to feel however you feel about how unfair and immoral it is for them to put that pressure on your free will. The point is you must never, ever confuse the pressure and force they use with taking away your free will.

2. Get into reality and accept what needs to be accepted as quickly as possible. When we are using our free will to resist what is, we have no power. It is wasted energy. We are always at the effect of others and are fighting the situation we are in, instead of making immediate adjustments in response to it. For example, if someone refuses to accept the reality that the economy is collapsing, the decisions and actions they will take will absolutely not serve them. It is as pointless as playing a chess game and spending your energy denying that someone has just made a move instead of seeing it, accepting it and based off of that, making a counter move . Reality is your only axis for power. But often we will not see, feel, hear or accept reality. You have got to surrender to the truth of the situation at hand. That is very different than surrendering to the situation itself. If you surrender to truth, you are able to start making decisions and start taking actions relative to the actuality of what is occurring.

3. When we feel powerless, all we are focused on is what we *can't* do. It is as if the situation itself is closing doors and windows in our face. We tend to bang against those doors and windows, hoping that if we do that, someone will somehow take mercy on us and decide

to open them. That's not going to happen unless
somehow the people who currently have power over
those doors and windows decide that it is in their best
interests to do so. You might be able to own your power
by trying to convince them it is in their best interests
to do so. This is the power of influence and persuasion
at work. But it may just benefit you much more to
put your energy towards looking for other doors and
windows that might be open. Long story short, to own
your power in any situation, you have to shift focus
towards what you CAN do. In whatever situation you
find yourself in, ask yourself: How and in what ways
can I create, direct, influence or do something so as to
bring about what I want?

4. Be true no matter what. To do this, you have to be
    honest with yourself. No one can control where you
    put your energy. Again, they can only put pressure on
    you to try to get you to decide with your free will to
    put your energy towards what they want you to put it
    towards. You have the control over what to put your
    energy and focus towards and into. You have control
    over your commitment because all commitment is, is
    to put your energy into something. Put your energy
    into what is true for you. Put it into what matters
    to you, what is meaningful and important to you.
    Commit your energy to your specific and individual
    values. Another way of saying this is that your power
    is really about staying as true as you possibly can to
    your values and what is important and meaningful to
    you specifically. This requires powerful authenticity.

5. Put yourself in your own hands. To understand this concept, I want you to imagine yourself in the middle of a deep pool with a bunch of larger people. Because you don't want to be responsible for swimming yourself and you see them as having more power in the situation than you do, you swim from person to person and with each one, you climb on top of them so that they can keep you afloat. The reason this diminishes your power is because *you are now in their hands*. It is up to them whether you sink or swim. You have made yourself *their* responsibility. If you sink, you can now make it their fault. This absolves you of pressure, but at the cost of your own power. See where you are doing this in your life. See where you are expecting them to be responsible for you and therefore putting yourself in their hands and simply hoping they do the right thing with you. For example, you might be doing this if you expect your abundance to come through a pay check from your boss instead of seeing your own skills as your venue for achieving abundance. You might be doing this if you expect your doctor to heal you instead of taking responsibility for your own health. You might be doing this if you expect other people to make decisions that affect your life. You might be doing this if you make your partner responsible for changing to be whatever way makes you feel good and powerlessly sinking into unhappiness in the relationship you are in, instead of actively taking steps to change the dynamic or choosing another partner. How can things related to your wellbeing be in your hands instead? Where do you think the power lies in this situation? How can you switch the situation so that it lies with you? People who intensely embrace responsibility have the most individual power.

6. Words have incredible power. Start using ones that honor your power instead of taking it away. For example, change "I can't" to "I choose not to" or "I wont." So often when we say "I can't," we are recognizing a limit that doesn't actually exist or not owning and taking responsibility for an actual limit we have. Change "he made me" to "he put pressure on me" or "I chose to." Your words shape the way you think about yourself and the world around you on a deeply subconscious level. This includes language where you are blaming or making excuses. When we are not owning our power, we always have an excuse for why something we want did not come about or is not coming about. Pay attention to the language you are using to convey your reasons for doing or not doing something, your choices and decisions. You might be surprised how many excuses you make. Whenever your language absolves you of responsibility or ability, it absolves you of power as well.

7. Recognize, feel and build your confidence. If you don't feel your personal power, it is because you are focused on what you have no confidence in, relative to the situation you are in. What do you have no confidence in relative to the situation that is causing you to feel you have no power? How could you increase your confidence in that situation? In what ways could you learn and grow in that area so as to build your confidence in the areas causing that lack of confidence? What do you have confidence in? Make a list. If you recognize where you have confidence in your life, the areas where you don't won't feel like they diminish you. For example, you may feel totally

confident with cooking or being able to work with someone's emotions or fix a car or paint or understand complex concepts or clean and organize. Really resource the confidence that you currently take for granted relative to those things. And remember, at one point in time, none of us felt confident walking. Now we are so confident about it that we take it so much for granted that we would not even think of putting it on the list of things we are confident about.

8. Get out of the position of the victim. The reality is that people are raped and murdered and taken advantage of and lied to and all of those things that fit into the category of being a victim. Those who hurt others were hurt themselves, so we are all victims of victims. You were the one who was hurt in the situation, but the rub of it is that doesn't change anything. It still happened and it can't un-happen. The only question you are left with is what are you going to do about it now? There is great value in expressing the emotions around being victimized and caretaking the part of you who has been victimized and continues to see itself as unable to get out of the position of being the one who is powerless and wronged. But once that has happened, complaining won't actually change anything at all. In fact, it keeps you powerless because it is a cry for mercy from others. It is an attempt to put yourself in their hands. It is an attempt to cause them to see you as innocent and good so that you can gain their sympathy. You want to gain their sympathy to the degree that they will put their energy towards creating, directing, influencing or doing something so as to bring about what you need and want. Face the very hard question

of what positive thing do I get or am I trying to get out
of complaining to people or telling them how badly
I was hurt by someone else? There has been so much
badness attached to considering yourself a victim or
victim mentality now that it is very hard for people to
resolve the very real parts of themselves that have been
victimized and it is very hard for people to look at and
admit to their emotional attachment to staying in this
role. I completely disagree with this shaming. There
is no shame in whatever answer you get when you ask
this question. There is only a decision to make about
whether you want to maintain that position or whether
a different approach serves you better. How might you
have power in the matter instead?

We assume that fault implies responsibility.
Perhaps one of the most important things to accept
about life is that it doesn't. Fault and responsibility
don't necessarily go together in a world where every
being has power. And taking responsibility is not an
admission of guilt. It is not letting someone who hurt
you off the hook. It is a recognition of your personal
power. It is an act of emotional self-preservation and
empowerment. It isn't a man's fault that he had an
abusive, alcoholic father. But even if it is his father's
fault, this doesn't mean his father will ever take
responsibility for picking up the pieces and righting
his wrongs and fixing the son he abused. This means
that if he wants a life that feels good, the ball is only
in his court to pick up the pieces of himself and find
new, fulfilling relationships and heal. It doesn't matter
if something in your life is someone else's fault, you
can't guarantee that they will take responsibility for
fixing it. This means the power and therefore the

responsibility is in your hands even if it isn't your fault to change the situation into what you want it to be instead. If you look at the word responsibility as if it is response-ability. You can ask yourself the question, how is it within my ability to respond? How do I have the ability and opportunity and capacity to respond to this situation so as to bring about what I want?

9. Wherever possible, commit to being in the position of cause instead of effect. This requires a mindset shift. We live in a universe based on the law of cause and effect. This means we will do things that affect others and others will do things that affect us. One of the best ways to own your power is to choose out of the position of being at the effect of others. This is something that entrepreneurs have figured out. If you are in the position to be fired, you are at the effect of your company and boss. Therefore, entrepreneurs have chosen to remove themselves from that position and be at the effect of themselves. A person who simply blames their partner in a relationship for the negative relationship pattern that is occurring, is at the effect of their partner. If however they recognize their own role in that pattern and change it, they have switched into the cause position in the universe, instead of staying in the effect position. Any time you are in a situation that feels like you are at the effect of someone or something else, ask how could I adapt to the reality of this situation so as to switch back into the position of cause instead of effect?

10. Follow the north star of your desires. Commit your energy to your desires, values, what is meaningful and what is important to you. Follow those things like a

compass pointing you due north. As I've said earlier, to fully commit to something is to put all of your energy into something. This means mental, emotional and physical focus and actions. Your personal power is about being able to bring about what you want. *This means commitment to following the north star of what you want, what is meaningful, important and what you value, is central to personal power.* Doing this makes you a driver of your life instead of a passenger. This means being willing to be different, go in a different direction and stand out from the crowd. This means staying pointed towards your north star when people put pressure on you to stray from your course or try to make you wrong for what you want.

11. Ask yourself the following questions:

- *How did I make myself a match to this?* (This does not mean to look for ways to blame yourself for it; it means to look for the power you had in creating it.)
- *What am I meant to learn from this?*
- *What is this pain causing me to know that I want?*
- *What positive things have come or could possibly come from this?*
- *What can I do to change things for the better right here and now?*

Stop Depriving Yourself

Self-deprivation is sabotage in the form of withholding enjoyment from ourselves. This form of sabotage is the direct result of thinking that you don't deserve whatever it is that you want. When we deprive ourselves, we operate from the belief that we don't deserve the best, we don't deserve to get what we want, and we don't deserve happiness and love.

If you struggle with self-deprivation, you are confused about the difference between self-love and selfishness. That topic was covered in Tool #17, so please review it so you can be clear on this. It is also important to recognize that self-deprivation is a way that people try to self-preserve. For example, depriving ourselves can be a way of trying to gain control over our needs if we feel that needing in and of itself makes us weak and vulnerable. It can be a way of protecting ourself from loss. By depriving ourselves, we might be trying to guarantee that we will not get used to having or depending on something that we may ultimately lose. It can also be a way of getting the hit of self-worth that people often get from feeling like they are a *good* or *disciplined* person for depriving themselves.

But don't let this feeling fool you: depriving yourself is ruining your life. And it is a poor substitute for true self-worth.

Don't Deny Your Self-Worth

Self-deprecation is self-sabotage in the form of belittlement where you deny your own worth. When we depreciate ourselves, we undervalue ourselves and hold a "less than" attitude toward ourselves. We also tend to invalidate anything that draws attention to our worth.

If you struggle with self-deprecation, it is important to understand that in many cases, this is just a way of manipulating other people's perceptions of you in order to avoid taking a "hit" to your self-esteem. The basic strategy behind this avoidance technique is to "get an attack in first." In other words, you launch a preemptive attack on your own failings before anyone else can do it to you.

If you have spent your life belittling yourself in front of others, it is most likely because you have noticed that if you attack yourself in front of others, they are no longer inspired to do so, and they may even give you a compliment. In this way, you may be using self-belittlement to get love from others. Until you recognize this pattern, and decide that the payoff is not worth the detriment, you will continue to do it.

In most cases, if we struggle with self-deprecation, we have spent time as a child around adults who had unreasonably high expectations of us. When we experienced failing to live up to their high expectations, we developed the idea that we were not good enough. Our early life experiences of being below standard caused us to feel fundamentally flawed and inadequate. Because of this, we have most likely developed our personality on top of a foundation of shame, living our life with the ever-present fear that we are inadequate. You may find that you struggle intensely with the idea that you deserve anything.

This fear of being seen as inadequate can lead us to chronically procrastinate. Procrastination protects us from the higher expectations that may come with succeeding. We procrastinate not only because we fear failure, but also because it keeps us safe from facing our true limits by avoiding challenges and putting things off. Because we fear being seen as inadequate, we chronically avoid drawing other people's attention and we try to lower other people's expectations of us, as well as our own expectations of ourselves. We may apologize for things in advance so that when we fail, there is no backlash. We fully believe in and identify with our own inadequacy to the extent that we don't believe that there is anything good about ourselves. We can't believe any compliment that we are given.

If you are someone who self-deprecates, it is important to find different, less detrimental ways to self-preserve. From there, focus on things that cause you to feel proud and good about yourself. If you feel tempted to undermine yourself before you have even begun a project, take a silent vow to let the results of whatever you are doing speak for themselves. You do not need to talk yourself up, and you certainly shouldn't talk yourself down. Just stay quiet and let the results unfold. And most important, engage in any activity that causes you to improve your opinion about yourself.

Pride Goes Before a Fall

The eighth form of self-sabotage I want to mention is self-pride, which often hides under the mask of narcissism. It is the belief that you are better than other people. Contrary to popular belief, pride and narcissism are not forms of self-love. They are actually quite the opposite. We develop pride when we feel deeply insecure about ourselves, as a way to overcompensate for how terrible we actually feel about ourselves.

This overcompensation becomes a form of self-sabotage because not only does pride silence the voice of the truth—the truth that we are scared, lonely, and insecure—but it also drives people away from us. Pride does not bring us love, attention, and adoration, but rather it causes others to reject us, leading us to feel abandoned.

If you struggle with self-pride, also known as arrogance or superiority, it is important to understand where this behavior comes from. Just like self-depreciation, self-pride is also a way of manipulating other people's perceptions of you in order to avoid taking a "hit" to your self-esteem. The basic strategy behind this avoidance technique is to divert people's attention away from your insecurities and weaknesses by going on about your specialness and perfection. The only way you can find to avoid feeling worthless is to coat your insecurity with a heavy coat of varnish, and the varnish you use is called boasting.

In most cases, those of us who suffer from self-pride have experienced direct criticism and disapproval from significant people in our childhood, usually our parents. Most of us who suffer from self-pride have discovered early on in our life that the rewards and punishments that are given out by adults are the direct result of how those adults perceive us. Because of this, we seek to manipulate the adults around us, and eventually everyone around us, to perceive us as perfect or amazing. We think this will bring us more love, and we may even put other people down in order to compete for what limited positive attention there might be.

Self-pride doesn't always come across in an overt way. For example, someone who struggles with self-pride may mask their pride with a complaint such as, "I'm so sick of people writing me all these love letters. At some point, enough is enough!" These covert statements are meant to make it seem as if we are not bragging, and that we might even potentially be humble. But the statement is really intended to cause the other person to come to the conclusion that we are amazing and special.

If you struggle with self-pride, the most important thing to do is to shine a light on your actual insecurities. Ask yourself, *What am I so afraid of?* Be honest with yourself and know who you truly are.

We can't really love ourselves if we only love what is perfect about ourselves, so we must learn to embrace what is imperfect. Other people actually like us better when we are open enough to admit to our imperfections. Plus, it's exhausting having to keep up a facade all day, every day.

Caring What Other People Think

It is not possible to stop caring what other people think about you. As social beings, not caring what other people think about you defies biology. Not caring what other people think about you has drastic consequences. But so does letting what other people think about you run your life. Instead of trying to stop caring what other people think of you, start considering how much you are willing to let the way that other people think about you control your life.

Everyone has negative thoughts about themselves and other people from time to time. So when you are worried about someone else's opinion, remember that they are also worrying about what someone else thinks of them. They may even be worrying about what you think of them. Ask yourself, *What am I afraid will happen if someone thinks a bad thought about me?* The answer to this question will show you what needs to be healed if you want to stop caring what other people think of you.

Letting your life be ruled by what other people think is a very common problem. It is a problem that stems from the need to be loved and accepted. So if you want to be stop feeling controlled by what other people think, and if you want to let go of self-pride, simply take incremental steps toward loving and accepting yourself.

When we set out to love ourselves, there inevitably comes a time when we must commit to living our life in line with our highest good. Inevitably, the time will come to let go of our self-sabotaging thoughts and behaviors, and that time is now.

It may not happen overnight, and you don't have to do it all at once. But if you begin to take incremental steps toward replacing self-sabotaging behaviors with self-supporting daily actions, you will get to the point where you no longer "sabotage" yourself.

One of the most amazing realizations that you will ever have is the realization that even when you think parts of you are doing things against you, they are really doing those things FOR you. This means, you are loving yourself even when you think you are hating yourself. When we are in a place of self-hate, we feel like we are living with an enemy inside our own skin. The power of understanding that there is no such thing as self-sabotage, is the power of understanding that there is no enemy. You cannot be your own enemy. Even those parts that at face value seem to be harming you, are doing what they are doing because they think it is in your best interests to do so. There is no enemy within. Only advocates that could find no better way to advocate for you until now.

TOOL #26

CLEARING OUT
THE CLUTTER

Making More Room for You

Do you have enough room in your life to love yourself? If not, take the pivotal step toward loving yourself by making space enough for this to happen. It's a very symbolic step, and it's like clearing out clutter. In this case, clutter can be defined as anything that stands between you and the vision you have for your ideal life.

It's not easy to clear your life of what doesn't serve you. It takes courage, but the truth is when your life is full of clutter, there is no room for self-love. Think of it this way: If there is any space that is occupied by something that doesn't serve your highest good, there is less space for things that do serve your highest good. This is true whether that space is your mind, your body, a closet, your whole house, or just a sock drawer.

Start by taking an objective look at your life. Is your body cluttered? Is your mind cluttered? Is your living environment cluttered? Is your schedule cluttered? What things in your life no longer serve your highest good? When you are looking over your life, ask yourself, *Does this thought, person, place, or object enable me to be closer to my vision of the life I want to live, or does it make me feel as if I am further away from it?* If the answer is yes, keep it. But many times, you will get a resounding *no*. If so, ask yourself this question honestly: *What is this doing in my life?* As soon as you get insight, act upon it! It's time to purge what you no longer need.

Once you clear out old objects, old habits, old beliefs, and people who do not add to your well-being—all the things and beings that no longer serve your highest good—you will create emptiness. All this new emptiness is an invitation for you to fill the space consciously with things that *do* serve you and that *do* support your well-being. The majority of this book addresses clearing out and replacing the internal things that no longer serve your consciousness and your body. So now it is time to address the external aspect of your reality.

Getting a Handle on Your Stuff

Start with the physical aspects of your life. Clear out the material clutter from around you. Again, it is important to remember that clutter can be defined as anything that stands between you and the vision you have for your ideal life. If your reality is physically cluttered, that is a reflection of your internal reality. If your physical reality is stark, controlled, and colorless, that is also a reflection of your internal reality.

Since your physical world mirrors your consciousness, it is profoundly self-loving to create an environment for yourself that supports your happiness and well-being. Maybe this task will be as simple as reorganizing your closet, painting your room a color that you love, cleaning a dirty car, sorting out a cluttered garage, or rearranging furniture. Maybe it will entail changing your entire living space. Be honest about what things serve your highest good and what things do not.

It can be overwhelming perhaps, but it is important to begin somewhere. Survey each item one by one in the space that you are clearing out and ask yourself, *Does this thing serve my highest good? Does this spark joy? Does this thing lend to my happiness? Does this thing make me feel closer to my vision of the life I want to live, or does it make me feel further away from it?* If the answer is yes, keep it. If the answer is no, it is time to let it go.

If you feel as if you aren't ready to entirely get rid of something yet, but you know that it doesn't fit your vision of your best life, put it in a box and put it in storage, out of view so you can decide later whether you want to keep it. Remember that your happiness right here and now is more important than all your "stuff."

Some of us surround ourselves with actual physical clutter, while others clutter our space with absence. This may sound like a contradiction in terms, but it isn't. Some of us can become obsessive-compulsive and instead of creating chaos, we create our worlds in the image of control, monotony, and lifelessness. If your environment is drab and lifeless, it is time to start bringing some life to it by adding things that cause you to feel positive emotions. Now is the time to create an external reality that mirrors the best life that you can envision for yourself.

People Can Cause Clutter

It's also time to survey the people in your life. When we don't love ourselves, we have a way of attracting all kinds of people into our lives who support self-hate. Which people in your life don't serve your highest good? Are there individuals who drain you or use you instead of supporting you? If you feel the need to end relationships with those who don't serve your highest good, now is the time to do so. In particular, it is very important to end relationships with people who are abusing us.

If it doesn't feel right to cut people out of your life altogether, you may want to simply express to them the way they make you feel. Be aware though that you may have attracted a great many people who are similar to you, insecure with themselves, and so receiving this message from you may cause them to go into defense mode.

Avoid blaming them when you speak to them. Simply tell them how they make you feel and why. They may not be receptive, and they may not respond in the way you wish they would. But at least you are creating the opportunity for the dynamic to change.

Stress Can Cause Clutter

Perhaps the most important thing to clear out of your life when it comes to self-love is stress because stress is clutter. Stress is pure resistance, and as we've mentioned before, ask yourself, *What is it that I am resisting?*

Contrary to popular belief, stress isn't caused by circumstances, such as having no time, not having enough room to put things away, not having someone to help us out, and so on. We blame many things for our stress, but stress is actually always the result of a thought that we are thinking about the circumstance we find ourselves in.

To let go of stressful thoughts, we must recognize them and then clear them from our minds. To do this, you first pay attention to how you feel. When you feel negative emotion, ask yourself, *What thoughts are going through my mind?* If it is difficult to tune in to your thoughts in this way, try to trace backward and identify the circumstances you encountered that caused you to start feeling bad. Then ask yourself, *What thoughts was I thinking about that circumstance?*

Once you have identified the negative thoughts, pick one of the thoughts to work on. The best way to mentally clear negative thoughts from your mind is to ask yourself, *Who would I be without this thought?* Ask yourself this question relative to the thought that you have chosen to work on, and spend some time really envisioning what your life would look like and how you would feel if you didn't even have the ability to think that thought.

The next step is to reverse the thought and ask, *In what way is this reverse statement as true or more true than the original thought?* For example, we could start with the thought *I have to get it all done today,* and you could reverse it and think, *I don't have to get it all done today.* Then search for all the evidence that you can find to support that second statement.

Here are some examples of ways you can support the fact that you don't have to get it all done today:

1. I am the only one putting this pressure on myself. I am the one who decided that I "have" to get it done, so I can choose to release myself from this expectation.

2. The minute I complete this task, I will inevitably find another thing that I have to get done and so in reality, I can never get it all done.

3. If I tried to get it all done today, I'd be so stressed that I'd get sick, and I couldn't get anything else done. So obviously, I don't have to get it all done today if it's not even in my power to do that.

4. I'm not going to die if I don't get it all done today, so this is not a life-or-death situation.

Try to think of as much evidence as you can that supports the reverse of a thought that is creating stress for you. It doesn't necessarily have to be evidence in support of the reverse statement. You could choose to simply come up with any thought that causes you to feel better about whatever it is that is causing you stress. Any thought that causes you to feel less stress is causing you to release resistance and is therefore contributing to your own well-being.

Anchor in the Present

Most of us have an addiction to the idea of productivity because we think productivity is what makes a person successful. We have been conditioned to think that success is what brings us self-worth, positive attention from others, and ultimately, love. Because of this, our lives become total chaos. We are constantly looking ahead to the next thing. It becomes a cycle of worry and stress that prevents us from experiencing and appreciating the only thing we really have control over, which is the present moment.

Focusing on the present moment is one of the best ways to clear your life of stress. When you are focusing on the present moment, you are clearing the clutter of the past and the future out of the now.

Practice coming back to the present moment every day. If you can learn to recognize the feeling of stress, then you can use stress as a trigger. The following is an exercise to help you do this.

1. When you feel the trigger go off—that is to say, when you recognize the first feeling of stress—use it as a reminder to come back to the present moment.

2. To come back into the present moment, simply withdraw your attention from whatever it is that you are thinking about and focus it on what's around you right here and now. Take a few really deep breaths while focusing only on your inhaling and exhaling. Focusing on the breath helps you to instantly align with the present moment.

3. Then, tune in to your senses. Look at what's right in front of you right now. Listen to the sounds around you. Smell the fragrances of your environment. Feel the fabric of your clothes and the pressure of your feet against the floor. Reconnect with the experience of the exact moment you are in.

4. Close your eyes, and focus on what is going on inside you in the present moment. For example, scan each part of your body and tune in to how each part of your body feels. Turn your attention to your feet, and work your way up your body, stopping your attention at your legs, your pelvis, your chest, your neck, your head, your shoulders, your arms, and your hands. Without judgment, just sit with the sensations that you are feeling when you tune in to each area of your body.

5. Next, tune in to the emotions you are feeling right here and now. Without judging them, just surrender to those emotions by sitting with them and observing the way they feel.

Simplify Your Life

Be aware that how you organize your life adds greatly to the stress that might be cluttering up your life. What's the solution? Simplify your life. Simplifying your life is more of a process than a goal, because to truly simplify our lives, we need to allow ourselves to reorganize our priorities and amend our decisions as time goes on. The initial goal when you are simplifying your life is to identify what is most important to you and deal with the highest-priority things first. Then you can eliminate everything that isn't important to you.

The more complicated your life is, the more stress you are going to experience, so be prepared to simplify every aspect of your life: your commitments, your tasks, your finances, your schedule, your relationships, your environment, and your goals. Trust your intuition. You most likely already know what areas of your life need to be simplified. If not, ask yourself what areas of your life cause you the most stress and those will be the ones that need to be simplified the most. The goal when you are simplifying your life is to clear your life of unnecessary things. But remember that things that add to your happiness are to be considered necessities! Those you are going to keep.

Many proponents of simplification would have you believe that in order to truly simplify your life, you must become a minimalist, but this is not true. What makes them happy is to live minimally, and that is the right choice for some people. It can be a noble way to live if that's what you like. But you may be happiest when you surround yourself with the luxuries that this world has to offer. Simplification is about living according to your top values and to what you deem to be truly important.

In summary, people who love themselves have no room for things in their lives that don't serve their highest good. When you take the time to clear your life of the things that no longer serve you, that do not lend to your happiness, and that do not line up with your best life, you are opening up space for things that *do* serve you. You will soon find that you are attracting new things, new ideas, and new people to take their place; and you will be surrounded with elements that do contribute to your happiness and create the best life you can envision for yourself.

TOOL #27

ADOPTING YOUR
INNER CHILD

Your Own Childhood Story

Once upon a time, each and every one of us was a child. When you were a child, you laid the foundation for your future life. It was a foundation that you built based on the lessons you learned, beliefs you adopted, and things that you experienced as a child. Some of these lessons, beliefs, and experiences were wonderful, but others were traumatizing and detrimental to your self-concept.

We eventually become adults, and we think that this is where the story of our childhood ends, but it isn't. Our child self remains alive within us. Its perceptions and beliefs affect the way we think, feel, and act today. Our childhood self is like a skipping CD within us. When we encountered things in our childhood that were painful, we ended up getting stuck in that pain with no knowledge of how to assimilate and heal it. The totality of who we were at that point in time could not move forward. That's how old thoughts, feelings, and experiences became frozen into our being, and so many of us continue to survive and keep functioning day-to-day by ignoring those feelings of pain and suppressing them.

In some cases, the feelings became so painful that in order to keep functioning at all, we disowned the part of us that first experienced that pain. In essence, as children, we buried our own inner self. It was a coping mechanism that served us well at the time, but stifling that pain can kill us in the end. The pain we hang on to can be healed and assimilated only when we become willing and brave enough to turn our attention back toward the child that is frozen in time within us; we need to listen to what that child has to say and love it like it needed to be loved back then.

Each and every one of us, regardless of how loving or unloving our upbringing was, holds within us the essence of the child that we once were. One part of us grew up, but the other part stayed a child. This inner child is the symbol of our emotional selves. The adult-you grew up despite not getting what it needed as a child. It is your adult self that holds the key to healing.

Child Care 101

We will always be orphans emotionally if we wait for someone else to parent the underdeveloped parts of ourselves in a loving way. We will always be powerless if we wait for someone else to rescue the part of us that needs to be rescued. And we will always be unhealed if we wait for someone else to take care of the parts of us that need to be cared for.

The best way to begin facilitating our own healing is choosing to consciously take care of the child self that is present within us on our own. We begin by loving the child part of ourselves that feels helpless, deprived, afraid, and unloved.

Here are some techniques that work well. Go through any old pictures you have of yourself as a child. Look very closely at them. How do they make you feel? What do these pictures tell you about yourself as a child? Do they represent the truth of how you felt back then? Do they reflect a facade that you had to maintain for the sake of the adults in your life?

It is often healing to select one of these pictures, frame it, and then keep it somewhere where you will see it every day as a reminder that this child is inside of you, and it needs love. If you do not have any pictures of yourself as a child, simply imagine yourself as a child. Try to imagine what you looked like. Try to remember what your world was like and how you felt.

Now, whether you have an actual picture or just a mental image, imagine that this child is with you at all times. Before you make decisions that could potentially be detrimental to you, practice asking yourself, *Would I do this to the child within me?* It is important to realize that you are doing to your inner child anything that you are doing to yourself on a daily basis.

It can also be very helpful to carry on an internal dialogue with your inner child. You can speak to the inner child throughout your day by periodically checking in with him or her. You can ask this child how he or she is feeling and thinking. You can ask this child what it needs or wants. You can even ask it for advice about what the adult-you should do.

Children have a very straightforward, fresh, and unclouded perspective. Because of this, their opinions can cut through our illusions and thus prove invaluable to us. When you are conversing with your inner child, you are giving the truth of your feelings permission to speak through the symbol of your inner child. If we adopted the habit of suppressing our thoughts and feelings, we can now allow our inner child to express them for us.

Really Get to Know This Child

Now it's time to take your work with your inner child even deeper with the following exercise:

Get two sheets of blank paper and a pen; keep them close to wherever you are sitting. Close your eyes and imagine a safe place. This place can be realistic, like a pristine meadow, or imagined, like a fantasy landscape. It can be indoors or outdoors. Imagine every little detail about this place that you can. Make sure that the place is safe and that it feels wonderful to you.

Now imagine that somewhere within this safe space is your childhood self. Imagine watching your childhood self from a distance. How old is your childhood self? What is your childhood self doing? What is your impression of your child? Is your child happy or sad? Just observe this child for a bit.

When you feel ready, imagine walking up to your child and introducing yourself. Tell your child how much you love him or her. Tell this child that they don't have to be afraid anymore, that they can tell you anything they have to say. Tell them that they can express what they need you to know through you. Then invite your child to merge with you. Ask the child for a hug. When the child hugs you, imagine this child blending with you so your body becomes its body, too.

Then open your eyes and pick up the first piece of paper and the pen. Place the pen in the hand that you do not usually write with, and invite the child within you, who is merged with you, to use your hand to draw you a picture of its life. Allow it to draw whatever it wants to draw. Step out of the way and just let this child express itself through its drawing. Don't expect the drawing to be an aesthetically pleasing masterpiece—it's just an expression. Don't judge what the child is drawing. Just let him or her draw by using your hand. When the child is done with the drawing, set it aside and pick up the second piece of paper.

Again, using the hand that you do not usually write with, ask the child within you to write you a letter telling you anything that it needs or wants to say. Never force your child to express itself to you, but encourage it to do so in whatever loving way that you feel inspired. If the child seems reluctant, you may need to coax them into trusting that they can express themselves.

When the child begins to write, just step out of the way and allow the words to flow through your hand. When it seems like the child is done writing what it needed to say, you can begin to ask any questions you may have. To do this, ask the question and allow the child to answer by using your less dominant hand. Some examples of questions you might ask are, *How are you feeling today? What are you thinking about? What are you afraid of? What do you need? What do you want? What do you think of Daddy? What do you think of Mommy? What do you think of your brother or sister? What do you want me to do differently? What do you need me to do for you?* Don't think about the answers. Just let them come out. The answers you receive may sound very childlike.

When your child is done answering your questions, close your eyes and imagine that you are back in your safe place. Now invite your child to separate from you. Imagine him or her once again standing in front of you. Kneel down to the child's level and hold their hands while you thank them for being brave enough to tell you what they told you. Tell them that it's all over, meaning anything that they are afraid of, and that they don't have to be brave anymore.

Then ask them if there is anything that they want. Give them whatever it is that they ask you for. For example, if what they want is for you to never leave them again, assure them of the fact that you won't leave them and that they can talk to you whenever they want to. If they want a toy, imagine giving them the toy, and watching them play with it. If the child is tired, imagine tucking them into a warm, cozy bed.

When you and your child feel ready to part until next time, tell them anything that you feel they need to hear. And then hug your child. Hold them for as long as they want to be held. Assure them that you will always be there to take care of them. Imagine them either falling asleep or running off to play.

Take four slow, deep breaths and then direct your attention back into the room. When you open your eyes, look over the drawing and the letter that your child wrote while you were doing this exercise. Look for the meaning that is hidden in the images or words that your child used. What are your impressions? Did you discover anything about yourself? How do you feel toward your inner child? Can you see the ways that the feelings of your childhood self have carried on into your adult life?

We can use this technique any time we are trying to gain clarity about how we feel, because the child is a symbolic representation of our emotional selves. The child will express exactly what we need to express on any given day.

Tests and Tantrums

On occasion, when we are first working with our inner child, we may run into their angry defense mechanisms or even get no response at all. They may even refuse to show themselves to us before they fully trust us. This is understandable seeing as how we have never connected with them before. They are used to not getting the love and care that they need, so it is natural that they are suspicious when we suddenly show an interest in them and their feelings.

Therefore, you may need to do this process several different times before your inner child trusts that you really care and that they are safe to express themselves. Keep at it. Your inner child may be testing your love. It may help for you to write your childhood self a letter telling them how sorry you are that you didn't come to save them or talk to them and take care of them sooner. Be as sincere as you can be in expressing yourself to your inner child. Your inner child can spot a lie a million miles away. Eventually, even the most hurt and distrustful inner child will come around and willingly express themselves as well as soak up the love that they have wanted to experience for so long.

Adopting your inner child allows you to connect with your feelings. It allows you to reintegrate the disowned parts of yourself. It also helps you to take care of yourself and provide for your needs. Deep within you is a part of you that retreated from the rest of the world. This childhood part of you retreated because it came to the conclusion that this was an unsafe world, where it had no ability to get its own needs met.

Without knowing it, you have been connecting to the world through the feelings of this inner child. Much of your life has been lived through the perspective of this wounded child who has been trying desperately to act like an adult. Give your inner child a little time each day to express itself and get its needs met. Give your inner child the love it has been wanting for so long. By doing this, you will be integrating this inner child with your adult self. The result will be a feeling of wholeness that you have not experienced in years or potentially ever. You will be providing your orphaned inner child with a loving home. Loving yourself is about providing for yourself today what you didn't receive in the past from others.

TOOL #28

Re-Own Your Shame

Shame is one of the most misunderstood aspects of social behavior. The reason for this is that most people think that shame is solely a mental and emotional response to self-diminishing experiences, beliefs, and thoughts. The truth is, shame is a biological affective reaction, much like the fight or flight mechanism. It happens at an instinctual level, without us having to think about it.

There are only two basic energetic movements within this universe: to push something away and to bring something closer. When we see certain things, such as something we perceive as cute, it triggers an instinctual reaction to bring it closer. But when we see images of threatening things, it triggers an instinctual reaction to push something away.

Love is an instinctual reaction to pull something closer to you and include it as part of you. So self-love could be seen as the act of pulling all parts of yourself closer to you so as to include them as part of you. And *shame is an instinctual reaction to push yourself away from yourself.* Therefore, shame could be seen as the exact opposite of self-love. Of course, you cannot do this physically because your consciousness experiences a singular embodiment. The only way to push *yourself* away from *yourself* is through fragmentation. For this reason, we could say that *shame is the mechanism for fragmentation* and shame creates *internal separation.* Shame makes it possible for you to have one part of you that opposes another part of you.

This shame reaction comes with a certain "feeling signature," meaning that you feel this reaction in your body as specific sensations. This is the same way you feel love as specific sensations. The most common feeling associated with shame is that your chest or heart area will ache intolerably. You may also experience flushing to your neck, chest, and cheeks, or the feeling of diminishing in size, along with the feeling of wanting to hide or contract.

As children, we are completely relationally dependent. We depend completely upon our closeness with the social group. If we perceive ourselves being pushed away by someone, like mom or dad, as a result of some aspect about us, we will triangulate internally. We will try to re-establish closeness with the person pushing us away by turning against whatever they have pushed us away for. For example, let's say that mom pushed us away because of our anger, we will immediately push away our own anger. We subconsciously disown, deny and reject it. But we can't do this physically; we have to do it within our own consciousness and we do so by creating a split in our consciousness. We feel a sense of shame when this occurs. We can say then that we are ashamed of our anger.

If we perceive ourselves to be pushed away enough in our childhood, that we either have to push away many parts of ourselves to be loved or could not find a way to push enough of ourselves away in order to be loved, we will carry the felt-based experience of ourselves as essentially bad, broken, defective, wrong, and undesirable at our core. The emotions we feel at that moment become embedded as the *feeling signature* that is the foundation of our self-concept. Essentially, our core self-concept is that of Shame. We want to push away our core.

The reason that everyone has been failing with shame is because most methodologies involving overcoming shame are aimed at trying to get a person to see their worth and positive attributes. They are aimed at trying to convince a person who is ashamed of his or her anger to see that he or she is not an angry person. This strategy only creates a greater split within them. The approach we have to take to resolve shame is to completely re-own and accept the parts of ourselves that we have tried to push away from ourselves. Owning your shame is the first key to ending shame. When we have pushed away aspects of ourself, we need to bring them back in.

People are usually terrified that when they re-own parts of themselves instead of continuing to push them away, they will become totally bad and unlovable. But have you ever noticed that it feels like you cannot overcome your problems no matter how hard you try? You cannot overcome your problems because; you cannot overcome what is inside you or part of yourself. As soon as you identify with something, it IS you. And from that point forward, to try to overcome those things, is to put one part of you at war with another part of yourself. Even negative traits (which are part of you) can never be eradicated from you. They can only be transformed into their highest aspect.

The solution is exaltation. The concept of exaltation is an ancient alchemy concept. Simply put, to exalt something is to transform something into its highest spiritual aspect. For example, the old alchemists thought that the exalted form of metal was gold. If we are to live better lives, where we are not continually made unhappy by our negative personality traits, we must take each personality trait we do not like and first recognize it within ourselves. We must then accept it by both owning it and finding a way to approve of it. And then we must find a way to amplify that personality trait into its most in alignment or exalted expression.

Here's an example of exaltation: let's say that someone is a master at mental chess. They play mind games with people. So, the highest aspect of that trait (what we call the exalted aspect) is to play mind games with people that benefit them. This person could become a brilliant counselor or psychologist. They could outsmart other people's egos and help them to see things about themselves that they are totally unaware of.

OR, for example, maybe someone is a bully. Bullies push people. The exalted form of being a bully could be that they push people to be their best. If they embrace their forceful energy and use it in situations where people could benefit by that force, such as when someone needs especially strong encouragement. Bullies establish dominance within a social group. The exalted version of this dominance is leadership. If this person embraces their leadership ability and takes charge when other people feel as if they need direction, they can rally people to cooperating with one another.

Any time we love something – which is to bring it close and include it as part of us, instead of push it away – we form a connection with that thing. When that thing feels connected to us, it can no longer hurt us without hurting itself and as a result, its expressions begin to take on a form that benefits us instead of hurts us.

Exalting your negative personality traits and problems is not about going to war with yourself. It is profoundly self-hating and counter-productive to want to rid yourself of those traits.

It is resistant and whatever we resist, persists. *So the key to solving your problems is to find the highest and best use for those so-called negative traits. Fall in love with what you hate about yourself.* Turn metal into gold on an internal level. Embrace and own the person that you are. Quit trying to turn yourself into something or someone else.

Describe yourself. What problems do you have? What do you feel are the negative parts of your personality? Be very honest about what traits you don't like about yourself. Once you have your list, spend some serious time thinking about what the highest and best use of those traits could be. What is the positive exalted form of those negative traits?

To take this practice deeper, try to see these parts you push away from yourself as a different person or being within you. Close your eyes and ask to see the part of you that you feel bad about. Allow whatever appears to appear, and then address this inner Shame Self with compassion. For example, you may be ashamed of the fact that you are a bully. So you're going to close your eyes and ask to see the part of you that is a bully. When you do this, you might see an image of a monster that looks like the incredible hulk. You can spend some time observing that part of you and then try to relate to that part within you.

I will give you a tip: compassion naturally arises as a result of relating to someone's suffering. Therefore, all you have to do in order to feel compassion for someone is to deliberately look at how you relate to their pain. So, relative to this exercise, you have to deliberately look at how you relate to the pain belonging to this hulk personality within you. How is your pain the same as it's pain? Can you identify with its pain? Look back over the course of your life. When did you experience pain similar to what that hulk aspect is feeling? Try to remember what that felt like and what you thought. What did you really need back then when you were in that same kind of pain?

If you are terrified of deliberately looking for how you relate to someone, even if that is a persona within you, you need to ask yourself "Why? What bad thing do I think will happen if I relate to this thing or feel close to this thing or if I am the same as this thing?" Using the example, you need to try to see into this hulk persona, feel into it, listen to it, learn about it and understand it completely. What are its needs and desires, and why?

The next step is to compassionately challenge the "push away" thoughts that arise as a result of asking these questions. For example, if you think a thought towards your hulk aspect like "this part is going to destroy people's lives," get into the mental space of philosophical debate. If you were a lawyer whose job it is to prove that this hulk personality is *not* going to destroy people's lives, what would your case be?

If you would like, you can also involve other people in this process so they can help you make a case for the parts of you that you have pushed away.

Next, picture yourself in your mind's eye. With this image in your mind, identify the parts about yourself that you don't approve of. In other words, identify the parts of you that you feel are not lovable. These parts could be personality traits, feelings, thoughts, parts of your body, or entire persona (such as the hulk aspect I was describing earlier), that you feel are unlovable aspects of you. Pick one of these parts to focus on. Now think of something that you love more than anything else. When that emotion is built up and intense, visualize permeating and surrounding that unlovable part that you chose with that feeling of intense love. You may want to visualize that love as a light that fully bathes the unlovable part of you in its essence to such a degree that the part of yourself that you chose is transformed.

Repeat this process with each part of you that you feel is unlovable. This visualization will help you release resistance to yourself. Remember, any disapproval you hold towards an aspect of yourself is resistance, and resistance to yourself is the opposite of self-love.

The understanding of fragmentation within the self; that your consciousness can separate into different aspects that we may call "selves," provides for us the most straightforward conceptualization of self-love. *To love yourself is to see, hear, feel, understand, see the value of, act in the best interest of and include all parts of your "self."*

TOOL #29

SETTING YOUR BOUNDARIES FOR SELF-TRUST

Boundaries Abound but Don't Always Work

Your individual perspective and experience is what is currently serving the expansion of this universe, so you naturally perceive a difference between yourself and the rest of the world. This individual perspective is a kind of boundary that defines us from everything else.

We have heard again and again from self-help experts and psychologists that it's crucial to our well-being to develop healthy boundaries. But what are boundaries really? Boundaries are guidelines for how someone relates the self to the rest of the world. They are rules of conduct built out of a mix of beliefs, opinions, attitudes, past experiences, and social learning.

So think about the word "boundary" as something that defines you – it is a preference not a fence.

A boundary is the imaginary line that uniquely defines your personal happiness, your personal feelings, your personal thoughts, your personal integrity, your personal desires, your personal needs, and therefore most importantly, your personal truth from the rest of the universe.

Boundaries get very complicated if we define them according to cerebral concepts of right and wrong, or wanted and unwanted, or according to the boundaries other people think are or aren't healthy. After all, there are physical boundaries, emotional boundaries, mental boundaries, spiritual boundaries, and sexual boundaries.

So right off the top, I'm going to simplify the concept and make them very easy to understand. Your boundaries are personal truths. They are defined by your feelings. Your feelings will always tell you whether a boundary of yours has been violated, no matter what kind of boundary it is.

For example, when someone asks you to a party and you feel as if you don't want to go, but you go anyway. You feel bad, which is your indication that you have violated your own boundary. This is why it is so crucial to be in touch with how you feel all day, every day. When we are ashamed of who we are and what we want, we have poor boundaries.

A person who does not listen to and respect what he himself feels is violating his own boundaries. If you don't listen to or respect what others feel, then you are violating other people's boundaries.

This is why it's so important to practice really listening to and feeling how things feel. Listen to what your feelings are telling you. They are speaking to your personal truth. Personal truth is something that cannot be defined by anyone other than you because no one can step into your body and feel for you.

But strangely, this is what so many people try to do. It's what society does all the time—try to tell people what their boundaries should and shouldn't be. In fact, the health or weakness of your boundaries has a great deal to do with the world around you, especially the world you grew up in.

Stop Abandoning Yourself

Most people who are embarking on the self-love journey expect to trust themselves and are frustrated when they don't. The thing is, it is super unfair to expect yourself to trust yourself if you have not demonstrated thus far that you can be trusted. The definition of trust is to be able to rely upon someone or something to capitalize your best interests. Honestly, think about whether your thoughts, words and actions thus far have demonstrated that you can be relied upon to capitalize your own best interests. Self-trust is something that is built over time by continually demonstrating that you will act in alignment with your best interests instead of against them.

The next important point here is that learning to trust yourself is a process, so let it be a process. If your life has been filled with difficult lessons, wrong turns, and all manner of hurts, then trusting yourself is not something that you can suddenly wake up and decide to do. Rather, it is the inevitable by-product of gradually making changes to the way you think and the way that you live your life so that you eventually come to love and trust yourself explicitly. On your journey to self-trust, one of the most important things you can do is set up healthy boundaries.

The reason that you likely don't trust yourself is because you have tended to abandon yourself. You do this by not listening to or honoring your feelings, an action that we call violating your boundaries, and you quite likely run from your negative emotions. The holy grail of self-trust is learning to STAY, which is an acronym for STop Abandoning Yourself.

How do you handle negative emotions? Do you run from them? Can you count on yourself to be there for *you*? For most people on earth, the answer is no. The reason is that whenever you start to feel negative emotions, part of you feels really worried and afraid because it knows that the other part of you is going to try to run away. You keep trying to get yourself to feel differently so you will want to be with yourself and not take off.

Let's face it. Most of us want to be with ourselves only when we feel good. If we feel bad, we will do anything we can to feel differently. Sometimes we even engage in destructive addictions in order to escape the way we feel and therefore escape from ourselves, which is the same as abandoning ourselves.

Can you trust someone who abandons you? No. In order to trust ourselves, then, we need to prove to ourselves that we won't try to escape ourselves when we feel negative emotion. We will sit with the emotion and be with ourselves exactly as we are, unconditionally.

If you can break the habit of abandoning yourself when you are experiencing negative emotion, you will come to trust that you will always be there for yourself. You will feel a deep sense of inner peace arise within you.

Defining Your Own Boundaries

As we discussed earlier, personal boundaries are really nothing more than the imaginary line that uniquely defines your personal happiness, your personal feelings, your personal thoughts, your personal integrity, your personal desires, your personal needs, and therefore most importantly, your personal truth from the rest of the universe. This means that if you asked me what my favorite flavor of ice cream is, and I said "coffee," that is actually a boundary of mine, because it uniquely defines me. But why so many self-help experts and psychologists and spiritual advisors are concerned with personal boundaries is that they help to define an individual by outlining likes and dislikes and what is right or wrong for them personally. Defining these things helps us to know what is right for us and wrong for us and how we will and won't allow ourselves to be treated by others.

Here are some signs that you have unhealthy boundaries:

Saying no when you mean yes, or saying yes when you mean no.

Feeling guilty when you do say no.

Acting against your integrity or your values in order to please someone else.

Not speaking up when you have something to say.

Adopting another person's beliefs or ideas so you are accepted.

Not calling out someone who mistreats you.

Accepting physical touch or sex when you don't want it.

Giving too much of yourself just to be perceived as useful.

Becoming overly involved in someone else's problems or difficulties.

Not defining and communicating your emotional needs in your relationships.

Making the feeling of closeness with someone such a priority that you are willing to deny, disown and reject parts of yourself in order to mirror and conform to their feelings, thoughts, desires, preferences, needs, and truths instead.

Boundary Violations

The biggest issue really isn't that other people violate our boundaries; it's that we violate our own boundaries. By letting someone violate our boundaries, we are in essence violating our own boundaries. This is self-betrayal. If you go against your personal boundaries, you violate yourself, you abandon yourself, and you allow self-hate to rule the day.

When most people think of boundary violation, they think only of intrusive violations, such as someone raping someone else. But there are also distancing violations that are very painful. A distancing boundary violation occurs when you have a connection with someone and they withdraw from you. Because this can be emotionally wounding to you, it constitutes as an emotional boundary violation as well.

Too many of us were shamed out of our true sense of self as children. In order to fit into our family and into society, we had to develop an identity that was acceptable to the people around us, a false self. It was a survival strategy to become the person we think we are supposed to be and shame the person who we really are. Those of us who had invalidating parents do not have healthy boundaries. Indeed, we may cross our boundaries all the time or not even have any.

Here is a common scenario. A child begins to feel angry because his parent is always working and never has time to be with him. The child expresses that anger and is invalidated. The parent says, "I spend more time with you than any other parent that I know spends with their child," and the child is shamed for being ungrateful. The child has learned that the way he feels is not true and that he should be ashamed for feeling the way he feels.

Likewise, the child has learned that anger is not acceptable, either. So the child creates a false self that does not express anger and that says "thank you" all the time. Over time, he believes that who he really is, is happy and grateful. He has never really admitted to the fact that deep down, he truly feels angry.

So how do you know if you have set up a false self? One way is if you fear other people thinking negatively of you. Ask yourself these questions: *Do I know what I really want? Or do I let other people tell me what to think or believe and how to feel? Do I do things I don't really want to do and say yes when I really want to say no or say no when I really want to say yes? Am I afraid to let people know how I really feel? Am I afraid of people thinking negatively of me?*

What Is Keeping Us Stuck?

Let's consider some of the reasons why it's so hard for people to set boundaries for themselves and keep to them.

First, we have been taught to put other people's needs and feelings before our own.

Second, we may not feel as if we have rights.

Third, we might not truly know ourselves.

Fourth, we could believe that setting boundaries will jeopardize a relationship.

Finally, perhaps we have just never learned how to have healthy boundaries.

The truth is most of us were told that how we felt was either not how we felt or was not an okay way to feel. Most of us were told that what we saw was not what we saw. Most of us were told that what we thought we wanted was not what we really wanted, or was not okay to want. In this way, we lived lives where our own personal truths were invalidated again and again. This made most of us feel crazy and as if we could not trust ourselves. This internal self-betrayal is what caused us to stop trusting ourselves.

How to Trust Yourself

For most people trust is an abstract concept, which sucks because trust is essential for relationships with others and self-trust is critical for personal happiness. If trust remains an abstract concept for you, you won't know what the hell to practically do in order to create trust in relationships or to create self-trust. So, I'm going to make trust simple for you. *To trust someone is to feel as if you can rely on them to capitalize (act in) your best interests.* This is as scientific as you can get with what trust actually is. For this reason, it's a good idea to sit with that definition for a moment and let it sink in. Keep in mind that I did not say that trust is about being able to rely on the fact that someone will put your best interests above their own. Nor is it making someone else fully responsible for your happiness. It is being able to rely on the fact that they will capitalize (act in) your best interests.

Taking the next conceptual step, to trust yourself is to *feel as if you can rely on yourself to capitalize (act in) your own best interests.* Even in a scenario where self-trust is about the assured reliance on your own character, ability, strength, and truth, this is true. For example, if you were to consider whether you trust yourself to be able to execute a task well, you would have already decided that executing that task well is in your best interests.

The reason self-trust remains so abstract for people, is because they see themselves as "one thing." I don't walk up to you and introduce myself by several different names. But this way of viewing yourself, is inaccurate. Consciousness itself functions like water. If you are looking at a river from above, you can see that a large river often branches off into smaller rivers. Over the course of your life, your consciousness splits, just like the river does. It is usually an act of self-preservation. When this happens, your sense of self becomes fragmented. So even though you have one body, within that body, you end up with multiple selves. The best way to picture this is to imagine that inside your body, you have a collection of Siamese twins. They are technically all conjoined because they all share one body. But each one has its own identity, its own desires, needs, perspective, strengths, weaknesses and appearance.

If you understand that you are not one thing that you call by one name, but that you are more like an ecosystem of different "parts," suddenly self-trust or the lack thereof makes sense. These internal "parts" of you can have any kind of relationship under the sun. All the way from super loving and supportive to violent and hating. The bottom line is, some parts of you *cannot currently be relied upon to capitalize (act in) the best interests of other parts of you.*

For example, if one part of you wants to go to a party and another part does not and the first part simply bulldozes and drags you to the party, the other part cannot trust it. Or for example, if one part of you wants to get rid of another part of you, that second part can't trust the first one. Or for example, if one part of you really wants you to become an artist and another part of you wants family approval (which it knows is not possible if you become an artist). And the part that values family approval makes the executive decision to do what the family wants, the part of you that wants you to be an artist cannot by definition trust the one who values family approval. And in all of these scenarios, you will feel that lack of self-trust emotionally in your whole being. You know what it feels like to be in a relationship where someone cannot be relied upon to act in your best interests. When you lack self-trust, that same relationship is taking place in your internal system.

But here's the good news: Trust can be rebuilt. If you have lost self- trust, that trust is rebuilt through parts of you demonstrating that they can be relied upon to be aware of and capitalize the best interests of whatever part they are currently opposed to. Building trust in any relationship, including those relationships taking place between your own parts, is really as simple as being aware of and capitalizing on each other's best interests. It is as simple as finding a meeting of minds about what a win-win scenario actually is.

So, now that you understand that, here is what you need to do in order to trust yourself:

1. **Start to work directly with the parts of yourself that are creating the self-distrust**. This means the parts within you that are opposed, that disagree, that are fighting, abandoning, suppressing, rejecting, denying, disowning, or

bulldozing each other and that are engaged in zero sum games. First, identify the part you are going to work with. To give you an example, lets imagine that a woman is overworked and her body is breaking down. But no matter what she does, she can't stop and relax. It is then safe to assume that the part that is creating an atmosphere of distrust within her is the part of her that will not let her relax. She is now going to pick a certain place in the room. She is going to go sit down in that place, but when she does, she is going to sit down AS only that part of her that won't let her relax. The best way to imagine this is to imagine that she is a method actor and, in that moment, she is only diving into the perspective of and becoming that one part of herself, as if it were the totality of her. Another way of thinking about this is that by sitting in that place, you are channelling only that one part of you and allowing it to take over your whole body and awareness. She is going to spend some time getting used to it as if she is in a foreign being. She will consider things like, "What do I feel like?" "How big or small am I?" "Do I feel female or male? Human or not human?" "How old do I feel?" "Where do I feel like I am?" Essentially, to begin with, you are simply becoming aware of it without asking it to express or questioning it.

From there, you have a choice to communicate in a written or spoken format as this part (keep in mind that some parts are less communicative and verbal than others). Some people choose to record themselves doing this if they are speaking. Others prefer to write. If you have chosen to write and find it difficult at first to simply let the truth belonging to one of your parts to flow through you, consider

writing with the hand you do not usually write with.
It doesn't matter if it is messy. Your non-dominant
hand is more connected to your subconscious mind.
This woman in our example will then begin to write or
speak as this part. What is its current truth? What does
it need to say or need you or others to hear? Seeing as
how the part this woman in our example just went
into, is the part that will not let her relax, it may write
or say things like, "I even hate the word relax. It just
makes me stressed out to sit around and do nothing.
We didn't come to this life to lounge around. We have
way more important things to do. All that's going to
happen if we relax is that we are going to feel guilty
and start stressing out more about everything that
we need to get done. No matter what, if we absolutely
have to do it, we can't let anyone see us. If they do,
they are just going to use the fact that we are being
lazy, to slack off themselves and then all hell is going
to break loose" etc. Let it express as much as it wants.
You may feel questions arise from somewhere deep
inside you. You can ask these questions to this part.
Things like, "When did this start or when did things
change for you?" Or "What are you trying to prevent?"
Or "What good thing do you think happens as a result
of the way you are doing things?" Or "What would
you be doing instead if you could do anything and
why?" Any question that arises can help you to gain
deeper clarity about this part of you. Two questions
that you need to remember to ask are how this part
feels about the central personality. For example, if it
were me, I would ask, "How do you feel about Teal".
Also ask how this part feels towards the part on the
opposite or other side of it (the other side of the split).

In our example, the part that is opposite of the part of her that won't let her relax is the part of her that desperately needs to relax. Don't be surprised if it has no awareness of this other part. Also understand that it can have any type of relationship with this other part. It may hate the other part, love the other part, consider the other part a protector, minimize the other part etc. Any relationship that is possible in the outside world is possible in the inside world.

When it feels like this first part has said what it wants and needs to say and you've explored it so as to have a good understanding of it, you are going to stand up from the place you were sitting. When you do this, imagine leaving that part of you sitting there. You are going to turn back around and look at the place you just came out of as if that part of you is sitting in front of you. Imagine, sense, or feel that part of you. Your perspective of it from this "middle point perspective" will often be different than the perspective you had of it when you were inside of it. What does this tell you about yourself? Using our example, the woman might notice that when she was inside this part and sitting in the chair, it felt older. It felt like a stressed-out version of herself but that when she stood up, suddenly that part sitting in the chair mentally looks like a soldier.

You can then repeat this process, but this time, with the opposite part. The one that is in conflict with the first. The woman in our example would pick another place in the room. She would then sit down in that place, but when she does, she would sit down AS only that part of her that desperately needs to relax. She will repeat the same process with this part, that she did with the first. Seeing as how the part that this woman in our example is now going into, is the part that needs to relax, it may write or say things like, "I can't do this anymore. I feel like crap. I just need to stop. I don't even know why the hell I'm doing most of the things that I am doing. My entire life is just about the daily grind. I'm going to get sick one day. I can feel it. I just feel like the other part of me is trying to run me into the ground, as if that is what it takes to be successful. But who the hell cares if you're successful if you're wrecked by the time you achieve anything" etc.

Really deeply seeing, hearing, feeling, and understanding the parts of yourself that are at odds, you will then seek to bring these parts into alignment with each other. When parts are in alignment, they decide together what the best decision, action and new way of being with each other is.

When you do this with parts that are creating an atmosphere of distrust in your being, you often need to make these parts of you aware that they are part of the same body and as such, they literally cannot play a zero-sum game. In other words, there is no "I win and you lose" for something that shares the same body. Each part needs to be made aware that it no longer works to capitalize on its own best interest to the detriment of the other's best interest. They will begin to look for a win-win situation when this is the case and begin to caretake each other's best interests. This creates an atmosphere of trust in the internal system. But stay open to this looking different than you would anticipate. When certain internal parts become aware of others, and really see, hear, feel, and understand them, their own perspectives and therefore estimation of their best interests often change. If you allow your awareness to touch these parts, the process of integration will already be occurring. The awareness that comes out of working directly with these parts of yourself will give rise to deep shifts in perspective and a deep understanding of what will actually work to resolve these internal conflicts that are leading to self-distrust.

2. **Become intimate with the part(s) of you that you don't trust**. This point goes in alignment with the last. But it must be a stand-alone point. If trust is about capitalizing on someone's best interests, you have to actually know what their best interests are. To know what someone's best interests are, you have to be willing to have intimacy with them. Intimacy is seeing into someone, feeling into them, hearing them and understanding them as deeply as you can. This means, you've got to be willing to face and create intimacy with the part of you that you think is the "bad guy" in the trust department. For example, if you lack self-trust because a part of you keeps taking drugs regardless of your desire to stay sober, you need to stop playing a zero-sum game with it and really see, hear, feel and understand that part; especially the WHY, so you can help that part of you to get its needs met and act in its best interests in alternative ways than the ways it is currently going about getting its needs met. "You" can't oppose, fight with, abandon, suppress, reject, deny, disown, bulldoze or engage in zero sum games with any part of yourself and create an atmosphere of self-trust in your being.

3. **Accept that there is no such thing as self-sabotage**. We covered this in depth in our previous chapter on self-sabotage. This understanding can go a long, long way towards developing self-trust. Usually when we don't trust ourselves, we become afraid of ourselves. But remember: If any of your internal parts or selves are resisting or opposing your desires, or if any of them are hurting other parts of you in any way, it is because they think it is in your best interest for them to do so. In other words, they believe they are saving your life by *not* going along with the plan. For this reason, we cannot say that they are *against* you. They just don't agree with the rest of you about how to be FOR you. For example: consciously, you may really want a relationship to work, but you keep pushing the other person away or doing and saying things to create conflict in the relationship. In this scenario, one fragment or part within you (the one we are consciously identified with) has made the decision to be in a relationship and make it work. Another part knows that relationships have been so painful in the past and that it has been abandoned and therefore thinks abandonment is inevitable. So, it is trying to save you from the pain of getting attached to something you are inevitably going to lose. No part of you, even the ones who "hate you" are actually against you.

4. **Build your self-confidence.** Self-confidence and self-trust are very good friends. When we use the word confidence, what we mean is *your ability to depend upon yourself*. When we understand that lack of self-trust, goes hand in hand with lack of self-confidence, we see that

not trusting ourselves is often a self-worth issue. It is an issue of devaluing and invalidating ourselves. One of the reasons that we do not trust ourselves, is that we do not *accept* our own abilities, talents, intentions, and value. This means, take time to recognize and acknowledge your abilities, talents, positive traits, and thus value.

Part of this confidence is *Allowing yourself to do what you are good at and what comes easily to you.* Everyone is good at something. We don't often allow ourselves to do what we are good at however because we have all been raised in societies with very specific values. Our strengths may not align with the values that those around us hold. And on top of this, most societies today value *effort*. Most of us think it is weak to do the things that come easy to us. But for us to learn how to trust ourselves, we need to allow ourselves to do what we are good at and what comes easily to us. If we always feel as if it is a struggle to do things, we will always feel behind the pack and lack confidence. So, own up to the things which *you* excel at, and then focus on designing your life around *those* things. Give yourself permission to take pride in them and give yourself credit for your successes. And remember that we have to look for the people who will value what we have to offer.

5. **Listen to your feelings. They always have important messages to share.** Most people view feelings as a menace; something to fight, something he or she is powerless to, a drawback, and even something to distrust. The average person does not know what purpose they serve. The result is, many people are living in a tug of war between being a slave to their emotion and flipping around to wage war

with their emotions. We have a multibillion-dollar pharmaceutical industry set up to make a profit from chemically aiding people to suppress their feelings and change them. This is especially sad considering that your feelings are the compass guiding you through this venture called life. Emotions are the carriers of personal truth. They never "come out of nowhere." They are the exact reflection of the truths belonging to parts of you. I am not saying that the thoughts, perspectives and opinions of parts of you are always accurate and a perfect reflection of objective truth. But they are always real and important and they always exist for a valid reason. You have to notice and listen to the truth being carried by a feeling to recognize that a part of yourself is activated and to hear that part of you out. You cannot do what is right for you or in your best interests if you don't "hear out" the truth being carried by your emotions. And consciously choose what to do given that information.

6. **Let go of the idea of "the" right answer and just look for "your" right answer.** People who don't feel as if they can trust themselves, often defer to others. They tend to become preoccupied with the idea of right and wrong and it paralyzes them. They tend to fear making the "wrong" choice so much, that they procrastinate making any choice, and they trust other people's opinions rather than forming and "owning" their own. *Gain perspective by eliciting other people's opinions, but do not "weigh them" in order to make your final decision. Instead, make your own decision. Use inquiry to question your current perspective and consciously choose a perspective, which serves your highest good.* Every

single person, experiences the world in their own way. So we make decisions about what is right based on our own individual assumptions, judgments, perceptions and past experiences. This is why no two perspectives will be the same. And no one can see the situation from *your* perspective. You are also never going to have *all* of the information that you would like to have in order to make "the perfect decision." You can't know everything and so sometimes you have to take a risk by making a choice anyway. If you are looking to develop self-trust, stop trying to find *the* right answer. Find *your* right answer and be open to it changing as you develop and become more and more aware and evolve.

7. **Take risks, even if taking those risks results in making "mistakes."** We have to be *willing to take risks and make mistakes* in life. One day during my sports career, I was in a panic about racing as usual. At that point in my life, my self-worth was completely tied up in performance. As a result, I had the habit of getting such bad performance anxiety that I did terribly in races and sometimes didn't even show up for them. But on a chairlift on the way to the starting gate, I had an epiphany. The epiphany was this: I have lost 100% of the races that I didn't run. This is the case when we don't take risks. We like to think that if we don't take risks, we don't fail. But the truth is the exact opposite of that. If we don't take the risk, we have already failed. While it can be scary for us to take risks in life, it is one of the best ways we can build our capacity for self-trust. Taking risks takes courage, and courage makes us feel better about ourselves. It allows us to see what we are *really* capable of, which in turn

helps us to trust ourselves. You won't know that you can trust yourself unless you take a risk and see that you can.

8. **Compile a list of all the ways that you *do* trust yourself.** Our level of trust is often different relative to different things. For example, we may trust our instincts relative to some things, like driving our car; while we doubt ourselves relative to other things, like making a good impression in an interview. Take some time to compile a list of all the ways that you currently know you *can* trust yourself. Compile this list by filling in the blank as many times as you can. "I trust myself to_____." For example, "I trust myself to be loyal to the person I have committed to." Or "I trust myself to be loyal to my own happiness regardless of whether or not that means breaking a commitment that I have made to someone." Some other examples might be, "I trust myself to care for my pets." Or "I trust myself to do exactly what I say I'm going to do." Or "I trust myself to make a breakfast which tastes good." Nothing is too small or too large to include in this list. Any kind of trust, no matter what it is in, is important because it is trust. We have the tendency to ignore the ways that we actually *do* trust ourselves, when we become aware of the ways that we don't trust ourselves. This corrodes our self-concept. It disables us by making us feel bad about ourselves, instead of simply allowing us to incrementally build trust in the things we don't currently have trust in.

Trusting yourself is a process. Let it be a process. Trusting yourself is not something that you can suddenly wake up and decide to do. It is the *inevitable byproduct* of gradually improving the internal relationships taking place within your system. Just remember that the better it gets, the better it gets.

In relationships, we deeply crave to be with someone who understands how we feel, but we don't even take the time to understand how *we* feel. We wind up having a relationship of convenience with ourselves. We only listen to our own personal truth when it doesn't cause trouble or difficulty. We don't realize that we are causing the very difficulty we are trying to avoid by not listening to our feelings and personal truth all the time regardless of whether it may cause difficulty or not.

The bottom line is that it's impossible to know who you are, what you like, what you believe, and what you want unless you know how you *feel*. People with healthy boundaries are able to have relationships without losing themselves. Remember, when our boundaries are vague to us, they will be vague to others.

Creating Healthy Boundaries

Healthy boundaries are nonresistant in nature and thus, they are in alignment with oneness. Healthy boundaries are not about controlling what other people do. They are entirely about you personally defining and then following your individual sense of happiness, desire, and personal truth. It is a state of self-awareness, integrity, and self-love. People who build walls against others are not exhibiting healthy boundaries—rather, they are in resistance to the world. An unhealthy boundary pushes against the world and tells others how they can and can't behave. Ultimately, we have no control over how anyone else behaves and what they do and don't do. We only have control over what we do and don't do and what we allow ourselves to experience at the hands of others.

So here's a technique to get you on the right track and honor your own boundaries. Say you are feeling badly about having said yes to something you don't really want to. You can reassess your boundary or reestablish it in this way. List ten things you'd like other people to stop doing around you, or to you, or saying to you. It may even help to list the people in your life one by one and write down how you feel around them.

Then, relative to every item on the list, ask yourself these three questions:

How am I violating my own boundaries by letting them violate my boundaries?

How do I really feel about this?

What do I really want?

Once you figure out what is true for you and what you truly want, take action to be in alignment with those boundaries. Firmly state your case to the people around you.

However, be aware that as time goes on, your boundaries will require updating. They don't always stay the same. For example, perhaps the time you can give to others is much more limited after starting a new relationship or having a baby. Redefining your boundaries throughout life is a crucial part of staying true to yourself and loving yourself, and you can use the three questions above at any time to reassess where you are at today.

In fact, we can all help to rehabilitate each other with regard to boundaries. We can do this by giving people around us permission to feel how they feel and admit to how they feel to us. This doesn't mean that we let go of how we feel and what we want. It means we make space for both our truth and their truth, so as to figure out what the highest and best option is, given the reality of both.

TOOL #30

STEPPING INTO YOUR PURPOSE

Creating a World You Love

At some point in our lives, we all end up asking ourselves the question, *What should I do with my life?* It's a decision we all must make and one that we do make one way or another. Everyone ends up "doing" something, consciously or unconsciously. You may not like it, you may not have even chosen it deliberately, but you are "doing" something. This chapter explores this topic in order to help you get closer to finding your true purpose, if in fact you are not there yet.

Within the bigger spiritual picture, your life path is meant to be a reflection of who you really are. This means that your life has no more limitations than the limitations that you, yourself, impose on it. In truth, you are truly free and your life can change at any moment. You are the one in charge. If you're not happy with your career direction or your life's purpose, it is up to you to take action to get back on track.

You may have already realized this, but in case you haven't, here is an undeniable truth: If you don't decide how you want to live, what you want to be, and what you want to do, then someone or something else will decide these things for you. If this has already happened to you, with some other forces having determined your place in life, chances are that you are not living according to your own inner values and enjoyment. Instead, I expect that you have probably yielded to any number of subconscious influences such as genetic predispositions, upbringing, social conditioning, environment, and the opinions of other people in your life.

This process can be a scary one because your true inner values may run counter to everything you've been led to believe. Your inner values may even run counter to the inner values of everyone else around you! But if you are brave enough to live according to your own inner values, the result will be a level of freedom, joy, and fulfillment that you have never before experienced.

Your Soul's Purpose

This is a good time to speak to you about your soul, which is your true, essential self. Your soul doesn't need to go searching for who you are, because it knows exactly who you are, what you love, and what your deepest desires are. We are not born upon this planet searching for our souls as if we have lost them. In fact, young children, for the most part, live entirely according to their souls. It's only when we become self-conscious enough to adopt external values, opinions, and advice that our own souls become suppressed and obscured to us. Many of us spend the rest of our lives seeking ways to get this inner awareness back, and the lessons I am sharing in this chapter deal with that process.

Until you uncover and accept your true desires and true self; it is not possible to be truly loved. True love is love that exists for the truth of someone, not a facade put on for the perceived benefit of anyone else or of society. There is nothing in this world that compares to being loved for what is real about yourself.

So when you are trying to decide what to do with your life, it is important to first find out where you are. Ask yourself in this very moment if you are happy. This is not a question that refers to mere contentment. Asking yourself if you are happy really means asking yourself, *Are you passionate about your life? Do you get more excited about going on vacation than you do about doing your day-to-day work? Are you in love with your existence? Are you delighted to be here on earth at this particular point in time? Do you like where you live? Do you enjoy your relationships?*

Once you have your answers, without calling them good or bad, you can begin to move forward to the place where you want to be, living the life you want to be living.

Finding your own values and priorities can take some risk. It takes being brave enough to remember who you really are again.

Rediscovering Your Natural Passions

One major reason people don't live the lives they wish to live is because of negative beliefs. We touched upon negative beliefs in many of the previous chapters. We develop beliefs because of conditioning and experiences, and many of these beliefs limit our reach with regard to our careers and our life purpose.

You may believe many of these familiar mantras—we have all heard them: "No one can make a living doing this or that." "Fun is just irresponsible." "You're worthless if you don't go to college." Many of us are turned away from our natural desires by adopting these kinds of limiting beliefs and values, which were drummed into us by authority figures at such a young age. Too many of us have lost touch with our desires completely, but here's a bit more good news: Your spark is still there. You just need to find it and reignite it.

One of the best ways to get back in touch with the real you is to think back to your natural inclinations as a child. Make a long list of things you knew you loved when you were a child. Make a list of your natural talents, and try to remember what you wanted to be when you grew up.

Now, after you make that list, make sure to ask yourself, *Why did I love those things? Why did I want to grow up to be those things?* Then ask yourself, *Do I still enjoy and practice these things today? If not, why not? Can I remember what caused me to stop? Was it because of someone else? Do I remember how it felt to stop doing those things?*

From this point, fast-forward to today. Ask yourself what has been your favorite part of your entire life so far and why. Get as detailed as you can in order to discover the true reason you enjoyed it so much. After that, ask yourself, *What am I passionate about in my life currently? Have I put my passions on the back burner, or are they the primary focus of my life?*

This process will help you understand what it is that you truly enjoy and separate these true passions from the ideas in your conditioned and logical brain which, being mechanical in nature, has often been taught to minimize feeling states such as joy and passion.

If you're a person who says that passion just isn't your personality, or isn't necessary in life, you should know that you have sacrificed too much. If you're living on purpose instead of by default, passion will be the normal state of your life. Following your passions will not suddenly transform you into an unbalanced, emotional wreck. Instead, it will push you to live up to your full potential.

In case you haven't noticed this either, in this world intellect can only get you so far. There's a difference between deciding to achieve a goal and actually achieving it. Your intellect can manage the former, but it's incapable of achieving the latter. You will feel passion directly as the emotional result of taking actual, tangible action to head in the right direction. If you find that the passion is gone from certain parts of your life, you will feel that lack and know that it's time to make a new decision. It's time to change directions.

Mining for Gold

When you allow yourself to be who you really are, then what you are meant to be doing will present itself without you even having to look for it. But it can be quite enlightening to play around with what your life's purpose might be. The following is a fun exercise designed with this very aim in mind, and it requires you to practice listening to your emotions.

Start by taking out a sheet of paper and writing down a list of all the different things you can think of that might be your life's purpose. Any answer that pops into your head should be written down. Repeat this as many times as you possibly can until you reach the answer that evokes a strong emotional reaction from you. In other words, the one on the list that makes you want to cry.

This usually takes some time to happen, as you clear all the other thoughts out of your mind; then the answer that really strikes a chord with you is the one that has been voiced by your true self. You may discover a few answers along the way that seem to give you a mini-surge of emotion, but they don't quite hit you in that epic way that the real answer does. Those others are just a bit off.

Make sure to highlight those other answers though as you go along, so you can come back to them to generate new permutations if needed. Each one that resonates with you reflects a piece of your purpose, but individually they aren't complete. When you start getting these kinds of answers, it means you're getting warm, so keep going. When you write the one that truly reflects your real self, you will know it.

Once you find the answer, ask yourself if you are living your life according to that purpose. If the answer is no, ask yourself, *What steps could I take right now in order to live according to that purpose? Is there a way that I could foresee incorporating the things that I enjoy and feel passionate about into the very life's purpose that I've just discovered?*

If you can, then take the risk of doing so. If not, put forth the intention for the opportunity to do so to come to you. It may come completely out of the blue. You don't need to know the complete picture of the "how" of things. The how will be incrementally presented to you in response to taking action in the direction of what you want. You simply need to know what you want and why you want it and then be brave enough to jump at ideas and opportunities as they come to you.

When it comes to finding your purpose, have no fear of making the wrong choice. If you take the risk to try something that you feel is in line with your true self, that action will bring you closer to your true purpose. And remember, you can always change your mind and try something new. Maybe you are one of those people who avoids risks at all cost, perhaps because you've been told that to play it safe is the intelligent thing to do. But ask yourself this: *Why? Why not take a chance?* We will all die one day. Our lives are not permanent. All too often people don't take risks only to arrive at death . . . safely. But anyone who lives this kind of life regrets it in the end.

The Mind-Set of an Explorer

If you feel completely and utterly cut off from your talents and your own sense of enjoyment, now is the time to start trying new things. Take a class or select a hobby that is completely out of your comfort zone. You may have something in mind that you are interested in trying, or you could just start trying things regardless of whether you are interested in them. If you're not sure what to try, ask other people for their suggestions and dive in.

Allow your friends to drag you to that event they've been trying to get you to attend forever. Do anything that you feel inspired to do. The worst thing that can happen is that you could decide you don't like something that you tried. And even if this were to happen, you'd be closer to knowing yourself. So adopt the mind-set of an explorer. Trying new things can wake up parts of you that you never knew existed.

Everything that is ever done is done for one reason and one reason only: the doer thinks they will feel better in the doing of it. If a person lives for fun, it's because they think they will feel better in the having of fun. If a person lives to help others, it's because they think they will feel better by helping people. If a person lives for purpose, it's because they think they will feel better if they have purpose.

So you see, everything ever done is therefore done in the quest for happiness. So why not cut right to the chase and make happiness the true goal of your life? If you begin to do this, you will find yourself on the path toward your ultimate desires, even if it is a path you never in a million years thought you would find yourself on.

How Our Life Purpose Really Works

Now is the time I can let you in on a little known secret. We very often make a mistake when we are searching for our life purpose because we look for what we are supposed *to do* or *to have* in this world when, in fact, our purpose comes instead in the form of what we are supposed *to give* to this world. It is only through the giving of this gift that we can ever receive, and allow our true self to express itself into this world.

Giving this gift should not feel as if you are losing anything. It should instead feel as if you are gaining more from life than ever before. And so here are the two questions you should be asking yourself every day: *What am I meant to give in this life?* and *What is trying to come through me and express itself today?*

Don't worry that you don't have anything to give, because embedded in the soul of every being who is born to this earth are a number of gifts that are intended to be shared with the world. For some of us, the gifts we came in with are obvious. We can't help but share them from the minute we touch down.

For other people, their gifts are less obvious. Some of us may even doubt we even have them at all. But I assure you, that there is not a soul born without a gift, waiting and ready to be discovered and shared. Each and every gift that is waiting to be expressed is an equally valuable part of the balance of this world. Each gift is a necessary part of the whole. Just remember, these gifts don't come in the package of duty; they are delivered in a package of joy. So as simple as this sounds, we are meant to share the things that bring us personal joy.

Therefore, finding your purpose is no more complicated than opening your heart to what you love and then sharing it with others. It is a gift to the world when an athlete performs a great jump shot during a basketball game. For that basketball player, the joy of playing the game is his indication that his gift to share with the world is the expression called playing basketball.

It is a gift to the world when a writer releases a new book. For the novelist, the joy of writing a story is her indication that her gift to share with the world is the expression called writing a book. It is also a gift to the world when someone conveys information. For the professor, his joy of verbally speaking his truth is his indication that his gift to share with the world is the expression called teaching. It is a gift to this world when one person offers a great meal to another person. To the chef, the joy of creating a really great dish is his indication that his gift to share with the world is the expression called cooking.

We may have one thing that we are meant to do here or many things. Purpose is not always expressed through a formal kind of profession. We may not receive money or be recognized for our purpose, but it is still part of our purpose. For example, for a mother, the joy of taking care of her children is her indication that her gift to share with the world is the expression called parenting. Fathers also feel this same sense of joy, purpose, and wonder when they engage with their children as an expression of their passion to be a father.

Other kinds of gifts come in more covert ways, like the gift of eloquence, the gift of abstract thinking, the gift of listening, the gift of mathematical comprehension, or the gift of perfect pitch. It just so happens that for many of us, our multitude of gifts tends to fit nicely within a specific profession or a hobby that we just love. Sometimes, a single gift that we possess fits nicely within a great many professions. In any event, your gifts are no less important if they do not line up with one profession. You are fulfilling your purpose any time you allow any gift to express itself.

Don't Minimize Your Purpose

The main reason that our purpose is often expressed through a profession is that our current society calls for us to make money and spend most of our day doing so. Since most of us would rather be happy than miserable while making money, the best scenario is that we would choose to make money in exchange for something that we love doing. When you think about it, this is definitely the choice that someone who loves themselves would make.

Don't let yourself be talked out of what truly causes you to feel joy and passion by your ego. The ego is really nothing more than your self concept. The ego is dissatisfied with the idea that purpose can be as simple as doing joy-filled acts each day, because the ego doesn't come into this equation and feels slighted that it doesn't have a role to play when it comes to true purpose. Because ego doesn't play a role and is not being validated, it loses control, and therefore, you will find that your ego will go to great lengths to minimize the importance of doing the things that you love. Your ego will try to convince you that if you are enjoying what you are doing, then your life must be meaningless and you aren't doing enough. Your ego will tell you that unless you're saving the world or engaging in some other special, heroic, significant act on a mass scale, that you are missing out on your purpose. But this is not the truth.

The ego loves to measure everything by quantity; the bigger the better, the more valuable. But universally it is powerful purpose to change a powerful act of legislature that effects the entire world and it is powerful purpose to hold a single person's hand when they are in pain. Every purpose is valuable.

A LOVE LETTER
FOR THE FUTURE

Becoming Butterflies

Caterpillars, who curl up inside of their cocoons in darkness, do not simply grow wings. Their metamorphosis first turns them into a primordial fluid. They dissolve completely and are reassembled to emerge as butterflies. This is how it goes for so many of us before the dawn breaks in our own lives and we can emerge as transformed people. We are disintegrated. We experience darkness so all-consuming that we fear we may never see the light of day again. But we will. I am living proof of it.

And so, in the name of self-love, there is only one way for me to end this book and that is with a new love letter from my future self to my current self. Like the first love letter that I wrote myself all those years ago, which I included in Tool #11, I will let this one weave the fabric of what is to become my future:

Dearest Teal,

The omnipresent dust of the past once covered your present and frosted your future with grief. Grief that with its disheveled hands pulled you back in time. You kept on breathing even when your world was shattered. And because of that bravery, I can tell you now that when the world is shattered like a window, no glass remains between you and the sunflower that was always there. No illusions, no barriers—just the opportunity to see it.

Hurt is the stopping point before life flows down a completely different road. If you resist the current of where life is now taking you, if you try to change what you cannot change because it has already been written in time, you are drowning. You are shutting life out, just as you once shut out the sunflower with the glass of your life. It is only when you let go and surrender to the current that you have a chance of taking in air. When the world was shattered by grief, you didn't take your own life like you thought you would; you were brave enough to go with the current and you didn't shut life out. Because of that bravery, you saw the sunflower. And that is what I love the most about you.

I can imagine you sitting with your paintbrush, drawing the colors across the canvas, wondering how it is all going to turn out. Well, I am here to tell you that it is all going to turn out fine. In fact, take your definition of fine and multiply it by a million. You will live to see every single one of your dreams come true. You have created a legacy of positive world change. You have started centers and programs in too many countries to mention. Headway Foundation took on the world and won. It pioneered changes in the food industry, the health-care industry, the justice system, the education system, animal welfare, environmental protection, child care, technology, and end-of-life care, just to name a few.

The best day of your life so far is when you walked into an office room full of stoic, impersonal men in suits, wearing your bright-colored spiritual attire and signed your name on the documents that were drafted to adopt your justice system programs into the mainstream jails. You always knew that day would be the best day of your life, and it happened. Sometimes it seems like everything you touch turns to gold.

Your son grew up to be an emotionally intelligent man who follows his joy no matter where it takes him, and he comes home of his own volition because he loves you and wants to eat your cooking. Your community is still around you. You have grown old together, and when they look back over their lives, they tell you that living with you made their lives epic and full of meaning, and there is nowhere they would rather be.

In truth, so many things have gone better than you wished for them to go that there are too many successes to mention in this letter. I will just have to let you experience it all for yourself over the years that are to come. I just want you to know that even though you have finally learned how to love yourself, the love that you feel for yourself today does not compare to the love that you will hold for yourself in the years to come. I love you more than you know—you are wonderful, and I am proud of you. I would love you and be proud of you even if you had spent your life curled up in an institution like they told you that you would. I would love you even if you had achieved nothing.

But your achiever personality took you all the way to the moon, which is ironic because when there is a full moon, you look up at the sky and you wish for two things: The first is to find freedom and happiness, and the second is to be able to teach others exactly how to find it, too. And that wish has come true. You have found happiness, and you have found freedom. You have taught people exactly how to find it, too. You taught them by example because freedom is in the reclaiming of self, in the turning of life's cyanide into honey, and happiness is the pinnacle of color sketched to a world full of petals, all of which grow from soil. Perchance the squalid circumstances of our given lives were none but a call to ripen. For the life within a life is transcendental, forever searching out the ways the world has bisected us. In order to unite us again with a kind of soundness so brave, it drowns out the throes, so you can see that beauty in its most absolute forms is not virgin to rancor. Instead . . . it comes from it.

With love always,

You

ABOUT THE AUTHOR

Teal Swan is an internationally recognized spiritual leader. She travels the world teaching people how to surmount their suffering, heal their wounds and awaken to an empowered, authentic life. As an international speaker and best-selling author, she inspires millions of people around the world towards truth, authenticity, freedom, and joy.

Website: www.tealswan.com

WATKINS
1893

The story of Watkins began in 1893, when scholar of esotericism John Watkins founded our bookshop, inspired by the lament of his friend and teacher Madame Blavatsky that there was nowhere in London to buy books on mysticism, occultism or metaphysics. That moment marked the birth of Watkins, soon to become the publisher of many of the leading lights of spiritual literature, including Carl Jung, Rudolf Steiner, Alice Bailey and Chögyam Trungpa.

Today, the passion at Watkins Publishing for vigorous questioning is still resolute. Our stimulating and groundbreaking list ranges from ancient traditions and complementary medicine to the latest ideas about personal development, holistic wellbeing and consciousness exploration. We remain at the cutting edge, committed to publishing books that change lives.

DISCOVER MORE AT:
www.watkinspublishing.com

Read our blog

Watch and listen to
our authors in action

Sign up to
our mailing list

We celebrate conscious, passionate, wise and happy living.
Be part of that community by visiting

 /watkinspublishing    @watkinswisdom

/watkinsbooks   @watkinswisdom